Table of Contents

About the Forms

Purchasers of this book may download, print, and/or photocopy Appendices 4.1–13.1, Appendix A, and Appendix B for professional and educational use. These materials are included with the print book and are also available at http://www.brookespublishing.com/downloads with (case sensitive) keycode: 53acDeW98.

Behavior Support for Students With ASD

Practical Help for 10 Common Challenges

by

Debra A. Leach, Ed.D., BCBA
Winthrop University
Rock Hill, South Carolina

Baltimore • London • Sydney

Paul H. Brookes Publishing Co.
Post Office Box 10624
Baltimore, Maryland 21285-0624
USA

www.brookespublishing.com

Typeset by Progressive Publishing Services, York, Pennsylvania.
Manufactured in the United States of America by
Sheridan Books, Chelsea, Michigan.

All examples in this book are composites. Any similarity to actual individuals or circumstances is coincidental, and no implications should be inferred.

Library of Congress Cataloging-in-Publication Data

Names: Leach, Debra, author.
Title: Behavior support for students with ASD : practical help for 10 common challenges / by Debra A. Leach.
Description: Baltimore, Maryland : Paul H. Brookes Publishing Co., 2018. | Includes bibliographical references and index.
Identifiers: LCCN 2017038737 (print) | LCCN 2017053187 (ebook) | ISBN 9781681252667 (epub) | ISBN 9781681252674 (pdf) | ISBN 9781681251998 (paperback)
Subjects: LCSH: Autistic children—Education. | Autistic children—Behavior modification. | Autism spectrum disorders—Patients | BISAC: EDUCATION / Special Education / General. | EDUCATION / Special Education / Mental Disabilities. | EDUCATION / Classroom Management.
Classification: LCC LC4717 (ebook) | LCC LC4717 .L42 2018 (print) | DDC 371.94—dc23
LC record available at https://lccn.loc.gov/2017038737

British Library Cataloguing in Publication data are available from the British Library.

2022 2021 2020 2019 2018

10 9 8 7 6 5 4 3 2 1

About the Author

Debra A. Leach, Ed.D., BCBA, Department of Special Education, Winthrop University, 701 Oakland Avenue, Rock Hill, South Carolina 29733.

Debra Leach is Professor of Special Education at Winthrop University in Rock Hill, South Carolina, and a Board-Certified Behavior Analyst. She is also the project director of the Winthrop Think College program, a fully inclusive postsecondary program for students with intellectual and developmental disabilities. Her areas of specialization are autism spectrum disorders, applied behavior analysis, multi-tiered systems of support, positive behavior interventions and supports, differentiated instruction, and inclusion from birth to adulthood. She is the author of *Bringing ABA into Your Inclusive Classroom: A Guide to Improving Outcomes for Students with ASD* and *Bringing ABA to Home, School, and Play for Young Children with Autism Spectrum Disorders and Other Disabilities.*

SECTION I

Understanding Students With ASD and Frameworks for Providing Behavioral Support

First things first: Students with autism spectrum disorder (ASD) are absolutely wonderful children to teach. Teachers receive great joy from their work when they have a solid understanding of ASD and know how to implement research-based practices to support children's unique learning needs. In fact, it is rare to hear a professional educator say, "I used to work with students with ASD." Once a professional has positive experiences teaching and supporting students on the autism spectrum, he or she will likely continue to seek opportunities to work with more children with ASD. The strengths of individual students with ASD vary, but many of these children have average or above-average intelligence, excellent rote memorization skills, and specialized talents and interests; they also have interesting perspectives to share, say and do funny things every day, and work quite hard despite the challenges they face.

By the nature of their disability, students with ASD are faced with many potential roadblocks as they progress through school. Although each child has an individualized profile of strengths and challenges, some common issues faced by students with ASD include deficits in social skills, language and communication skills, fine and gross motor skills, and academic skills. These students may also have cognitive differences in the way they learn and process information, sensory processing problems, heightened levels of fear and anxiety, difficulties regulating emotions, problems with focus and attention, and executive functioning challenges. They also often have a restricted range of interests, repetitive behaviors, and an intense need for sameness. In addition, some students with ASD have medical issues to deal with, such as side effects of the medications they must take to manage their ASD symptoms, gastrointestinal problems, sleep issues, seizures, or food allergies.

Although not every student with ASD has all of these challenges, most have to deal with some of them on a daily basis. If teachers do not understand these characteristics and difficulties, then it is likely students will not receive the supports and interventions they need to be successful in the classroom. Challenging behaviors will ultimately arise when children with ASD are not adequately supported. The challenging behaviors are not necessarily characteristics of ASD but, rather, the lack of understanding on the part of educators, ineffective teaching approaches, and overuse of teacher-directed approaches that do not consider the needs and perspectives of the individual child.

The purpose of this book is to help readers understand how the characteristics of students with ASD can affect their behavior in school settings and provide assessment and intervention planning tools that take this information into consideration. Long-lasting positive outcomes are likely to occur when research-based behavioral interventions and supports get to the heart of the matter, which requires educators to think beyond basic classroom management principles and practices. Simply setting behavioral expectations, explicitly teaching expectations, delivering positive reinforcement when students meet expectations, and using consistent consequences when they do not meet expectations will not adequately address all of the behavioral challenges of students with ASD. Trying to get these children to fit into school is like putting a square peg in a round hole because of their multitude of social, communication, emotional, physical, medical, and adaptive behavior challenges. Teachers who start with that understanding and are open to using a more child-centered approach to planning and delivering behavioral interventions are able to support their students better and effectively address their behavioral challenges.

Section I contains three chapters. Chapter 1 provides readers with an understanding of the characteristics of students with ASD and how they may affect behavior in the classroom. Chapter 2 provides an overview of multi-tiered systems of support (MTSS), explaining how these frameworks can be used to address the needs of students with ASD to prevent challenging behavior and intervene as early as possible after the onset of behavioral challenges. Chapter 3 includes step-by-step functional behavioral assessment (FBA) procedures to follow when intensive behavioral interventions and supports are needed for students with ASD. Section II of this book (Chapters 4–13) provides guidance for determining the reason behind 10 common behavioral challenges of students with ASD. Each chapter in Section II includes sample intervention plans and classroom vignettes to illustrate how to link assessment and intervention planning to achieve positive outcomes for students with ASD.

CHAPTER 1

Characteristics of Students With ASD

This chapter discusses the characteristics of ASD that may affect behavior in the classroom. Although many issues and challenges will be covered, each student has a unique profile. Although some students with ASD may display all the characteristics discussed in this chapter, most students will exhibit only some of these traits. The purpose of sharing this information is to help teachers better understand the complexities of ASD so that they do not simply view the student as having behavior problems when challenging behaviors occur. These challenging behaviors are most often the result of one or more of the characteristics of ASD affecting the student's behavior. This is important because hopefully it will change the mind-set of teachers and how they approach behavioral issues in the classroom.

CORE DIAGNOSTIC FEATURES

According to the *Diagnostic and Statistical Manual of Mental Disorders, Fifth Edition* (*DSM-5*; American Psychiatric Association, 2013), the core diagnostic features of ASD include social-communication impairments and restricted, repetitive patterns of behavior, interests, or activities. The following sections describe each characteristic and how it may affect classroom behavior.

Social-Communication Impairments

Social-communication impairments in students with ASD can be quite complex. There are often deficits in broad areas such as joint attention and social reciprocity as well as weaknesses in the development of specific nonverbal communication skills and social skills. These deficits and weaknesses can negatively affect a student's ability to communicate with others and develop and maintain relationships. The following sections explain these various social-communication impairments students with ASD may face.

Deficits in Joint Attention

Problems with joint attention are one of the key defining features of ASD (Mundy, Sigman, Ungerer, & Sherman, 1986; Wetherby, Watt, Morgan, & Shunway, 2007). Joint attention involves the coordination and sharing of attention between two or more people and an object or event (Bakeman & Adamson, 1984). This can involve several observable behaviors, such as looking back and forth between a communication partner and an object, following a person's gaze or point, showing something to someone, or pointing to something to share attention with someone. The purpose of joint attention is to engage in a sharing experience with another person or group of people (Hobson, 1989). Simply put, it is the feeling that you get when you are truly connected with another person during a common experience. Students with ASD may have difficulties responding to joint attention initiations from others, initiating joint attention from others, and sustaining joint attention with others for an extended period. Deficits in joint attention can certainly affect behavior in the classroom. Students with ASD who have problems with joint attention may not always follow directions, participate during group instruction, or play and interact as expected with peers.

Deficits in Social Reciprocity

Deficits in social reciprocity is another core diagnostic feature of ASD. Individuals who demonstrate social reciprocity are aware of others' emotional and interpersonal cues, appropriately interpreting those cues and responding to what is interpreted, and they are motivated to engage in social interactions with others (Constantino et al., 2003). To simplify, social reciprocity involves long chains of verbal and nonverbal back-and-forth interactions. Students with ASD typically have great challenges with social reciprocity. It can affect their ability to have conversations with others, ask and answer questions during group instruction and assessment activities, and have meaningful social interactions with their teachers and peers.

Deficits in Nonverbal Communication

Children with ASD often have skill deficiencies in the area of nonverbal communication. These students may not effectively use gestures, facial expressions, eye contact, and body language to communicate with others. They also may not be able to read nonverbal communication behaviors in others. Deficits in this area may affect behavior in the classroom in various ways. Students with ASD may not be able to adequately communicate with others to get their wants and needs met, resulting in frustration and challenging behaviors. They may not be able to read the social cues of their teachers and peers and, as a result, continue engaging in challenging behaviors. For example, they may stand too close to a peer, miss the peer's irritated facial expression, and not notice that the peer is physically leaning backward to try to create more space between them. Consequently, the peer may avoid interacting with the students in the future.

Deficits in Developing and Maintaining Relationships

Several reasons explain why students with ASD may struggle with developing and maintaining relationships with others. In addition to having deficits in joint attention and social reciprocity skills, students with ASD also exhibit weaknesses in specific social skills that are necessary for developing relationships with others. Turn-taking, sharing, waiting, giving and accepting compliments, initiating and responding to greetings, imitating others, using appropriate volume, accepting constructive criticism, knowing how to start and end a conversation, staying on topic during a conversation, taking the perspective of other people (also referred to as *theory of mind*) (Baron-Cohen, Leslie, & Frith, 1985), understanding the emotions of other people, and offering and accepting help are examples of skills in which students with ASD often have deficiencies.

In addition, students with ASD often have challenges when it comes to learning the hidden curriculum, which are the expected social behaviors and norms that typically developing children learn without instruction from others. Examples of these skills include showing appropriate behavior in public bathrooms, keeping negative comments to oneself if they will hurt others' feelings, maintaining personal hygiene, and knowing when and when not to report challenging behavior of others to the teacher. Children with ASD may damage relationships (or potential relationships) with others because they simply did not learn the countless social skills their peers learn naturally through everyday experiences.

Restricted, Repetitive Patterns of Behavior, Interests, or Activities

The behavior, interests, and activities of students with ASD often tend to be restricted or repetitive; they may have intense interest in just a few topics or activities or desire to engage in the same behaviors and routines consistently and dislike novelty. These characteristics can affect both learning and behavior. Educators need to keep these characteristics in mind when planning how to engage learners with ASD.

Rituals and Insistence on Sameness

Students with ASD may have nonfunctional rituals that affect behavior in school (Rodriguez, Thompson, Stocco, & Schlichenmeyer, 2013). For example, some students with ASD may have rituals such as repetitively asking a specific question or series of questions, enjoying the predictable nature of the responses they receive from others; insisting on sitting in the same seat in the cafeteria each day, eating the exact same food for lunch every day; or repeating play routines using a very specific sequence of events. The student may engage in challenging behavior when these rituals are interrupted or prevented.

Similarly, insistence on sameness is a common characteristic of children with ASD. This means they thrive on predictable routines and may get very upset when changes to their normal routines occur. They may also prefer instructional activities in the classroom that follow a very familiar format as opposed to new and varied activities. It is possible that students with ASD will become upset, anxious, or fearful when the teacher delivers a new type of lesson or assigns an authentic assignment and engage in challenging behaviors as a result.

Restricted Range of Interests

Students with ASD may have a restricted range of interests (Szatmari et al., 2006), which means they do not have the same broad and various areas of interest as most of their typically developing peers. Instead, they often have passions and fascinations for very specific topics (e.g., weather, trains, sports statistics, computers, dinosaurs, superheroes, animals, cars, music). Having such special interests may affect behavior in the classroom if the student lacks motivation to engage in activities unrelated to these specific topics. Special talents can sometimes be drawn from these restricted interests, however, leading to specialization in academic achievement and employment if these interests are tapped into and utilized to excite and engage learners. Also, their areas of interest can certainly change and expand over time if teachers use a strengths- and interests-based approach to teaching and learning instead of always focusing on the students' weaknesses and ignoring their individual fascinations and passions.

Repetitive Behaviors

There are various repetitive behaviors that students with ASD may display (Turner, 1999). Some students use stereotyped or repetitive speech, such as repeating certain sounds, words, phrases, or lines from television shows, commercials, or movies. Repetitive motor movements are also common, such as hand flapping, rocking back and forth, repeatedly waving their fingers in front of their face, lining things up, repeatedly building the same toy structures, repetitive spinning of the wheels of toy cars, repetitively drawing the same pictures, or any other nonfunctional repetitive movement or activity. Students with ASD may also have repetitive visual behaviors, such as visually focusing on the rays of light coming through the blinds for extended periods of time, holding objects at a certain angle and staring at them, or repeatedly watching the same video clips. Other terms used to describe these repetitive behaviors include *self-stimulatory behavior* (often abbreviated as *stims*), *stereotypic behavior*, or *stereotypies*. *Repetitive behaviors* is the primary term used in the chapters that follow to describe the various topographies of stereotypic behaviors.

Sensory Processing Problems

Many students with ASD suffer from sensory processing problems or sensory integration dysfunction (Baranek, David, Poe, Stone, & Watson, 2006). Basically, this means that children with ASD may have hypersensitivity or hyposensitivity to sensory stimuli (Tomchek & Dunn, 2007). If they experience hypersensitivities, then they deal with sensory overload and have a difficult time processing the various sensory information in the environment and filtering it so they can focus on what is relevant to them at the moment. This can affect behavior in schools if students are unable to process all the sounds, sights, smells, movement, and other sensory experiences that are present across settings. If students are hyposensitive, then they may be underreactive to sensory stimuli and/or seek out sensory input, which is commonly referred to as *sensory-seeking behavior* and can often look like the repetitive behaviors previously described; however, not all students who demonstrate repetitive behaviors are seeking sensory input. Students with ASD may be both hypersensitive and hyposensitive to stimuli in the environment, depending on the situation (Baranek, 2002).

Getting first-person accounts whenever possible is the best way to learn about the sensory processing difficulties faced by individuals with ASD. For example, Carly Fleischmann, a young adult with ASD who coauthored a book with her father, explained that she often engages in what appears to be verbal stims to create output to help her deal with so much input during periods of sensory overload (Fleischmann & Fleischmann, 2012). This information is priceless to educators because most teachers would immediately try to stop the verbalizations, thinking they were getting in the way of the student's learning. The opposite is true, however, for Carly. She needs to express herself verbally to cope with and maintain involvement in sensory rich environments.

OTHER COMMON CHARACTERISTICS OF STUDENTS WITH ASD

In addition to the core diagnostic features previously described, students with ASD almost always have one or more of the following co-occurring conditions: expressive communication impairments, language impairments, heightened levels of anxiety and fear, executive functioning challenges, emotional regulation difficulties, problems with focus and attention, academic and cognitive deficits, deficits in fine and gross motor skills, and medical conditions. Information about the prevalence of specific co-occurring conditions in people with ASD is provided in the following sections.

Impairments in Expressive Communication Skills

In addition to the social-communication impairments discussed earlier in this chapter, some students with ASD also have expressive communication impairments. Students may be completely nonverbal or minimally verbal (meaning they use just a few one-word utterances, short phrases, or simple sentences), or they may have verbal communication limitations that inhibit their ability to fully function in academic and social situations. Approximately 25%–35% of individuals with ASD are nonverbal or minimally verbal (Rose, Trembath, Keen, & Paynter, 2016).

Language Comprehension Difficulties

Students with ASD may have receptive language comprehension difficulties that make it difficult for them to understand verbal directions and instruction (Ellis Weismer, Lord, & Esler, 2010). They may not fully grasp the academic language and vocabulary used by teachers during instructional activities. Although they may understand when teachers use consistent, clear, and concise language, students may not be able to comprehend language when its complexities increase. In addition, children with ASD may not understand figurative language and interpret information literally when it is not intended as literal. These deficits can affect the student's ability to follow directions and meaningfully participate during group instruction. Challenging behaviors may arise if the student gets frustrated during activities that require understanding complex language.

In additional to having problems understanding language, students with ASD may also have difficulty processing oral language. A student may understand the individual words and phrases used during a lesson, but he or she may have trouble processing all the language when it is presented quickly and in long, complex sentences. Students may need teachers to deliver small chunks of information and provide time to process before moving on in the lesson. Instead of having information presented to them only verbally, these students may need to have it written down or need visual instructional supports. When these supports are not in place, students who have language processing issues may demonstrate challenging behavior when they get frustrated because they are unable to adequately and efficiently process verbal directions and instruction.

Heightened Levels of Anxiety and Fear

Approximately 40% of individuals with ASD meet clinical diagnostic criteria for anxiety disorders (Van Steensel & Bogels, 2011). As many as 84% of people with ASD have symptoms of anxiety, however (White, Oswald, Ollendick, & Scahill, 2009). Heightened levels of anxiety can trigger challenging behavior such as tantrums, aggression, and self-injury (Canitano, 2006). Students with ASD may also have specific phobias and fears that can be quite debilitating (Leyfer et al., 2006), such as a fear of loud noises, dogs, and dark places. It is important for teachers to recognize anxiety and fear with compassion and support the student accordingly. If this does not happen, then the student's emotions are escalated even more when teachers get angry or impose punitive consequences for challenging behaviors that occur as a result of anxiety and fear.

Students with ASD may have heightened levels of anxiety and fear because they do not feel in control of their environment. Others often make all their choices for them (Clark, Olympia, Jensen, Heathfield, & Jenson, 2004; Wehmeyer & Metzler, 1995), giving directives instead of options. Their sensory needs may be disregarded, resulting in the students continually worrying about being put in situations that are uncomfortable, restricting, or painful. Students trying to gain more control over their environment is often viewed by teachers as a challenging behavior opposed to a basic human need because students often do not have the expressive communication skills needed to effectively negotiate with others to advocate for themselves. Instead, they engage in negative behaviors as a means of communicating their desire for more control in their lives.

Executive Functioning Challenges

It is well documented that many children and adults with ASD have difficulties with executive functioning (Corbett & Constantine, 2006; Hill, 2004; Kenworthy et al., 2005). In a broad sense, *executive functioning* refers to brain functions that help individuals regulate their behavior and carry out goal-directed tasks (Cannon, Kenworthy, Alexander, Werner, & Anthony, 2011). Specific executive functions include inhibition, flexibility, working memory, organization, planning, and self-monitoring (Rogers & Bennetto, 2000).

Problems in these areas may result in the following challenges for students with ASD in the classroom. They may have difficulty controlling their impulses due to problems with inhibition. Issues with flexibility can result in becoming upset by unexpected changes in their routine and environment. They may also have difficulties handling transitions throughout the school day, shifting their thoughts, and accepting flexible interpretations of classroom or school rules. Problems with working memory may make it difficult for students with ASD to follow multistep directions. If they have organizational deficits, then they may have trouble keeping track of their assignments and materials. Impairments in planning may make it difficult for them to initiate and complete individual tasks when attempting to complete projects. Students with ASD who have limitations in self-monitoring skills may have problems with managing time and altering their own behaviors to ensure they meet behavioral, social, and academic demands.

Emotional Regulation Difficulties

Many students with ASD experience challenges with emotional regulation (Laurent & Rubin, 2004; Mazefsky et al, 2013), which is a process in which positive or negative emotional arousal is redirected, controlled, modulated, or modified to enable a person to function adaptively (Cicchetti, Ganiban, & Barnett, 1991). Emotional regulation abilities are crucial for optimal functioning and development because they enable appropriate responses in social situations and facilitate the use of coping strategies in new or changing situations (Gross, 2007; Silk, Steinberg, & Morris, 2003). The inability of students with ASD to regulate feelings of extreme negative or positive emotions can detrimentally affect attention, communication skills, and problem solving (Prizant, Wetherby, Rubin, Laurent, & Rydell, 2006), ultimately having a negative impact on their classroom behavior.

Problems With Focus and Attention

Approximately 50% of students with ASD also meet the diagnostic criteria for attention-deficit/hyperactivity disorder (ADHD) (Rommelse, Franke, Geurts, Hartman, & Buitelaar, 2010). This means many children with ASD will likely have challenges with impulsivity, hyperactivity, or the ability to focus and attend during group instruction and independent activities. This almost always results in challenging behavior in classrooms because school expectations often require children to be quiet, sit still, and pay attention. Also, students with ASD often have difficulty shifting their attention (Courchesne et al., 1994). When they are focused on a specific activity and the teacher gives a direction that requires them to stop what they are doing and do something else, they can have great difficulty doing so. This is not defiance but a neurological difficulty students with ASD may have when it comes to shifting their focus of attention.

Deficits in Academic Skills and Cognition

Students with ASD may demonstrate challenging behaviors due to frustration related to academic skills deficits, cognitive impairments, or cognitive differences. Although the estimated rates of individuals with ASD who also have intellectual disability (ID) vary between 25% and 70%, results of a study of 253 children with ASD between the ages of 2 and 5 years showed that 36.8% met the criteria for ID (Rivard, Terroux, Mercier, & Parent-Boursier, 2015). ID is determined by IQ testing and adaptive behavior measurements, which include skills needed to function in everyday life such as social skills, daily living skills, and occupational skills.

The problem with identifying a co-occurring ID in students with ASD is that even high-functioning students with ASD who have above average IQs often have deficits in adaptive behavior (Kenworthy, Case, Harms, Martin, & Wallace, 2010). Thus, many individuals with ASD will meet the adaptive behavior deficits requirement for an ID diagnosis. Also, it is not always possible to get an accurate IQ measure for children with ASD because they may have problems demonstrating their abilities within the strict constructs of testing protocols due to their deficits in social-communication and other potential co-occurring conditions (i.e., problems with focus and attention, executive functioning challenges, sensory processing problems, anxiety). Therefore, let's make the least dangerous assumption: We do not always know whether a student with ASD has ID. Do not assume that a student has ID because the student is nonverbal, does not have alternative functional communication skills, demonstrates a high frequency of repetitive behaviors, or has severe weaknesses in joint attention and social reciprocity. Many students with ASD prove otherwise once they find ways to communicate and show what they know and what they can do. For example, although Carly Fleischmann had no functional communication skills and had severe sensory processing problems, repetitive behaviors, and excessive behavioral meltdowns as a young child, after she began typing to communicate and meaningfully participated in IQ testing, it was found that she was actually intellectually gifted (Fleischmann & Fleischmann, 2012).

A student with ASD may have academic weaknesses that affect challenging behavior in the classroom, regardless if he or she has ID. Students' reading comprehension and written expression skills may be impaired because of language deficits, which may also affect their ability to solve math word problems. Students with ASD also may process information differently and have difficulty when instruction is presented at the abstract level. They may be more concrete in their thinking and require scaffolding to move beyond thinking literally to understanding abstract concepts and ideas. Students with ASD may continually be faced with challenges because academic expectations often require students to use reading comprehension skills, writing skills, and abstract reasoning, which may lead to the occurrence of challenging behavior.

Deficits in Fine and Gross Motor Skills

Students with ASD often have poor fine or gross motor skills (Lloyd, MacDonald, & Lord, 2013; Provost, Lopez, & Heimerl, 2007) along with coordination and balance problems (Dunn, Myles, & Orr, 2002). This can pose behavioral challenges when students are expected to participate in activities and complete assignments that require the use of well-developed motor skills. Students with ASD may engage in challenging behavior in physical education classes to avoid activities involving gross motor skills, coordination, and balance if they have impairments in these areas. Students who seem to be displaying aggressive behaviors may be doing so because of difficulties with proprioception (i.e., one's sense of where one's body is located and how it is oriented in space). For example, a student may push another student down by accident when getting in line because of problems with sensing his or her own position and movement. Thus, he or she is unable to adjust his or her behavior accordingly when approaching others so as to not bump into them. Fine motor skills may also be an area of weakness that affects classroom behavior. Writing assignments are a common trigger for challenging behavior for students who have fine motor skills deficits. Although they may be able to write one-word responses with some ease, lengthy written responses can be quite taxing, especially when weaknesses in fine motor skills are paired with potential difficulties with language and written expression.

Medical Conditions

A multitude of medical conditions can potentially affect the classroom behavior of students with ASD. Approximately 8%–30% of students with ASD have epilepsy (Spence & Schneider, 2009). Following the occurrence of seizures, children may have extreme lethargy and difficulties engaging and complying with teacher directives. Epilepsy can also cause problems with focus and attention, challenging behavior, and mood disorders (Simonoff et al., 2008).

Also, between 23%–70% of individuals with ASD suffer from gastrointestinal (GI) problems (Chaidez, Hansen, & Hertz-Picciotto, 2014), including abdominal pain, bloating, diarrhea, and constipation. Certainly, if a student is experiencing GI problems, then it can negatively affect behavior in school due to the pain and discomfort associated with the condition. The behavioral challenges can be intensified for students who are unable to communicate when they are not feeling well. This is also true for more common illnesses such as colds, other illnesses resulting from viruses, sinus infections, and allergies.

Furthermore, because many students with ASD take medications for conditions such as anxiety, ADHD, repetitive behaviors, epilepsy, or aggression, challenging behaviors can also result from side effects to medications. Finally, the prevalence of sleep disorders in individuals with ASD is very high, with estimates ranging from 50% to 80% (Krakowiak, Goodlin-Jones, Hertz-Picciotto, Croen, & Hansen, 2008). Most people can agree that they are not necessarily on their best behavior when they do not get enough sleep. Thus, consistent sleep problems paired with the other characteristics of ASD can result in significant behavioral challenges in the classroom.

SUMMARY

This chapter provided an overview of the core diagnostic features of ASD and other co-occurring characteristics these students may also display. It is important to note that each of these characteristics has a greater affect when different characteristics occur in conjunction with one another. For example, a student who has severe anxiety and fear and also struggles with emotional regulation will have a very difficult time remaining calm when feeling worried or afraid. A student who has problems with focus and attention and also has executive functioning challenges will have increased difficulty completing multistep tasks because these tasks require the ability to focus and attend as well as organization and planning skills. Students who exhibit many of the characteristics discussed in this chapter are likely to exhibit behavioral challenges in the classroom. Yet, if you begin to understand that these problems are a result of ASD characteristics and not necessarily maladaptive behaviors, then you will be able to plan better interventions and supports. This in turn will help students cope with the challenges they face and learn new skills to improve their ability to thrive in academic and social settings.

CHAPTER 2

Multi-Tiered Systems of Support for Students With ASD

This chapter provides an overview of MTSS with explanations for how the MTSS framework can be used to address the academic and behavioral needs of students with ASD. Evidence-based practices that can be used to prevent behavioral challenges of students with ASD and remediate problems as early as possible after onset are introduced and explained. This chapter includes additional resources readers can gain access to for more information on the various practices that are also included in the sample intervention plans in later chapters, indicated in bold, italicized font. Thus, as you read subsequent chapters in this book, you can use typographical cues for easy reference back to this chapter any time you want to review specific information and gain access to the recommended resources.

INTRODUCTION TO MTSS

The MTSS framework combines the positive behavior interventions and supports (PBIS) framework that was developed to support students with challenging behaviors and the response to intervention (RTI) framework that focuses on the academic needs of struggling learners. The PBIS and RTI frameworks use tiered intervention models, which means that different levels of research-based intervention and support are given to students, with the intensity of supports and frequency of data collection for progress monitoring purposes increasing at different tiers (Vaughn & Linan-Thompson, 2003). Tier 1 instruction and supports are research-based approaches used with all learners in the classroom to prevent challenging behavior and optimize learning. Students who need more than Tier 1 supports to address their behavioral and academic needs, receive additional specialized interventions to address areas of weakness (Tier 2). Intensive, individualized Tier 3 interventions and supports are provided if a student continues to struggle behaviorally or academically. Because behavioral needs and academic needs occur in conjunction with one another, it does not make sense to have two separate frameworks (RTI and PBIS). This means the problems of many students with behavioral challenges are related to their academic deficits. Likewise, students' academic needs may be a result of their challenging behaviors. Thus, separating behavior and academic interventions and supports into two systems is not the most efficient and effective way to address challenges.

The MTSS model combines academic and behavioral supports into one comprehensive framework. Differentiated instruction using research-based practices is provided through tiered intervention and supports for purposes of preventing academic and behavioral challenges or remediating problems as early as possible after onset, as opposed to using reactive procedures after the severity of students' behavior or academic challenges become extremely problematic. Second, the intention of MTSS is to deliver supports within the context of the general education classroom to the maximum extent appropriate, using layered supports and collaboration among general and special education teachers, related services providers, families, and the student whenever possible. This collaboration and team approach is essential to the intervention process because there is no other way to fully understand the various strengths, interests, and needs of the student without considering various perspectives. The collaboration should be ongoing and occur both formally through individualized education program (IEP) meetings as well as teacher planning meetings, parent conferences, e-mails, telephone calls, communication logs, and informal assessments in the classroom. The team must be knowledgeable about the student's passions, areas in which the student excels, present levels of academic and functional performance, and ways in which specific ASD characteristics discussed in Chapter 1 affect the student.

MTSS FOR STUDENTS WITH ASD

Students with ASD may have various academic and behavioral challenges due to their unique characteristics (see Chapter 1). It is important that teachers recognize that many of their challenges can be addressed at the Tier 1 and Tier 2 levels without needing the most intensive behavioral and academic interventions and supports at the Tier 3 level. The following sections explain a multitude of evidence-based and research-supported practices that can be used in classroom settings to be preventative at the Tier 1 level and offer immediate remediation and support at the Tier 2 level. Chapter 3 focuses on providing Tier 3 supports through FBA, leading to the development and implementation of comprehensive behavioral intervention plans.

As you read the specific strategies discussed next, keep in mind that it often is most effective to use two or more strategies in conjunction with one another when planning and implementing a comprehensive intervention, rather than relying on one strategy alone. Using a combination of strategies is often more effective in getting a student to learn a specific replacement behavior or reach a desired outcome.

Tier 1 Supports and Interventions for Students With ASD

Many practices can be used by teachers for all students that will prevent challenging behaviors for students with ASD. These are the approaches that are part of Tier 1 interventions and supports. If teachers utilize the interventions and supports explained next, then the frequency and intensity of challenging behaviors for students with ASD and other students in the class will certainly decrease. Although these approaches do require planning and time allotted for the delivery of the supports and interventions, the intent is that these are part of the everyday planning and instructional practices in the classroom. Progress should be monitored by collecting data once a week on general classroom expectations to document the behavioral outcomes for students with ASD. These can be simple measures, such as rating scales that document the level at which the students are meeting classroom behavioral expectations. Figure 2.1 shows an example of a Tier 1 progress monitoring tool.

Set Clear Expectations

Be sure to clearly define academic, behavioral, and social expectations for various school contexts. Although having three to five positively stated classroom rules is part of this, many expectations beyond what is stated in classroom rules will need to be explained to students with ASD. For example, the expectations for one-to-one instruction, small-group instruction, whole-group instruction, independent work, and group work are often quite different. Students may be expected to raise their hands and wait to be called on during whole-group

Directions: Highlight or circle the appropriate rating for each expectation. Create a line graph by connecting the ratings each week to determine if the student is progressing, making no progress, or regressing.

Expectations	Week of ____	Week of ____	Week of ____	Week of ____	Week of ____	Week of ____
Follow teacher directions	4 3 2 1	4 3 2 1	4 3 2 1	4 3 2 1	4 3 2 1	4 3 2 1
Participate during group instruction	4 3 2 1	4 3 2 1	4 3 2 1	4 3 2 1	4 3 2 1	4 3 2 1
Complete independent classwork	4 3 2 1	4 3 2 1	4 3 2 1	4 3 2 1	4 3 2 1	4 3 2 1
Respect others	4 3 2 1	4 3 2 1	4 3 2 1	4 3 2 1	4 3 2 1	4 3 2 1
Make transition appropriately in and out of the classroom	4 3 2 1	4 3 2 1	4 3 2 1	4 3 2 1	4 3 2 1	4 3 2 1

Use the following key to indicate a rating for each behavioral expectation:
1: Maximum teacher support and prompting
2: Moderate levels of teacher support and prompting
3: Minimal levels of teacher support and prompting
4: Little or no teacher support needed

Figure 2.1. Sample Tier 1 progress monitoring tool.

instruction and during independent work, but it may be acceptable to give answers and ask questions without raising hands during one-to-one instruction and small-group instruction. Without direct teaching of these differences in expectations across situations, students with ASD often do not naturally pick up on them.

Explicitly Teach Expectations

Although some students with ASD can learn the expectations through verbal instruction, most need other instructional formats to fully understand expectations and be able to demonstrate what is expected. Using the "I Do It," "We Do It," "You Do It" instructional format is one way to provide the ***explicit instruction*** necessary and involves the following: 1) telling the students the expectation and modeling the expected behavior during the "I Do It" phase of instruction; 2) providing opportunities for supported guided practice using appropriate levels of scaffolding with immediate positive and corrective feedback during the "We Do It" phase; and 3) providing independent practice opportunities during the "You Do It" phase for students to demonstrate the expectations during naturally occurring situations and receive immediate feedback.

Students with ASD may need additional instructional supports if verbal instruction and physical modeling and guided practice is not enough. The "I Do It" phase may need to include ***visual supports***. Visual supports help students who have language comprehension difficulties, problems with focus and attention, and executive functioning challenges and include pictures or symbols, cue cards, lists, and video clips. To teach the expectation of only speaking when called on by the teacher during group instruction, you can provide a picture of a child raising his or her hand and waiting to be called on, a cue card that says, "Raise your hand," or a video clip that shows another student or the student with ASD raising his or her hand and waiting to be called on during group instruction. ***Video modeling*** is when you use video clips of another student demonstrating the desired expectation. ***Video self-modeling*** is when the video is of the student him- or herself (Bellini & Akullian, 2007). Of course, behind the scenes prompting and video editing is often needed to create video self-modeling clips because the student may not independently perform the expectation prior to ***explicit instruction***. Information about using this technique and other recommended techniques in this chapter is available through training modules provided by the Autism Internet Modules web site (see the Resources section at the end of this chapter for links to this and other resources).

Using ***social narratives*** is another way to enhance the "I Do It" phase of instruction. Social narratives are visually presented stories that describe expectations for specific situations using language at the student's level of understanding. Examples of social narratives include Social Stories (Gray, 2010), comic strip conversations (Gray, 1994), or Power Cards (Gagnon, 2001). See the training module provided by the Autism Internet Modules web site listed in the Resources section at the end of this chapter for more information about social narratives. Although video modeling and social narratives are typically used at the Tier 2 and 3 levels, they can also be used at Tier 1 to help all students in the class more efficiently and effectively learn the academic, behavioral, and social expectations. Using these supports at Tier 1 may prevent problems that could arise and need to be addressed at Tier 2 or Tier 3.

Reinforce Students Who Meet Expectations

It is important to deliver ***positive reinforcement*** when students meet the expectations that have been clearly stated and explicitly taught. Most students with ASD respond very well to social positive reinforcement (e.g., smiles, specific praise, high-fives, fist bumps). Keep in mind, however, that positive reinforcement is only positive reinforcement when it is delivered immediately following a behavior and increases the likelihood that the behavior will continue or increase in the future (Alberto & Troutman, 2012; Cooper, Heron, & Heward, 2007). Thus, if the student does not maintain or increase the desired behavior when social reinforcement is used, then you may need to use token reinforcement, activity reinforcement, or tangible reinforcement. See the training module provided by the Autism Internet Modules web site listed in the Resources section at the end of this chapter for more information on the different types of positive reinforcement and reinforcement schedules.

Use a Hierarchy of Supportive Consequences When Students Do Not Meet Expectations

If students with ASD do not meet certain behavioral, social, or academic expectations, then teachers should use consequences that help redirect the student to the desired behavior. This can be done using a hierarchy of supportive consequences such as the following:

1. ***Proximity control:*** Stand near the student to promote positive behavior.
2. ***Planned ignoring:*** Provide specific praise to the peer closest to the student performing the desirable behavior, provide an opportunity for the student to adjust behavior accordingly, and positively reinforce the student if positive behavior is demonstrated.
3. ***Provide a visual reminder:*** Use a gesture, cue card, picture, or symbol to remind the student of the expectation.
4. ***Provide a verbal reminder:*** State the behavioral expectation positively and with encouragement.

5. ***Provide assistance:*** Help the student meet the behavioral expectation by modeling the behavioral expectation and having the student imitate or helping the student get started with an academic task.
6. ***Provide a safe place for deescalation:*** If the student is unable to meet the expectations and gets emotionally distressed, then allow the student to calm down in a specially designed area of the classroom. The student will return to the ongoing classroom activities once regulated and calm.

Explicit Instruction of Academic Skills

Students with ASD often require explicit, systematic instruction when learning new academic skills. This is also true for students with other disabilities and many typically developing students. The basic structure for ***explicit instruction*** is the "I Do It," "We Do It," "You Do It" format described earlier in the chapter. Many elements of instruction may be altered, however, when using ***explicit instruction***. *Explicit Instruction: Effective and Efficient Teaching* (Archer & Hughes, 2011), is an excellent resource for teachers who want to learn how to improve the quality of their instruction for all students. The book provides a comprehensive framework for delivering quality instruction and includes many evidence-based practices. Some of the practices discussed that will improve instruction for students with ASD at the Tier 1 level (and are referenced in sample intervention plans in later chapters of this book) include ***increased opportunities to respond; think-pair-share; promote high levels of success; use clear, consistent, and concise language; prompting/fading procedures; graphic organizers, choral responding;*** and ***response cards***. Visit the Explicit Instruction web site listed in the Resources section at the end of this chapter for more information about ***explicit instruction***.

Use Concrete Examples

When teaching new skills to students with ASD, it is important to use concrete examples the students can understand before moving directly into teaching abstract concepts. The ***concrete-representational-abstract (CRA)*** strategy is commonly used to teach mathematical skills by first teaching a new skill using manipulatives, then moving on to pictorial representations, and finally teaching the abstract concept (Miller & Mercer, 1993). Although this approach should certainly be used for mathematics instruction, it can also be applied to other content areas. Students with ASD often struggle with social studies content because too often it is primarily taught at the abstract level with a heavy focus on reading to learn utilizing texts that may be quite challenging to comprehend (Gersten, Baker, Smith-Johnson, Dimino, & Peterson, 2006). This may also be true for science and language arts content. It is important to first teach concepts using concrete approaches because students with ASD often think literally and have trouble understanding abstract concepts. This may include using manipulatives and models, but it can also include connecting to things that are familiar to the student to teach abstract concepts. For example, a teacher who is talking about conduction may bring in a pan and talk about what would happen if you touch the pan when it is hot (as opposed to relying on sharing a definition and giving one or two verbal examples).

Tier 2 Supports and Interventions for Students With ASD

Although some students with ASD may only need high-quality Tier 1 instruction and supports, most of these children will need additional interventions due to their various characteristics and needs. The following sections provide an overview of a multitude of evidence-based practices that can be used to address their behavioral, academic, and social needs. More information and guidance for many of the strategies and approaches described is available through the National Professional Development Center on Autism Spectrum Disorders web site and the Autism Internet Modules web site, both listed in Resources section at the end

Targeted objective: The student will complete independent work with little or no support from the teacher.

Criterion for mastery: The student completes at least 75% of independent classwork assignments each week with little or no support from the teacher.

Interventions and supports provided: ***Task analysis, self-monitoring, least-to-most prompting and fading procedures, positive reinforcement***

Directions: Divide the number of classwork assignments completed with little or no support from the teacher for the week by the total number of assignments given that week to get a percentage. Highlight the percentage to determine if the student is progressing, making no improvement, or regressing.

	Week of 10/1	Week of 10/8	Week of 10/15	Week of 10/22	Week of 10/29
91%—100%					
81%—90%					
71%—80%					
61%—70%					
51%—60%					
41%—50%					
31%—40%					
21%—30%					
11%—20%					
1%—10%					
0%					

Figure 2.2. Sample Tier 2 progress monitoring tool.

of this chapter. The interventions discussed are intended to be embedded within everyday instructional and noninstructional routines and activities to add an additional layer of support to what is already being implemented at Tier 1. Progress should be monitored by collecting data once a week on targeted objectives to document the outcomes of Tier 2 interventions and supports for the student with ASD. These can be simple measures, such as rating scales that document the level to which the student is meeting behavioral expectations in the classroom, or more objective measures, such as percentage data, interval data, and frequency data. Criterion for mastery should be set for each targeted objective to determine when the desired outcome has been reached. Figure 2.2 shows an example of a completed Tier 2 progress monitoring tool.

Provide Visual Supports

It is common for teachers to deliver the majority of their instruction using verbal directions, lectures, and discussions, which can be a barrier to students with ASD considering their potential language and social impairments. Students with ASD benefit from the use of ***visual supports*** to promote learning and positive behavior. Examples of visual supports include ***visual schedules, activity schedules, graphic organizers, pictures, symbols, charts, graphs, maps, cue cards, scripts,*** and ***visual boundaries***. More information about creating and using these supports is available through the Autism Internet Modules web site listed in the Resources section at the end of this chapter.

Increase Active Engagement

Students with ASD typically cannot just sit and get information. They need to be actively engaged in instructional activities to optimize learning and prevent challenging behaviors from occurring. Examples of ways to increase active engagement include, but are not limited to, the following:

- Provide opportunities for students to draw to represent information they are learning.
- Provide ***guided notes*** for students to complete during lessons (e.g., notes or outlines with blanks to fill in, graphic organizers to complete during instruction).
- Plan for opportunities for movement during the lesson.
- Use increased questioning.
- Embed their passions and fascinations into the lesson.
- Use hands-on learning activities.
- Show video clips to demonstrate concepts.
- Conduct experiments.
- Use cooperative learning activities.

Following the student's lead is another way to increase active engagement. This is a good strategy to use with students who have significant deficits in joint attention. The teacher initiates engagement with something the student is focused on to establish joint attention and reciprocal exchanges. You can also follow the student's lead by positively responding to comments the student makes and questions he or she asks during group instruction even if they seem off of the topic. Try to find a way to respond that acknowledges the ideas shared by the student but also connects to the lesson. (The web site of Dr. Paula Kluth, an educator who has worked extensively with students with ASD, provides strategies for doing this; see the Resources section at the end of this chapter for more information.)

Arrange the Environment to Address Student Needs

Classroom environments can be quite overwhelming for students with ASD. There are ways to make ***environmental arrangements,*** however, to adjust to student needs. Stimuli in the classroom needs to be considered for those students who have sensory processing problems. They may need modifications to lighting if fluorescent lighting causes discomfort or overstimulation, removal of excess clutter, noise reduction, modified materials to adapt to sensory needs, and so forth. Students who have difficulties with focus and attention may need preferential seating, an individually constructed study area when intense focus is needed, and clearly defined work spaces. If a student has emotional regulation difficulties, then it would be helpful to create a safe space or cool down area that the student can use if emotionally distressed.

In addition to the special area for emotional regulation, the student may also need ***emotional regulation strategies***. For example, using an emotional thermometer or rating scale helps students identify their emotional states and choose coping strategies or calming activities to implement before returning to their task. The Incredible 5-Point Scale (Buron & Curtis, 2003) is one example, and a training module about this approach can be found on the Autism Internet Modules web site in the Resources section at the end of this chapter. In addition, *Exploring Feelings: Cognitive Behaviour Therapy to Manage Anxiety* (Attwood, 2004) discusses various strategies to help students with ASD regulate their emotions, such as physical, social, cognitive, special interest, or relaxation activities that may be calming for the student.

Prompting and Fading Procedures

Using prompting and fading procedures can help ensure student success. Prompts can be physical, gestural, visual, or auditory (Wolery, Ault, & Doyle, 1992). ***Modeling/request imitation*** is another form of a prompt that involves showing the student what to do and immediately giving the student an opportunity to imitate your model and receive feedback (Buffington, Krantz, McClannahan, & Poulson, 1998). Two main ways to use prompting and fading procedures are ***least-to-most prompting*** and ***most-to-least prompting*** (or graduated guidance) (Alberto & Troutman, 2012; Cooper et al., 2007). When using least-to-most or most-to-least prompting, you develop a hierarchy of prompts that would be necessary to support a student in successful responding. If you are using least-to-most prompting, then you begin with the least intrusive prompt you think the student needs to be successful and increase the prompting supports if necessary. If you are using most-to-least prompting (graduated guidance), then you begin with intensive prompting and fade it out with successive opportunities. In either case, the goal is to eventually fade all prompts until the student responds independently. More information about these prompting systems is available through the Autism Internet Modules web site listed in the Resources section at the end of this chapter.

Time-delay is another strategy used in conjunction with prompting and involves systematically waiting for a student to respond before delivering a prompt for purposes of decreasing prompt dependency. Zero-second time-delay (or simultaneous prompting) is used when you are asking the student to do something he or she has not done before to ensure immediate success. Constant and progressive time-delay are used to encourage student responses without necessitating prompts (Browder & Snell, 2000). Constant time-delay uses a set waiting period (e.g., 5 seconds) before delivering a prompt. Progressive time-delay gradually increases the waiting period from 2 seconds up to 6 seconds with successive trials (Wolery, Bailey, & Sugai, 1988). Teachers should use expectant, positive affect and body language while waiting for a response to encourage a response from the student.

Use Motivational Strategies

Using a ***strengths- and interests-based approach*** is one way to increase the motivation of students with ASD. Students with ASD often have a restricted range of interests and may have skill deficits in communication, social, and academic skills (see Chapter 1). Much of what is presented to them at school is uninteresting (or boring) and difficult. No wonder many of these children have problems with motivation. Teachers can create a real game changer when they shift from a deficits-based model to a strengths- and interest-based model, which means the majority of instruction taps into the strengths and interests of the student, addressing skill deficits within activities that are also enjoyable and have easy tasks included. *Just Give Him the Whale: 20 Ways to Use Fascinations, Areas of Expertise, and Strengths to Support Students with Autism* (Kluth & Schwarz, 2008) is an excellent resource for considering creative ways to motivate students with ASD by tapping into their strengths and interests.

Teachers can use the ***behavioral momentum*** strategy (also referred to as ***high-probability instructional sequences***) (Mace et al., 1988) to increase the motivations of students with ASD to attempt difficult tasks. This means using a repeated pattern of easy-easy-difficult-easy-easy-difficult to support student motivation. Students with ASD often get anxious and fearful when presented with challenging tasks and have difficulty regulating their emotions, which may result in challenging behaviors. Presenting two or three easy tasks prior to each difficult task, however, can reduce anxiety a great deal. Academic success is one of the most natural reinforcers available to students. Thus, students with ASD are naturally reinforced by quick success when they are given two or three easy problems to solve or tasks to complete. This builds the momentum they need to attempt a more challenging problem or task that comes next. This approach can also be applied by using a repeated pattern of preferred-preferred-nonpreferred-preferred-preferred-nonpreferred tasks to address the motivational needs of students with a restricted range of interests.

Teachers can also use ***increased choice making*** to increase the motivations of students with ASD. Many people describe the purpose of challenging behavior of students with ASD as a need for control. Considering that many students with ASD have no control over their own bodies due to sensory processing problems, have limited opportunities to make choices due to communication deficits, and are often unable to effectively negotiate to have more input into decisions made on their behalf, it makes sense that they would engage in challenging behavior to try to have some control over their own lives. This is not a behavior problem, but a basic human need. Therefore, provide as many opportunities as possible for students with ASD to make choices throughout the school day to fulfill this need and improve motivation in the classroom. This can entail choosing study topics, materials, or ways to learn new material (e.g., read, listen to an audio clip, watch a video, have a small-group discussion); choosing who to work with during partner and group activities; choosing how to demonstrate learning (e.g., write an essay, answer multiple-choice questions, draw a picture, give an oral response, deliver a presentation, create a model); choosing scheduling of tasks, and so forth.

Prepare Students in Advance

Many students with ASD get extremely anxious and fearful when a change in the normal routine occurs because their need for sameness, sensory processing problems, social impairments, and other skill deficits. They are able to handle changes much better, however, when they are prepared in advanced using a strategy called ***priming*** (Koegel, Koegel, Frea, & Green-Hopkins, 2003). Teachers can explain an upcoming change verbally, in writing, or using ***social narratives***.

Priming can also be used to prepare students in advance for upcoming lessons and activities in the classroom. Teachers can preteach skills and concepts in small-group or one-to-one contexts to prepare the student for an upcoming whole-group lesson. This will provide the student with essential content and understanding of the lesson format, ultimately reducing the likelihood of challenging behaviors when the actual lesson takes place. Parents can also be involved in priming by preparing the student at home for an upcoming lesson or schedule change.

Make Sure Academic and Behavioral Expectations Are Developmentally Appropriate

Students with ASD may require extensive differentiation of instruction to address their needs, depending on their present levels of academic and behavioral performance. Teachers cannot simply set the same objectives for all students in the class without considering whether the objectives are appropriate and feasible for each student. Using the ***shaping*** strategy is one way to differentiate. *Shaping* means you reinforce success approximations of a desired behavior (Alberto & Troutman, 2012; Cooper et al., 2007) by first determining the student's baseline performance for a particular behavior or skill (e.g., works independently for 1 minute). Then you set an achievable target (e.g., works independently for 2 minutes) and positively reinforce the student when that target is reached. You continue this pattern until the student reaches the desired outcome (e.g., works independently for 15 minutes).

Partial participation is another way to involve the student in developmentally appropriate instructional activities (Ferguson & Baumgart, 1991). This is primarily used for students with more severe cognitive impairments who can benefit from participating in instructional activities but require adaptations or individualized objectives that will be focused on during the activity. For example, during a science experiment, the students may be required to write a hypothesis statement, conduct the experiment, record the results, and analyze findings. If a student with ASD is unable to meet all of those expectations, then the student can still participate by verbally predicting what will happen, gathering materials for the experiment, conducting specified steps of the experiment, and drawing a picture to show what happened.

Break Down Multistep Assignments Into Sequential Steps

Students with ASD often need support learning how to complete multistep directions and assignments because of problems with executive functioning and attention and focus. Teachers can use ***task analysis, chaining,*** and ***self-monitoring*** to address this need. Task analysis involves breaking complex assignments or directions down into simple, sequential steps and then teaching the steps using forward chaining, backward chaining, or total task presentation (Alberto & Troutman, 2012; Cooper et al., 2007). A teacher using forward chaining teaches the first step, then the second step, and so forth until the student can put it all together and complete the entire task independently. A teacher using backward chaining teaches the last step, then the second-to-last step, and so forth until the student can complete the entire task without support. A teacher using total task presentation involves the student in the entire task, increasing independence with whatever steps the student is ready to perform. ***Self-monitoring*** tools can be used by students with ASD to provide a visual representation of the individual steps of the task (either in words or pictures) because they often require visual supports to learn due to language impairments, executive functioning challenges, and problems with focus and attention, and students can check off each step as it is completed (Coyle & Cole, 2004). More guidance on implementing task analysis and self-monitoring tools is available at the Autism Internet Modules web site listed in the Resources section at the end of this chapter.

Point-of-view video modeling is another way to help students learn how to complete multistep tasks and involves showing a video clip of the task being performed from the student's perspective (Hine & Wolery, 2006). A video clip that removes all extraneous information and purely focuses on the steps of the task can be quite effective in teaching students with ASD how to perform complex tasks because they often have focus and attention problems. The video can be shown in its entirety, or ***video prompting*** can be used to show each step in isolation, and the student can perform the step before the next step is shown (Cannella-Malone et al., 2006).

Refrain From Positively Reinforcing Challenging Behavior

It is quite natural for teachers to respond negatively when students engage in challenging behavior. They may deliver reprimands, show negative facial expressions, remove the child from the activity or classroom, and so forth. Although most would call these things punishment, *punishment* means that consequences are delivered immediately following a behavior that decrease the likelihood that the behavior will occur again in the future. If teachers are honest, then they will admit that these punitive consequences are not decreasing the challenging behavior and actually increase the challenging behavior in many cases. This occurs because the consequences intended as punitive actually serve as positive reinforcement for students who are seeking attention and for those who enjoy the predictable reactions they observe due to their need for sameness. You may think students would not enjoy negative attention, but the truth is that negative attention is more consistently delivered than positive attention in classroom settings without the implementation of teacher training to turn that around (Cook et al., 2017). Thus, students quickly learn that engaging in challenging behavior is the most effective and efficient way to get teacher attention. Teachers should use ***differential reinforcement*** to address this issue (Alberto & Troutman, 2012; Cooper et al., 2007). You completely refrain from attending to challenging behaviors while increasing your positive reinforcement for desirable behaviors. More information about the multiple ways to utilize differential reinforcement is available through the Autism Internet Modules web site in the Resources section at the end of this chapter.

Provide Expressive Communication Supports

Students with ASD who have expressive communication skills deficits will require support to effectively communicate in the classrooms through the use of ***augmentative and alternative communication (AAC).*** AAC can be low tech or high tech. Low-tech AAC includes communicating using arrays of pictures or symbols, response cards, and simple switches with prerecorded words or messages. High-tech AAC includes communication devices such as the Dynavox or apps on the iPad or other tablets, such as Proloquo2go. Whether your student is using low-tech or high-tech AAC, it is important that the student has opportunities to do more than make requests. Students also need to be able to meaningfully participate in academic and social activities using AAC. Contact the assistive technology (AT) specialist(s) in your school district or state for more support. An AT evaluation may be necessary to determine which AAC supports are best for your student. Students with ASD often need AT supports for written expression because of their language and fine motor skills deficits. They may need to type using computer software or specialized devices instead of writing. Although you can use a ***scribe*** (i.e., have someone write what the student says) you do not want to rely on a scribe alone because it reduces independence. More information on AAC tools is available through the Autism Internet Modules web site in the Resources section at the end of this chapter.

Utilize Peer Supports

Teachers cannot deliver all of the instruction and supports that students with ASD need because they often need intervention in many areas. Peers can be a great source of support for students with ASD, however, if teachers know how to effectively facilitate ***peer-mediated interventions*** (DiSalvo & Oswald, 2002; Odom & Strain, 1984). Peer-mediated interventions occur when teachers provide training to peers on strategies and approaches to use to engage students with ASD and encourage the use of specific skills. It is important that teachers set up situations using ***balanced turn-taking*** (Landa, 2007) so that peers can support students with ASD in learning social reciprocity skills. This means that the interactions are designed with clear procedures for facilitating long chains of back-and-forth interactions. Steps for peer-mediated interventions are provided at the Autism Internet Modules web site listed in the Resources section at the end of this chapter.

Embed Social-Communication Intervention Within Existing Routines and Activities

It is important to continually take advantage of naturally occurring opportunities to enhance the social-communication skills of students with ASD. ***Incidental teaching*** is one way to do this and involves using the student's motivation to encourage the use of targeted social-communication skills (McGee, Krantz, & McClannahan, 1986). For example, if the student wants to play with a soccer ball during recess and runs to go get it, then get there first to provide an opportunity for the student to ask for it instead of just grabbing it. Here is a more advanced example: if the student likes to research different breeds of dogs on the Internet after finishing seat work, require the student to ask for permission to do so, and have a brief conversation about what information will be explored prior to allowing access to the computer.

Teachers can also embed ***discrete trials*** (Lovaas, 1987) during ongoing routines and activities to teach targeted social communication skills. This involves three basic steps:

1. Provide an antecedent (e.g., ask a question, make a comment, give a direction).
2. Deliver a prompt (if necessary) to support a successful response.
3. Provide positive reinforcement after the student successfully responds.

If the student does not successfully respond, then the third step should involve error correction procedures followed by positive reinforcement after the student is able to correctly respond. For example, the teacher asks the student to name his or her favorite kind of pet during guided reading of a book about adopting a pet. The teacher prompts the student by showing a picture with several pets from which to choose. The student says, "dog." The teacher delivers positive reinforcement by smiling, giving the student a high-five, and saying, "Great! You would love to have a dog!" Several training modules relevant for social-communication intervention are provided at the Autism Internet Modules web site listed in the Resources section at the end of this chapter.

Teach Functional Communication Skills

Many students with ASD engage in challenging behavior because they are not equipped with the functional communication skills needed to express themselves in various situations. For example, children with ASD often do not naturally learn how to say phrases such as, "I don't know," "Can you help me?" "What do you mean?" "I don't feel well," or "I can't do this right now." They may resort to using challenging behaviors to communicate those messages because of this deficit. Thus, it is important to teach functional communication skills based on individualized needs. Many students temporarily lose the ability to use their expressive communication skills when they get upset due to emotional regulation difficulties. Use expressive communication supports, such as visuals and AAC options, to address this fact for students who are nonverbal as well as those who are verbal. More information about teaching functional communication skills is available at the Autism Internet Modules web site listed in the Resources section at the end of this chapter.

Teach Social Problem-Solving Skills

Students with ASD often do not have the social problem-solving skills needed to effectively handle a situation in which they are in conflict with a peer or group of peers. They may resort to aggression or other challenging behaviors because they cannot see a feasible alternative. ***Social autopsies*** (Lavoie, 2006) and the ***SOCCSS*** (Situation, Options, Consequences, Choices, Strategies, Simulation) strategy (Myles & Simpson, 2001) are two strategies that can be used or adapted to teach students how to engage in social problem solving. These two strategies are typically used after a problem occurred and was not handled positively to help the student think about alternative choices that could have been made that would have led to desired outcomes without the use of problematic behavior. You involve the student in a dialogue in a social autopsy to identify the following:

- What happened?
- What was the social error?
- Who was hurt by the social error?
- What should be done to correct the social error?
- What could be done next time?

The SOCCSS strategy is used to engage the student in a dialogue to identify the who, what, when, where, and why of the situation; the desired outcome; and various options for alternative ways to handle the situation with associated consequences for each option. The student then chooses the best option(s) for future situations and participates in simulations to practice the selected option(s).

Although the social autopsy and SOCCSS strategies are typically used after a social problem has occurred, these strategies can also be used when a student does utilize positive social problem-solving skills to highlight what the student did well and positively reinforce the student for making good choices. In addition, the strategies can be used during role-play scenarios as a means of explicitly teaching social problem-solving skills. Additional information and resources related to these strategies are available at the Ohio Center for Autism and Low Incidence (OCALI) web site's Autism Center Resource Gallery, a link to which is provided in the Resources section at the end of this chapter.

Provide Scripts to Support Reciprocal Social Interactions

Because many students with ASD have significant deficits in social reciprocity and conversational skills, the script-fading strategy can be quite helpful when the students are working and socializing with peers (Krantz & McClannahan, 1993). This strategy involves creating a script of what the student and the peer should say in specific situations. Parts of the script are then systematically faded out until the student no longer requires the script to engage in reciprocal interactions during the activity. This can be used during social activities or academic activities.

SUMMARY

This chapter provided information about the MTSS framework and how it can be used to deliver support and intervention to students with ASD in classroom settings. Suggestions for Tier 1 and Tier 2 evidence-based practices that can be used within an MTSS framework to address the unique characteristics and needs of students with ASD were provided. These same strategies and supports can also be used at the Tier 3 level with increased individualization, intensity of intervention, and progress monitoring. When planning comprehensive interventions, it is often best to use many of the strategies included in this chapter in conjunction with one another to achieve desired outcomes. For example, using social narratives, video modeling, self-monitoring, and positive reinforcement to teach a specific replacement behavior would likely be more effective than just using one of those strategies alone. Chapter 3 discusses procedures for conducting FBAs to develop comprehensive behavior intervention plans at the Tier 3 level.

RESOURCES

The following print and online resources provide additional information and tools that will help you implement the recommendations discussed in this chapter.

Print Resources

See *Exploring Feelings: Cognitive Behaviour Therapy to Manage Anxiety* (Attwood, 2004) to learn more about helping students learn to regulate their emotions.

See *Just Give Him the Whale: 20 Ways to Use Fascinations, Areas of Expertise, and Strengths to Support Students with Autism* (Kluth & Schwarz, 2008) to learn more about creative ways to motivate students with ASD by tapping into their strengths and interests.

Online Resources

The Autism Internet Modules web site (http://www.autisminternetmodules.org) provides a wealth of information through training modules that address in depth many of the strategies introduced in this chapter and listed next. Access the home page using the URL provided, use the Module List link to navigate to a list of modules, then follow the link for the specific strategy. Module topics include

- Antecedent-based interventions
- Video modeling
- Social narratives
- Visual supports
- The Incredible 5-Point Scale
- Prompting
- Task analysis

- Self-management/self-monitoring
- Differential reinforcement training
- Picture Exchange Communication System (PECS) and speech-generating devices (SGDs)
- Peer-mediated instruction and intervention
- Discrete trial training, pivotal response training, and naturalistic intervention (used for social-communication intervention during classroom routines and activities)
- Functional communication training

Visit the Explicit Instruction web site at http://www.explicitinstruction.org for more information about explicit instruction.

Visit the National Professional Development Center on Autism Spectrum Disorder web site at http://autismpdc.fpg.unc.edu/evidence-based-practices for more information about evidence-based practices.

Visit educator Paula Kluth's web site at http://www.paulakluth.com to access various resources to learn how to increase the active engagement of students with ASD.

Visit the Resource Gallery of Interventions page of the Ohio Center for Autism and Low Incidence web site at http://www.ocali.org/project/resource_gallery_of_interventions to learn more about social autopsies and the SOCCSS strategy and download related free worksheet templates.

CHAPTER 3

Functional Behavioral Assessment for Students With ASD

Chapter 2 presented various interventions and supports that can be used within an MTSS model to support students with ASD at the Tier 1 and Tier 2 levels of intervention. Providing appropriate individualized interventions and support for students needing Tier 3 interventions involves conducting an FBA to determine why a given behavior is occurring before teaching a more adaptive replacement behavior. Thus, Chapter 3 includes step-by-step FBA procedures to follow when Tier 3 interventions and supports are needed for students with ASD. Although the main functions of challenging behavior are to gain access to something or to escape from or avoid something, this chapter discusses the necessity for thinking beyond these basic functions when examining challenging behaviors of students with ASD in classroom settings. It is important to consider the various characteristics of these students and how these unique traits may affect their behavior in school.

FBA PROCEDURES

When students with ASD continue to display significant behavioral challenges with Tier 1 and 2 supports in place, it is necessary to move to Tier 3 interventions by developing an individualized behavioral intervention plan (BIP) with intensive interventions and frequent data collection for progress monitoring purposes. It is important to conduct an FBA to develop a comprehensive BIP to address the student's unique needs. The FBA approach is built on the premise that information about the nature of the challenging behavior and the environmental contexts in which the behavior is observed is essential before planning intervention (Sugai et al., 1999). Although there are two major functions for challenging behavior—to gain access to something or to escape from or avoid something (Scott & Caron, 2005)—it is important to uncover as much information as possible to determine why a student is trying to get, avoid, or escape from something. The purpose of this book is to help you consider the unique characteristics of students with ASD when determining why a challenging behavior may be occurring. The only way to do so is by gathering meaningful data during the FBA process to learn as much as possible about the student and the student's behavior within the context of the school environment. The following sections discuss each step of the FBA process.

Step 1: Select a Target Behavior

FBAs generally address one target behavior (selected challenging behavior) or class of behaviors. A class of behaviors would be several topographies of one category of behavior. For example, physical aggression may include the following class of behaviors: kicking, spitting, biting, and pushing. Behaviors can also be grouped together if, based on informal observation, the educator predicts that they probably serve the same function. For example, a student may hit others, use self-injurious behaviors, shout out, engage in repetitive behavior, cry, or run out of the room when dealing with problems associated with emotional regulation. List all the challenging behaviors the student exhibits to determine what target behavior or group of behaviors to select for the FBA. The behaviors included on the list need to be specific, observable, and measurable. For example, instead of writing that the student is disruptive, explain the specific disruptive behaviors, such as shouting out, walking around the room, or having tantrums involving crying and screaming. Of course, if there are many disruptive behaviors, then you can group them together as a class under the disruptive behaviors category.

After you list all the challenging behaviors the student exhibits, the next step is to prioritize them to decide what to target first. Certainly, if any of the behaviors are dangerous to the student or others, then it is important to target those first. Do not always assume, however, that the most severe behaviors need to be targeted first. You want to choose the target behavior that could have the greatest impact on the child's classroom performance if it is adequately addressed. For example, suppose a student's behaviors include running around the room instead of completing independent work, using foul language when upset, shouting out during group instruction, and engaging in repetitive behaviors such as vocal self-stimulatory behavior, hand flapping, and rocking. In this scenario, it may be best to begin with the running around the room behavior. If you can effectively support the student in learning how to work independently, then some of the other behaviors may decrease as a result.

Step 2: Collect Baseline Data

After selecting a target behavior, baseline data should be collected. The purpose of collecting baseline data is twofold: 1) to make sure the behavior is occurring frequently enough or with sufficiently high levels of intensity to warrant going through the FBA process and 2) to be able to compare preintervention data with postintervention data to determine if the interventions and supports put in place are resulting in positive outcomes. Baseline data can be collected using any of the following types of data: frequency, rate, percentage, whole-interval or partial-interval recording, time-sampling, rating scales, scatterplot, latency, or duration data. Many of these may already be familiar to you through your work as an educator. In-depth discussion of data collection and types of data is beyond the scope of this book. Information is available online, however, if you wish to learn more. One valuable resource is the Technical Assistance Center on Positive Behavioral Interventions and Supports, established by the U.S. Department of Education's Office of Special Education Programs, and a link to their web site is included in the Resources section at the end of this chapter.

Step 3: Conduct FBA Interviews

After baseline data is collected, interviews should be conducted with teachers, support staff, or related services personnel, as well as the family and (whenever possible) the student, to gather information about why the target behavior may be occurring. It is amazing how much time you can save during the FBA process by asking the actual students why they engage in the challenging behavior. Of course, they may not always be able to respond to interview questions due to deficits in social-communication. Even if they can respond to questions, they do not always know why they do what they do. It is important to interview the students, however, because you may get useful information. Commonly asked questions during the FBA interview include the following:

- When, where, and with whom is the behavior most and least likely to occur?
- What usually happens right before, during, and after the occurrence of the behavior?

- What purpose do you think the behavior is serving for the student? Or, what do you think the student is trying to communicate by engaging in the behavior?
- What behavior or skill can the student learn to replace the challenging behavior?

It is just as important to examine the contexts in which the target behavior is not occurring as it is to examine situations in which it is occurring. By doing so, you will learn what types of variables, interventions, and supports are currently in place in situations in which the challenging behavior does not occur that may be replicated in the environments in which the behavior is occurring. (See the Resources section at the end of this chapter for a link to a sample FBA interview form.)

In addition to the commonly asked questions, it is also important to determine what skill deficiencies and challenges a student with ASD may face that could be affecting the occurrence of the target behavior. Figure 3.1 depicts an example of a data collection tool that can

Does the student have . . .	Yes	No	Notes
Problems with joint attention?			
Problems with social reciprocity?			
Problems developing relationships with peers?			
Nonverbal communication impairments?			
Deficits in specific social skills?			
Repetitive behaviors?			
Nonfunctional rituals that are followed?			
A strong need for sameness?			
Sensory processing problems?			
Language comprehension problems?			
Deficits in expressive communication skills?			
Heightened levels of anxiety and fear?			
Emotional regulation difficulties?			
Problems with focus and attention?			
Executive functioning challenges?			
Academic or cognitive deficits?			
Fine or gross motor skills deficits?			
Medical conditions? Reactions to medications?			

Figure 3.1. Example of a tool to assess the characteristics of autism spectrum disorders during the functional behavioral assessment interview process.

be used during the FBA interview process to gather this information. Refer to Chapter 1 as needed for explanations of each of the items included in the table.

Finally, it is important to gather information about the student's strengths and interests during FBA interviews because it will allow the team to tap into these strengths and interests when developing a comprehensive BIP. Sample questions include the following (Leach, 2010):

- What is the student passionate about?
- What does the student like to do?
- What makes the student happy?
- How does the student prefer to spend unstructured time?
- What are some of the student's favorite things?
- What is something the student would never want to give up?
- In what areas does the student excel?
- What about the student makes you proud?
- What can the student do that many others cannot do?
- What are the student's favorite times of day?
- What keeps the student's attention?
- What are the student's favorite places to go?

Step 4: Conduct Direct Observations

Based on the information gathered during the FBA interviews, plan direct observations to examine the contexts when the behavior is most and least likely to occur. The purpose of these observations is to find out what variables are affecting the student's behavior and what function the behavior is serving for the student (Calloway & Simpson, 1998). There are several ways to record information during these observations, including scatterplot data, A-B-C data, and anecdotal records.

Scatterplot Data

Recording scatterplot data allows you to determine when the behavior is most and least likely to occur. If this information was unclear during baseline data collection and during the FBA process, then it is important to find out. A scatterplot is a grid that includes the different periods, subjects, activities, or times of the day along the left side, with boxes to place tally marks each time the behavior occurs (see Figure 3.2). Thus, it is one format for collecting frequency data that also gives information about when the behavior is most and least likely to occur. If you can collect scatterplot data during baseline data collection, then it will save you time during this step.

A-B-C Data

It is important to collect A-B-C data to gather information about what happens before and after the target behavior occurs. Collect data each time the target behavior occurs, documenting the following: the setting events, the antecedents, the behavior, the consequences, and why the behavior may have occurred (see Figure 3.3). Setting events are the precipitating activities leading up the immediate antecedent (e.g., students are called to the circle for read aloud, the students are waiting in line for 10 minutes to get their pictures taken, recess was

Directions: Use the key below to record the frequency of behaviors. Write the letter for the behavior that occurred during the specific activity. Put as many letters in each box as needed to show the frequency of each behavior. Total the number of occurrences for each activity adding up the number of entries in each box each day.

H: hitting K: kicking B: biting S: spitting at others

	Date:	Date:	Date:	Date:	Date:	Total
Arrival						
Morning work						
Guided reading						
Centers						
Math						
Related arts						
Lunch						
Recess						
Science/social studies						
Dismissal						

Figure 3.2. Sample scatterplot data sheet.

Date/time	Setting events	Antecedent	Behavior	Consequence	Why did the behavior occur? What purpose did it serve?
3/10 8:45 a.m.	Students were working in centers while teacher was working with a small group. A teacher assistant typically supervises students working in centers, but that person was pulled out of the class for an emergency.	The student was using crayons to complete a center activity. A peer working on the same activity took the red crayon from the student's pile of crayons.	The student tried to grab the crayon back, but the peer would not give it back. The student then punched the peer on the arm.	The peer yelled and told the teacher. The student took the red crayon and began coloring with it while the peer was telling the teacher. The teacher gave the peer a red crayon to use.	The student has expressive communication deficits and did not know how to ask for the crayon back. The student has emotional regulation difficulties and got very upset when the red crayon was taken. The student has not yet learned social skills such as sharing and turn-taking. The student gained access to the crayon.

Figure 3.3. Sample A-B-C data sheet.

ended early due to rain). The antecedent is what happens right before the behavior occurs. The behavior section explains the topography of the target behavior. The consequence section includes what happened immediately following the behavior. The last section can be used to analyze the information to suggest a reason why the behavior may have occurred or the purpose it served for the student.

Anecdotal Records

Although not always necessary, you may find it useful to collect anecdotal records during direct observations in addition to A-B-C data. Create a transcript with the exact observable details that occurred prior to the occurrence of the challenging behavior and what happened after the behavior occurred. Although the A-B-C data is usually a summary, anecdotal records include the exact words stated by individuals and clear descriptions of what was happening in the environment. Observers often collect anecdotal records and then summarize the information therein using A-B-C data sheets.

Step 5: Triangulate the Data to Form a Hypothesis

After all of the FBA interviews and direct observations are completed, you should analyze all of the information to formulate a hypothesis for why the challenging behavior may be occurring. This is called *triangulating the data* because you should have at least three sources of information to compile and analyze. (See the Resources section at the end of this chapter for information about locating a sample data triangulation form online.)

A hypothesis should address the purpose the behavior serves for the student and how the behavior is related to setting events, antecedents, and consequences, and it may also include information about skill deficits (see Figure 3.4) (Scheuermann & Webber, 2002). It may also be helpful to include information about when the target behavior does not occur because this may help the team tap into the student's strengths and interests when developing the BIP.

Step 6: Test the Hypothesis

Although school-based professionals may be tempted to skip this step, it is quite helpful to actually test out your hypothesis to make sure it is accurate before developing a BIP based on a faulty hypothesis. This process is called *functional analysis* and involves manipulating variables in the environment to prove or disprove your hypothesis. For example, suppose you hypothesize that a student with ASD will follow directions when they are given using nonverbal methods (e.g., giving the direction in writing; showing the student what to do using ***pictures, symbols,*** or video clips; ***modeling*** what the student is supposed to do and having the student imitate your model; providing a checklist) as opposed to relying on auditory directions. You can conduct a functional analysis to test your hypothesis using the following steps:

1. Give five directions that rely on understanding the verbal (oral) language. Record the percentage of directions the student followed independently (without prompting). Get a percentage by dividing the number of correct, independent responses by the total number of directions given.
2. Give five different directions of comparable complexity using nonverbal methods. Record the percentage of directions the student followed correctly and independently.
3. Compare the two percentages: successful compliance when directions were given using purely verbal methods versus successful compliance when directions were given nonverbally. The hypothesis can be confirmed if the percentage of compliance is higher when directions are given nonverbally.

Student A The student has difficulty following directions due to language comprehension issues. The student is able to follow directions when they are given using very simple sentences or are familiar to him or her. When directions are given using more complex language or if they are unfamiliar, then he or she may not follow directions or may follow directions incorrectly due to receptive communication deficits.
Student B The student has difficulty working independently due to deficits in reading, writing, and math skills as well as weaknesses in fine motor skills. For reading tasks, the student is able to follow directions to read independently, but he or she often has trouble with reading comprehension assignments that include answering multiple-choice questions or writing short responses to comprehension questions. For math assignments, the student is able to complete up to 10 computation problems when the problems contain previously mastered skills, but he or she is unable to work independently when the problems contain skills he or she is currently working to improve. The student is able to fill out graphic organizers independently when given writing assignments, but he or she is unable to transfer those thoughts to write a full paragraph. If the student is permitted to type, then he or she can produce one or two sentences using the graphic organizer as a guide.
Student C The student has difficulty working independently when he or she is overly anxious, fearful, or emotionally distressed. If the student is mildly upset or worried, then he or she is able to work on independent tasks as long as the teacher is in close proximity. The student is unable to attempt the work tasks, however, when he or she is extremely distressed, and instructing him or her to do so results in meltdowns. The following situations increase his or her anxiety and fear: tasks that are new or difficult, tasks that require working with a peer, tasks that require writing, and tasks that have multiple steps.
Student D The student engages in repetitive motor movements and vocal self-stimulatory behavior when the environment is extremely loud or cluttered with excessive materials and when there is chaotic movement. Certain environments, such as the cafeteria and school assemblies, are often too much for the student to process, resulting in continuous loud verbalizations and repetitive motor movements.
Student E The student engages in repetitive, loud vocalizations, hand flapping, or rocking when unable to focus and attend to instruction or a work task or when he or she loses focus and attention that was initially established. The student is able to focus and attend without the use of repetitive behaviors when there are multiple opportunities for him or her to respond during instruction and when work tasks involve various hands-on activities as opposed to writing tasks. The student will often lose focus and attention and begin engaging in repetitive behaviors when the teacher has extended periods of verbal instruction without student engagement.

Figure 3.4. Sample hypothesis statements based on the unique characteristics of students with autism spectrum disorders.

It is also possible to conduct functional analysis activities during the FBA process to better inform the hypothesis as opposed to doing so after a hypothesis is already developed. For example, if you are conducting an observation during the FBA process for a student who is having difficulty working independently, and you think the problem may be due to executive functioning challenges, then you can provide a visual checklist of the steps required for the task the student is expected to complete. Quickly model how to use the checklist and observe if the student can complete the task with increased focus and independence. This type of analysis allows you to test your predictions early in the assessment process as opposed to waiting until after you formulate a hypothesis statement based on observation alone.

DEVELOPING COMPREHENSIVE BEHAVIOR INTERVENTION PLANS

The purpose of conducting an FBA is to develop a comprehensive BIP that encourages the individual to engage in alternative prosocial behaviors (replacement behaviors) that serve the same function as the challenging behavior and that helps you make necessary environment arrangements to prevent the challenging behavior from occurring (Horner, 1994). BIPs should have a heavy focus on antecedent (i.e., preventative) interventions as opposed to simply focusing on consequence interventions (e.g., ***positive reinforcement,*** punishment procedures).

It is helpful to consider the three I's (ineffective, inefficient, irrelevant) when putting together BIPs (Horner, 2000). Making the target behavior ineffective means that it does not work to get the desired outcome anymore. Making the behavior inefficient means that a learned replacement behavior helps the student get the desired outcome much more easily than the target behavior. Making the behavior irrelevant requires that you alter the environment or the behaviors of others in the environment that may be causing the challenging behavior. Consequence interventions are what you implement to make the behavior ineffective, whereas antecedent interventions are used to make the behavior inefficient and irrelevant. This model is similar to the Prevent-Teach-Reinforce (PTR) model (Dunlap et al., 2010). You put antecedent interventions in place to prevent the challenging behavior from occurring, you teach new skills to serve as replacement behaviors for the target behavior, and you ***positively reinforce*** students when they demonstrate desirable behaviors and refrain from exhibiting challenging behaviors. The following sections include the necessary components of BIPs.

Environmental Modifications

Students with ASD often require modifications to the environment to address their sensory needs, problems with focus and attention, and social-communication impairments. This may include reducing environmental stimuli, restructuring the environment to promote students' understanding of expectations, making environmental arrangements to promote communication and social interaction, and making changes to the environment to address problems due to setting events. Table 3.1 provides examples of each of these environmental modifications.

Table 3.1. Examples of environmental modifications

Types of environmental modifications	Examples
Reduce environmental stimuli.	Remove distracting stimuli, minimize the amount of materials that are available at any one time, reduce noise level, adjust lighting.
Restructure the environment to promote students' understanding of expectations.	Utilize visual schedules; arrange furniture in an organized fashion; provide visual cues for behavioral, social, and academic expectations; simplify tasks.
Use environmental arrangements to promote communication and social interaction.	Place desired items out of reach to encourage the use of communication and social interaction skills, give small amounts of desired or needed items to encourage the use of communication and social interaction skills, use flexible grouping.
Make changes to the schedule.	Alter the schedule so that preferred activities follow nonpreferred activities, alter the schedule to provide opportunities for movement and active participation following activities that are more passive.
Make changes to the environment to address problems due to setting events.	Provide food if the child is hungry, seek medical attention if the child is in pain, provide a drink if the child is thirsty, allow the child some time to adjust to a new environment before making demands.

Table 3.2. Examples of changes to teacher and staff behavior

Examples of ways teachers and staff can change their behavior to address challenging behaviors of students with autism spectrum disorder	
Antecedent interventions	Simplify verbal directions. Use positive affect when giving a direction or redirection. Use a variety of cues and prompts to ensure success. Follow the child's lead or focus of attention when attempting to engage in social interactions. Use positive redirection at the first sign of frustration. Give the student more choices. Embed the student's strengths and interests into learning activities. Increase opportunities for the student to respond. Plan for movement and other sensory activities.
Consequence interventions	Increase positive reinforcement for desired behaviors. Use more specific praise (as opposed to general praise). Eliminate positive reinforcement for inappropriate behaviors. Use shaping to support the student in moving toward age- and grade- appropriate desirable behaviors.

Changes to Teacher/Staff Behavior

Teachers and staff can alter their behavior in many ways to decrease the occurrence of the target behavior and increase positive behaviors. Decisions about how to do this are made by analyzing the antecedents and consequences of the target behavior. For example, if a child is displaying a specific behavior to avoid challenging tasks, then the teacher may need to alter the tasks being given so they are at the appropriate developmental level. Using a specific teaching strategy is another change the teacher can make. For example, if a child is displaying escape-motivated behavior, then implementing the ***behavioral momentum*** strategy of giving tasks that are easy prior to giving a challenging task may be appropriate, and you can continue the pattern of easy-easy-difficult-easy-easy-difficult. Table 3.2 provides additional examples of ways teachers and staff can change their behavior to get the desired outcomes in the student.

Changes to Peer Behavior

Peer-mediated interventions can be used to teach peers how to alter their behavior to reduce the challenging behaviors of the student with ASD and increase positive behaviors. They can be taught how to use ***differential reinforcement*** by letting them know what behaviors to ignore and what behaviors to ***positively reinforce.*** They can also be taught how to make more initiations to increase the engagement of the student with ASD and how to respond to the initiations made by the student with ASD. Too often, the need for positive peer interaction is not addressed in FBAs and BIPs, leaving a huge void in the intervention plan. Students with ASD have basic human needs, including a sense of belonging with a peer group.

Replacement Behaviors and New Skills

BIPs also need to include replacement behaviors or new skills that will be taught to the student to eliminate or reduce the need for the target behavior. These can be skills related to social interaction, communication, language, emotional regulation, executive functioning, focus and attention, and so forth. They should be positively stated and written so that they are specific, observable, and measurable, including a criterion for mastery. Detailed plans for teaching the replacement behaviors or new skills should be developed, including progress monitoring procedures.

Crisis Plan

A plan should be developed if the target behavior involves severe challenging behavior that may result in a crisis. This plan should list the steps to follow if and when the student requires deescalation procedures. Ethical protocols must be followed, including avoiding physical restraint and seclusion if possible.

Progress Monitoring and Evaluation

Finally, plans for monitoring student progress and evaluating the effectiveness of the plan should be clearly written. Include the responsibilities for implementation, data collection, and consultative support for each team member. BIPs should be reviewed and evaluated approximately every 6–8 weeks so that any necessary changes can be made.

SUMMARY

This chapter provided an overview of FBA and BIP procedures. It explained the six steps of the FBA process: 1) select a target behavior, 2) collect baseline data, 3) conduct FBA interviews, 4) conduct direct observations, 5) triangulate the data to form a hypothesis, and 6) test the hypothesis. It also described how to form a comprehensive BIP that is designed to make the undesirable target behavior ineffective, inefficient, and irrelevant and addresses the antecedents and consequences for the behavior. Components of the BIP include environmental modifications, changes to teacher/staff behavior, changes to peer behavior, plans for teaching replacement behaviors or new skills, a crisis plan, and a plan for progress monitoring and evaluation. (See the links provided in the Resources section at the end of this chapter for more information on conducting FBAs and developing BIPs.)

Section II of this book focuses on 10 common behavioral challenges of students with ASD, providing tools for assessment and intervention planning that consider their unique characteristics. The information and tools provided can be used at the Tier 2 level to address challenging behaviors as early as possible after onset or to enhance the FBA and BIP process at the Tier 3 level.

RESOURCES

Visit the Technical Assistance Center on Positive Behavioral Interventions and Supports web site at https://www.pbis.org/training/coach-and-trainer/fba-to-bsp for more information about the different data collection processes and methods mentioned in this chapter.

Visit the Virginia Department of Education's Technical Assistance and Guidance web site at http://www.doe.virginia.gov/special_ed/tech_asst_prof_dev/topic_specific_resources/index.shtml for a sample FBA interview form. See the links under the Behavior and Discipline section.

Visit http://www.cesa7.org/sped/discoveridea/topdocs/cecp/problembehavior2/appendixf.htm to access a sample data triangulation form.

Visit the IRIS Center's training module of FBA at https://iris.peabody.vanderbilt.edu/module/fba/ or PBIS World's Tier 3 Interventions page at http://www.pbisworld.com/tier-3 for more information on conducting FBAs and developing BIPs.

SECTION II

Ten Common Behavioral Challenges of Students With ASD

The rest of this book will help teachers address common behavioral challenges of students with ASD using a child-centered approach to understanding and treating the challenging behaviors. Chapter 1 referenced the problems with theory of mind that many students with ASD display, which means they have trouble understanding the perspectives of other people. Although this is certainly true in many cases, the bigger problem is that educators often do not understand and consider the perspective of students with ASD. Instead, they may set standard behavioral expectations that all students are expected to follow without putting supports in place that students with ASD may need to learn those expectations or without considering why students with ASD may have trouble meeting certain expectations. The purpose of Chapters 4–13 is to help teachers understand that challenging behaviors are almost always associated with specific ASD characteristics; they are not pure challenging behaviors due to noncompliance, apathy, disrespect, or any other negative intentions or maladaptive behaviors. The specific behaviors that the chapters address include the following:

- Chapter 4: Following directions
- Chapter 5: Engaging during group instruction
- Chapter 6: Working independently
- Chapter 7: Repetitive behaviors
- Chapter 8: Aggressive behaviors
- Chapter 9: Working with partners and groups
- Chapter 10: Attempting unfamiliar or difficult tasks
- Chapter 11: Engaging in nonpreferred tasks
- Chapter 12: Transitions
- Chapter 13: Shouting out

Each chapter begins with an overview of the specific behavioral challenge and a list of characteristics of ASD that may be at the root of the problem. The sections that follow include an in-depth look at each characteristic that may be affecting a student's behavior. Each of these sections has three parts: Understanding the Problem, Assessing the Problem, and Supporting the Student. In Understanding the Problem, you will learn how the specific characteristic can affect the behavior that is the focus of the chapter. In Assessing the Problem, you will learn how to use the FBA Checklist provided in that chapter's appendix to determine if the characteristic may be relevant to your student. In Supporting the Student, suggestions for strategies and supports that treat the underlying issue related to the specific ASD characteristics are provided. These suggestions include various research-based strategies that were explained in Chapter 2; these strategies are in bold, italicized type to indicate that you can revisit Chapter 2 if you need more information about the specific strategy.

The supports and strategies suggested focus primarily on antecedent interventions (i.e., what can be done to prevent the challenging behavior from occurring). It is also crucial for teachers to regularly deliver positive reinforcement when students with ASD meet behavioral expectations to increase the likelihood that those behaviors will continue and communicate that is exactly what you are looking for because expectations are not always easily understood by your students with ASD. Each chapter concludes with a vignette that illustrates how to use the FBA Checklist to formulate a hypothesis for the challenging behavior addressed in the chapter to plan successful behavioral interventions in the classroom.

The FBA Checklist included in each chapter appendix is a useful tool that allows teachers to quickly assess which ASD characteristics may be affecting the specific behavioral challenge. The checklist can be helpful in narrowing down the function of the behavior and formulating a working hypothesis for what is causing the trouble; it can also guide the teacher in designing classroom interventions that are sensitive to that child's unique challenges and characteristics associated with ASD. Check off one or more boxes on the FBA Checklist that pertain to your student. If you are unsure whether one of the items is relevant for your student, then set up conditions described on the checklist to test if those scenarios may be true for your student by conducting a brief functional analysis (see Chapter 3). When students with ASD exhibit a particular challenging behavior, the behavior often has more than one function. Thus, it is likely that you will check off boxes in more than one domain when using the form for a specific student. There is also an Other section that allows you to indicate any additional potential reasons why the challenging behavior may be occurring, considering other ASD characteristics or environmental considerations. The FBA Checklists can be used to plan Tier 2 interventions (see Chapter 2) or used during a formal FBA process (see Chapter 3). The vignettes at the end of each chapter illustrate how to use the FBA Checklists for Tier 2 interventions.

You may find it helpful to first gather general information about your student's ASD characteristics so you can use that information when completing the FBA Checklists provided in Chapters 4–13. The Characteristics of ASD Assessment included in Appendix A is a simple tool you can use to gather information about your student's unique profile. It is best to complete the assessment with the caregivers and professionals who know the student the best.

Appendix B includes a Characteristics of ASD FBA Template because students with ASD may present other challenging behaviors besides those specifically addressed in Chapters 4–13. This can be used for assessing any challenging behavior. Appendixes A and B include two completed samples of the Characteristics of ASD FBA Template.

CHAPTER 4

Following Directions

Students with ASD often have difficulties following directions in classrooms and other school settings. They may simply be noncompliant or may demonstrate challenging behaviors such as crying, yelling, leaving the work area or classroom, and so forth when directions are given. Although the reasons why students with ASD demonstrate noncompliance vary depending on each child's unique profile, some common characteristics associated with ASD explain why these students are challenged in this area. This chapter discusses nine challenges faced by students with ASD that may explain why they do not regularly follow directions:

1. Language comprehension difficulties
2. Deficits in expressive communication skills
3. Anxiety, fear, and emotional regulation difficulties
4. Social skills deficits
5. Sensory processing problems
6. Problems with focus and attention
7. Executive functioning challenges
8. Academic, cognitive, or motor skills deficits
9. Medical conditions

LANGUAGE COMPREHENSION DIFFICULTIES

Some students may have difficulty following directions due to language comprehension problems or deficits in receptive communication skills.

Understanding the Problem

Students with ASD may not understand the language that teachers use when giving directions, and, consequently, they may be unable to follow through with teacher requests. Some students with ASD not only have difficulties comprehending the language used when teachers give directions, but they also struggle with auditory processing problems. This means their difficulties following directions may stem from the trouble they have with processing what they hear when directions are spoken by the teacher. For example, when a teacher gives a direction such as, "Put your finished work in the red basket next to the sink," the student may not be able to process all the words to figure out what the teacher is asking. The student may hear and process some of the words, such as *basket* and *sink*, but is unable to take in all that was said and quickly process the request and respond accordingly.

Assessing the Problem

If you think language comprehension problems may be affecting your student's ability to follow directions, then complete Section 1 of the FBA Checklist for Difficulty Following Directions in the appendix at the end of this chapter. The following sections describe tips for assessing each item in Section 1 of the checklist.

1a: The Student Can Follow Directions Only When the Directions Are Given Using Very Simple Sentences

If the student can follow very simple directions but not directions that involve more complex language, then comprehension problems may be at the root of the problem. For example, if the student does not respond or responds incorrectly when the teacher says, "Quietly stand up, push in your chair, and line up at the door," but is able to respond appropriately when the teacher says, "Time to line up," then you can predict that the underlying problem is associated with understanding or processing the directions given. You can assess this by comparing the student's responses when simple directions are given with responses when the directions involve more complex language.

1b: The Student Often Performs the Incorrect Behavior as an Attempt to Follow Directions

If a student does not understand the language of directions given but is aware that a response is required and is motivated to respond, then he or she may perform the incorrect behavior in an attempt to follow the directions. Compare the student's percentage of attempted compliance with directions (even if the responses are incorrect) with the percentage of accurate responses to determine if this may be the case for your student.

1c: The Student Can Follow Directions Only When the Teacher Slows Down the Rate of Speech When Giving Directions

This would indicate that the student's noncompliance with directions is primarily an auditory processing issue that occurs because the student is unable to process so much language at one time. Compare the student's responses when directions are given using a slower rate of speech with responses when a normal rate of speech is used to figure out if this may be a relevant issue for your student.

1d: The Student Relies on Environmental Cues to Follow Directions

If a student follows some directions but not all, then the student may be relying on environmental cues to respond to directions as opposed to truly understanding the language of the directions given. Here are some examples:

- If the teacher tells the class to take out their math notebooks, then a student who does not understand the language may still respond to the direction after seeing other students take out their math notebooks.
- If the student sees the teacher writing a math problem on the board as he or she tells the class to take out their math notebooks, then the student may figure out what to do simply by seeing what the teacher is writing on the board.

- If a teacher usually displays a visual timer when the students are expected to clean up, then it may be that the student is responding to the presence of the timer to know it is time to clean up instead of the verbal direction.

It may be difficult to know when students are relying on environmental cues to respond to directions. Test this by purposefully eliminating environmental cues and examining the student's ability to continue to follow directions without those cues present, comparing this with how well the student follows directions when such cues are present.

1e: The Student Can Follow Directions Only When Directions Are Familiar and Given Daily

If the student follows directions that are given on a regular basis but does not follow unfamiliar directions, then this can be an indication that language comprehension difficulties are causing the problem. When directions are repeatedly given, students have multiple opportunities throughout the school day to learn the meaning of the words and process the directions given. When a direction is new or unfamiliar to the student, however, then language comprehension issues may impede the student's ability to comply. Thus, compare the student's compliance to familiar directions with the student's compliance to unfamiliar directions to assess if this may be an issue for your student.

1f: The Student Follows Directions Only When They Are Given Nonverbally or When Oral Directions Are Paired With Visual Supports

If the student is only able to follow directions given nonverbally or when oral directions are paired with ***visual supports,*** then a language problem may be the primary barrier. Examples of nonverbal methods for giving directions include 1) modeling the expectation and giving the student an opportunity to imitate your model (***modeling/request imitation***), 2) pairing the verbal direction with gestures, such as pointing to the door when telling the student to line up or using hand motions to indicate that the student should sit down, 3) showing a picture or sequence of ***pictures*** to communicate the expectation, or 4) showing a video clip to demonstrate the expectation and asking the student to imitate what was shown in the video clip. Compare the student's responses when he or she must rely solely on comprehending verbal directions with responses when directions are given nonverbally or paired with ***visual supports*** to test if your student's ability to follow directions is improved by giving directions nonverbally.

Supporting the Student

Consider the following strategies and supports to increase a student's compliance with directions when language comprehensions difficulties are the problem:

- Use ***time-delay*** to provide the necessary wait time the student needs to process the request.
- If the student can read, then provide written directions to allow the student time to read and process the directions at a developmentally appropriate pace. If the student cannot read, then give visual representation of the directions when possible. See Figure 4.1 for examples of visual representations of directions.
- Use consistent language when giving directions to provide the familiarity with the language that the student needs to improve comprehension.
- Use ***shaping:***
    - Slow down your rate of speech when giving directions to give the student more processing time. Then use ***shaping*** by gradually increasing the rate of speech to allow the student to improve auditory processing skills.

Direction	Visual representation
Arrange the coins from greatest to least value and count the total amount.	 Quarters  Dimes  Nickels  Pennies Total: ________
Write three facts that you learned about elephants.	 1. ______________________ 2. ______________________ 3. ______________________

Figure 4.1. Examples of visual representations of directions.

- Increase compliance by using very simple sentences when giving all directions. Then use ***shaping*** by gradually increasing the complexity of the language or the number of words in the directions to allow the student to improve receptive communication skills at the appropriate instructional level. Continue using ***clear, consistent, and concise language,*** however, even as the sentence structures become more complex.
- Use any of the following strategies to support the student when directions cannot be given using simple sentences:
    - ***Modeling/request imitation***
    - ***Most-to-least prompting/fading procedures***
    - ***Visual supports***
    - ***Video modeling***

- If the student attempts to follow a direction but performs the incorrect behavior, then ***positively reinforce*** the student for the attempt and follow this reinforcement with supportive error-correction procedures to help the student respond appropriately.

DEFICITS IN EXPRESSIVE COMMUNICATION SKILLS

Impairments in expressive communication skills can be another factor affecting a student's difficulty with following directions.

Understanding the Problem

When a typically developing student is given a direction to follow but does not understand the direction or needs help in some way, that student can ask the teacher to explain the direction again, give an example, or provide assistance. If a student does not have the expressive communication skills necessary to ask for clarification or assistance, however, then he or she may simply be unable to follow the direction. It is not only students who are nonverbal who may have difficulty asking for help or clarification. Verbal students with ASD may also have trouble due to limitations in the use of expressive communication.

Assessing the Problem

If you think deficits in expressive communication skills may be affecting your student's ability to follow directions, complete Section 2 of the FBA Checklist for Difficulty Following Directions in the appendix at the end of this chapter. Following are some tips for assessing each item in Section 2:

2a: The Student Does Not Follow Certain Directions Because He or She Is Unable to Ask for Help or Clarification When Directions Are Not Understood

If you are unsure if expressive communication weaknesses are preventing a student from asking for clarification or assistance, resulting in noncompliance with directions, then provide the student with a nonverbal way to request help. The student can be taught to use a picture to ask for help, use a card that has the word *help* written on it, or use a color-coded cup or card system in which green means no help is needed and red means help is needed; or, quite simply, the student can be taught to raise his or her hand when help is needed. Once the student understands how to request help and can do so, note whether you see an increase in compliance. If so, it is likely that deficits in expressive communication skills were affecting the student's ability to comply with directions.

2b: The Student Does Not Follow Directions Because He or She Does Not Have the Expressive Communication Skills Needed to Negotiate and Advocate for Accommodations Needed to Comply

Students with ASD may require accommodations to increase their ability to comply with certain directions due to their various needs. For example, some students may need to draw a picture about an experience before writing about it so they can use the drawing as a visual support to facilitate their written language. If the teacher tells the class to start writing without considering this necessary accommodation, then the student would need to have the expressive communication skills to explain why it is important for him or her to draw first. Many students with ASD unfortunately do not have this level of sophistication when it comes to expressive language, resulting in noncompliance with directions because of their inability to communicate needs for an accommodation or support.

2c: The Student Does Not Follow Directions Because He or She Does Not Have the Expressive Communication Skills Needed to Ask for a Break When Necessary

Some students with ASD require breaks to get calm and regulated before continuing with ongoing classroom activities due to sensory and emotional regulation issues. If a student does not have the expressive communication skills needed to ask for breaks when needed, however, then he or she may be unable to comply with directions. If a student cannot ask for a break and get to a regulated state, then following directions may be very difficult.

Supporting the Student

Consider the following strategies and supports to increase a student's compliance with following directions when deficits in expressive communication difficulties are the problem:

- Use ***explicit instruction*** to teach the student how to ask for help or a break.
- Provide ***visual supports*** for asking for help or a break (see Figure 4.2).
- Use ***video modeling*** to teach the student how to ask for help or a break.

Figure 4.2. Visual supports for asking for help or a break.

- Use the following ***least-to-most prompting hierarchy:***
    1. Use proximity and ***time-delay*** to encourage the student to ask for help.
    2. Gestural prompt: Point to the visual support to prompt the student to ask for help.
    3. Verbal prompt: "Remember to ask for help if you need it."
    4. Verbal prompt: "Do you need help?"
    5. ***Modeling/request imitation***: Model how the student should ask for help, and have the student imitate.
- Use ***priming*** to remind the student how to ask for help or a break prior to giving a direction that may be difficult for the student to follow.
- If you think the student is not complying with a direction because of the inability to request a needed accommodation, then approach the student in a supportive way and say something such as, "Is there something you need to get started?" If the student expresses incomplete thoughts, then attempt to figure out what the child is trying to say and ask questions to find out if you are correct about what the child is trying to communicate (e.g., "Are you saying that you want to sit in the beanbag while you read instead of staying in your seat?"). Once you figure out what the child is trying to communicate, use ***modeling/request imitation*** by saying what the student should say and having the student imitate. Whenever possible, allow the student's request to be granted to ***positively reinforce*** the expressive communication skills demonstrated.

ANXIETY, FEAR, AND EMOTIONAL REGULATION DIFFICULTIES

Some students may have difficulty following teacher directions due to high levels of anxiety and fear they experience when given directions.

Understanding the Problem

Students who have this problem are typically students who struggle with feelings of fear on a regular basis, and receiving directives from teachers can elevate their anxiety and fear, causing them to be noncompliant. This may be because they are not sure if they can accurately do what was asked or because the direction may require the student to do something new or unfamiliar. Students who have a strong need for sameness may get very fearful when asked to do something that is not part of the typical classroom routine. Many students with ASD also have difficulties with emotional regulation. So, it is a chain reaction for these students—as their anxiety and fear increases, they have difficulty regulating those emotions, which causes them to get very upset and ultimately impedes their ability to follow directions that were given.

Assessing the Problem

If you think anxiety, fear, and emotional regulation difficulties may be affecting your student's ability to follow directions, then complete Section 3 of the FBA Checklist for Difficulty Following Directions in the appendix at the end of this chapter. Following are some tips for assessing each item in Section 3:

3a: The Student Follows Directions When Given Time to Comply and Some Personal Space as Opposed to When a Teacher Demands an Immediate Response

Some students may get very anxious when teachers give directions and then hover over them, waiting for a response and often continuing to repeat the direction. Instead of doing this, try giving a direction and walking away, providing an opportunity for the student to calm down and comply when ready. If the student can have some time to deal with the increased anxiety or fear without an adult hovering and continuing to state the demand, then the student may be able to effectively regulate emotional responses and comply with the direction given. You may also want to try writing the direction in a note to the student instead of giving a verbal directive. Verbal directives may cause more feelings of anxiety than written directions for some students because they place more social demands on the student and indicate the need for an immediate response.

3b: The Student Follows Directions When Someone Uses a Positive, Supportive Tone of Voice and Warm Facial Expressions as Opposed to a Stern, Directive Voice and Flat or Negative Facial Expressions

In some situations, it may be the teacher's affect and tone of voice when giving directions that is causing fear and anxiety in the student. Give directions to the student using a positive tone of voice paired with warm facial expressions and refrain from using a stern, directive tone paired with flat or negative facial expressions to test if this may be a factor. For example, instead of the teacher saying, "You need to start writing," paired with a harsh facial expression, the teacher may say, "When you are finished thinking about what you want to write, let me know, and I will help you organize your thoughts," paired with a gentle smile and encouraging facial expression. Teachers may not realize they are using a certain tone or facial expression that is causing anxiety and fear in the student. Thus, it may be worthwhile to record the teacher–child interaction on video when directions are given so the teacher can determine if the way they are given may be negatively affecting the student's ability to respond.

3c: The Student Follows Directions Better on Thursdays and Fridays as the Student Gets More Comfortable With the Weekly Routines

Take note if the student typically follows directions more willingly toward the end of the school week as opposed to Mondays and Tuesdays. Some students have a hard time adjusting to school expectations after the weekend break and may have increased anxiety and fear. You may notice improved performance with following directions when the student reestablishes comfort with the daily routines as the week continues.

3d: The Student Has Difficulty Following Directions That Do Not Follow the Typical Routine or Schedule (Need for Sameness)

Some students with ASD have a very strong need for sameness. Thus, they may get very fearful and anxious when directions are given that do not follow the typical daily routine. Compare the student's ability to follow directions that are predictable and part of a structured routine with the ability to follow directions that break away from a familiar routine to assess if this may be the case.

Supporting the Student

Consider the following strategies and supports to increase a student's compliance with following directions when anxiety, fear, and emotional regulation difficulties are the problem:

- Use a calm, supportive tone of voice and positive affect when giving directions.
- Be more responsive and less directive when giving directions. For example, instead of saying, "You need to get in line," say, "Go ahead and choose your place in line." Instead of saying, "You need to get started," say, "I am looking forward to reading what you write about your beach trip."

- Give the student fewer directions on Mondays and Tuesdays, make the directions easier for the student to follow, and include more interest- and strength-based activities to ease the transition back to school after the weekend.
- Use ***priming*** to let the student know if something is going to be altered in the typical schedule. Refrain from using words such as *change* or *different,* however, if those words increase the student's anxiety. Simply state what will occur (e.g., "After reading group we will be going to the media center to take our class picture").
- Use ***shaping*** to get the student more comfortable following directions when there are changes in the schedule. Begin by making one small desirable change each day that is desirable for the student (e.g., "Instead of writing today, you are going to watch a science video on your tablet"). Gradually increase the amount of desirable changes each day. Then make one small change that is undesirable once a week, gradually increasing the amount of undesirable changes until the student can tolerate them and comply with directions.
- Use ***most-to-least prompting*** after giving new or unfamiliar directions to prevent fear and anxiety and increase confidence.
- Use ***video modeling*** for new or unfamiliar directions.
- Allow the student to have a brief observational period of watching peers respond before expecting the student to comply with a new direction.

SOCIAL SKILLS DEFICTS

All students with ASD have deficits in social skills. Each individual has unique strengths and challenges, however, when it comes to social interaction and engagement. In some instances, a particular social skills deficit or combination of social skills deficits may impede the student's ability to follow directions.

Understanding the Problem

Students who have the most significant social impairments have extreme deficits in joint attention and social reciprocity. If a teacher gives a direction without first establishing joint attention with the student, then the student is likely to have difficulties fulfilling the request. For example, if the student's mind is focused on something different from what the teacher is talking about, then the student is not likely to hear and process the direction. Even if joint attention is established, if a student has deficits in social reciprocity, then it may be very difficult for the student to process the direction and have the internal motivation to respond to it.

Although joint attention and social reciprocity impairments are the most debilitating social impairments when it comes to following directions, students who have acquired joint attention and social reciprocity skills may still have trouble following directions due to other social limitations. Some students with ASD have deficits in specific social skills, such as offering or accepting help, turn-taking, engaging in conversations, perspective taking, imitation, sharing, and so forth. If a direction requires the use of a specific social skill that the student has not yet acquired, then that gap may be the reason why the student does not comply. For example, if the teacher says, "Face your partner and take turns asking one another questions about the story," then the student will not be able to comply if he or she does not have the required conversational skills.

Assessing the Problem

If you think social skills deficits may be affecting your student's ability to follow directions, then complete Section 4 of the FBA Checklist for Difficulty Following Directions in the Appendix at the end of this chapter. Following are some tips for assessing each item in Section 4:

4a: Due to Significant Deficits in Joint Attention and Social Reciprocity, the Student Is Often Not Engaged Socially When Directions Are Given, Making It Difficult to Hear, Process, or Respond to the Directions

To determine if joint attention deficits are affecting a student's ability to follow directions, get yourself at eye level with the student and establish joint attention prior to giving the direction. If you discover that the student can comply with directions when you do this but otherwise cannot, then it is safe to say the problem is related to joint attention weaknesses. Even if the student appears to hear the direction, social reciprocity deficits may affect the student's ability to fully process the request and have the motivation necessary to follow through. Remember, this is a result of the way ASD affects the student, not a random challenging behavior. The student is not being lazy or defiant. Social reciprocity deficits cause somewhat of a social paralysis for some students, inhibiting their abilities to fulfill requests that require a rapid request–response sequence.

4b: The Student Has Problems Following Directions That Require the Use of One or More Social Skills the Student Has Not Yet Acquired

Sometimes it is necessary to assess if deficits in specific social skills such as sharing, waiting for a turn, taking the perspective of others, initiating greetings, initiating conversations with peers, using appropriate voice volume, or imitating others are affecting a student's ability to follow directions. Compare the student's responses to directions that do not require the use of such social skills with responses to directions that do. For example, give the student directions such as, "Please throw away all the scraps on the floor," or "Write your name on the top of the page," and document whether the student complies. Then give directions that require specific social skills, such as, "Whisper your answer to your partner," or "Give one of the crayons to each student at your table," to determine if there is a difference in compliance.

4c: The Student Has Problems Following Directions That Require Perspective Taking

A student may not be able to comply with academic directions that require perspective taking, such as answering questions about an author's perspective after reading a selection. Likewise, if a direction is given within a social context, such as, "Tell me how you would feel if you were Jamie," then the student may not comply because he or she has difficulty taking the other student's perspective.

It is a related and even greater challenge when a student will not follow directions that he or she does not view as necessary or important. If a student thinks a directive has no purpose or meaning, then he or she may refrain from following it. It is very important for teachers to fully explain the rationale for the directive. Some teachers may have the "because I said so" mindset. That does not go over well, however, with a student on the autism spectrum who has difficulty with perspective taking. It is worth the teacher's time to explain why a certain direction must be followed from the various perspectives of people who will be affected if it is or is not followed. This requires that teachers take the perspective of students with ASD and understand that they sometimes need things fully explained that others pick up on incidentally. For example, suppose a high school student with ASD is painting with acrylics during art class. The student may not see the purpose of the teacher's direction to wash out paintbrushes at the end of the class period and therefore not complete this task. The teacher may need to state explicitly that if this direction is not followed, then the unwashed brushes will become stiff with dried paint and other students will not be able to use them.

Supporting the Student

Consider the following strategies and supports to increase a student's compliance with following directions when social skills deficits are the problem:

- Get face to face with the student and establish joint attention prior to giving a direction.
- If the student is focusing on something else when you are about to give a direction, then ***follow the student's lead*** by first engaging with the student during the present activity. This will help the student shift attention to the direction because the student will be interacting with you at the time the direction is given.
- Restate the direction and use ***time-delay.***
- Use the following ***least-to-most prompts*** hierarchy:
    1. Pair the verbal direction with a ***visual support*** such as a gesture, picture, symbol, or ***cue card*** with the direction written on it.
    2. Use ***modeling/request imitation*** by showing the student how to follow the direction, and then have the student imitate your model.
    3. Provide gentle physical assistance, and fade out the physical support once the student can comply.
    4. Give directions using ***video modeling*** when feasible.
- It the student has deficits in imitation skills, then use ***modeling/request imitation*** during parts of the lesson that require the student to imitate gestures, words, or actions. Use ***peer-mediated interventions*** to teach peers how to use ***modeling/request imitation*** with the student during instructional activities. Make sure directions that require imitation are developmentally appropriate for the student (i.e., check that the student has the academic, verbal, or motor skills needed to imitate).

SENSORY PROCESSING PROBLEMS

Students who struggle with sensory processing problems may have difficulty following directions that make them feel physically uncomfortable. Some students with ASD may need sensory input to stay regulated and on task and have difficulty complying with directions that interrupt this flow of sensory input.

Understanding the Problem

Some students have adverse reactions to certain sounds, smells, textures, excessive movement around them, lighting, and so forth, and they may have a difficult time complying when directions put them in situations that force them in these sensory experiences. What may seem like a simple request for most students can be a sensory nightmare for students with ASD. For example, if a student with sensory processing problems is told to wait in the line at the cafeteria, get a tray, select food items, sit at the designated lunch table, and eat with the class, then the student may have major discomfort with the various smells in the cafeteria, the fluorescent lighting, the loud volume of student chatter, and the ongoing movement taking place, resulting in an inability to follow the set of directions.

Although sensory differences can cause discomfort when certain stimuli are present, some students will seek specific sensory input to help keep them regulated. A student may have difficulty complying to directions that take away the needed sensory input or do not allow access to it. Teachers often give directions that take away the need for movement that some students with sensory differences require to actively engage. For example, teachers often give directions such as "sit down," "sit still," "quiet hands," "stop rocking," and "be quiet." Students may have problems following such directions because they need the movement to help them process all the sensory information around them.

Assessing the Problem

If you think sensory processing problems may be affecting your student's ability to follow directions, then complete Section 5 of the FBA Checklist for Difficulty Following Directions in the appendix at the end of this chapter. Following are some tips for assessing each item in Section 5:

5a: The Student Has Problems Following Directions That Require Facing Increased Levels of Sensory Input

Students with ASD may have difficulty following directions when presented with extensive sensory input, such as environments that are loud or bright, have a lot of people moving around, or contain a lot of materials to see and touch. These students may be able to follow directions when settings are quiet, dim, or dark, when there is limited movement occurring around them, or when there are fewer materials to see and manipulate. If your student has advanced expressive communication skills, then ask him or her if certain things in the environment cause discomfort. If the child cannot answer that type of question, then observe the student in different environments, noting the different types of sensory input and the student's compliance with directions or lack thereof. Here are some examples:

- The student follows directions in various school environments such as the library, the gymnasium, and the art room but has difficulty following directions in the music room due to sensory discomfort with the sounds of the instruments.
- The student will follow directions to wash hands, blow his or her nose, or clean up the area but will not follow directions to go to the bathroom due to sensory discomfort with the sounds of the toilets flushing.
- The student will follow academic directions when natural light is used to brighten the room but does not do so when the overhead lights are turned on in the classroom.
- The student will follow a direction to draw a family picture when seated with one other peer at a table, with each student given three crayons and one piece of paper; however, the student is unable to do so when seated with a larger group of peers at a table with many drawing materials.

5b: The Student Has Problems Following Directions That Require the Use of Certain Materials With Specific Textures or Odors

If possible, ask the student if certain learning materials cause discomfort. If the child cannot answer that type of question, then observe the student's responses when directions are given to use various materials. Here are some examples:

- The student complies with directions that include the use of crayons, pencils, and markers but has a difficult time following directions that include the use of finger paints.
- The child complies when asked to draw with crayons or colored pencils, but he or she is unable to comply with requests to use markers because of the strong odors.
- The student complies with directions to play with a kickball or basketball but does not follow directions to play in the sand box.

- The student does not comply with directions during multisensory literacy activities, such as writing letters in shaving cream or running one's fingers along sandpaper letters to learn the letter formations.

5c: The Student Has Difficulty Following Directions That Take Away Opportunities for the Student to Get the Sensory Input Needed (e.g., Sit Still, Be Quiet, Hands in Lap)

In some cases, a student will not follow directions because doing so would take away much needed sensory input or output. Here are a few examples:

- A teacher tells a student who is rocking to sit still, but the student does not comply because he or she needs the movement to be able to attend during the lesson.
- A teacher tells a student during an assembly to put his or her hands in his or her lap when he or she is flapping his or her hands, but the student does not comply because the hand flapping is helping him or her take in and process all the sensory input.
- A student may follow directions to unpack his or her backpack, turn in homework, and work on morning work but will not follow the direction to take off his or her jacket due to the sensory input and comfort that the jacket provides.
- A student may follow directions to complete math problems, answer reading comprehension questions, or draw a diagram of the heart but will not comply when told to be quiet because creating vocalizations helps the student deal with the sensory experiences in the classroom while completing the required tasks.

Supporting the Student

Consider the following strategies and supports to increase a student's compliance with following directions when sensory processing problems are the issue:

- Use environmental arrangements whenever possible to minimize sensory input (e.g., use natural lighting instead of fluorescent lighting, use preferential seating to avoid exposure to certain odors in the cafeteria).
- Use ***priming*** to prepare the student for the sensory experiences that will occur in a specific environment or situation. Sometimes knowing what to expect will ease stress and enable the student to comply with directions. If a new environment will present many sensory stimuli (sensory rich), then preexpose the student to the new environment prior to the scheduled event or activity, if possible.
- Use ***shaping*** by gradually increasing the amount of time the student is exposed to a specific sensory-rich environment, delivering ***positive reinforcement*** each time the student can function and follow directions in the environment for a little bit longer than the previous time.
- Preteach the directions in sensory-rich environments at times when there is less sensory input (e.g., go to the cafeteria when lunch is not being served to practice following directions going through the lunch line).
- Allow accommodations when necessary (e.g., allow the student to eat in the classroom instead of the cafeteria, allow the student to wear noise-reduction headphones during music class).
- Do not restrict the student's coping mechanisms. For example, if the student engages in stereotypic verbalizations or physical movements in sensory-rich environments, then

these behaviors may provide the output the student needs to filter out some of the sensory input. Thus, these behaviors may help the student follow directions because they help to limit stress in a particular environment.

- Allow for movement with balance balls, wobble cushions, or bouncy bands for classroom desks.

PROBLEMS WITH FOCUS AND ATTENTION

Some students with ASD may have difficulty following directions due to issues with focus and attention.

Understanding the Problem

Students with ASD are often either paying attention to everything around them or are hyperfocused on one thing due to the nature of their disability. Either way, this can cause significant problems with following directions. The student may not follow directions given to the class because he or she was paying attention to something else. Also, some students may begin to follow directions but then lose focus; they get distracted by something else and cease following the direction. Many students with ASD have difficulty shifting their attention. Thus, if they are very engaged in one task, then they may not easily be able to shift their attention from it to listen to the teacher and follow the next direction.

Assessing the Problem

If you think problems with focus and attention may be affecting your student's ability to follow directions, then complete Section 6 of the FBA Checklist for Difficulty Following Directions in the appendix at the end of this chapter. Following are some tips for assessing each item:

6a: The Student Follows Directions That Are Given One to One and at Eye Level but Has Difficulty Following Directions Given to the Group

Compare the student's success with following directions that are given one to one and at eye level with the student's success when directions are given to the whole class or group. If the student can follow directions when they are given one to one but not when given to the whole group, then it could be a result of focus and attention challenges.

6b: The Student Begins to Follow the Direction but Gets Distracted by Something

Some students may hear the direction, understand it, and even begin to comply, but they get distracted and are unable to follow through. It is important to note that the student appears to hear and understand the direction, but difficulties with focus and attention impede full compliance.

6c: The Student Has Difficulty Following Directions When He or She Is Heavily Focused on Something and the Direction Requires the Student to Stop That Activity and Do Something Else (Difficulty Shifting Attention)

Observe what the student is doing prior to giving directions. If the student follows directions when he or she is not actively engaged in another task but is unable to follow directions when focused on something else, then difficulties with shifting attention can certainly be the root of the problem.

Supporting the Student

Consider the following strategies and supports to increase a student's compliance with following directions when focus and attention problems are the issue:

- Provide ***visual supports*** when giving directions to the whole group to support the student's focus and attention.
- Get the student's attention before giving instructions to the whole group.
- Use key words and phrases to cue the student that an important direction is being given to the whole class or group (e.g., "All eyes on me," "Time to listen").
- Ask the student to repeat the direction that was given to the whole class or group. If the student cannot do so, then say the direction again and restate the request to repeat the direction.
- Involve the student in demonstrating the expectations of the direction to the whole group.
- Use ***shaping*** using the following sequence:
  1. ***Positively reinforce*** the student if directions are followed when given one to one before they are given to the whole class or group.
  2. Provide ***positive reinforcement*** when the student follows directions that are given to the whole class or group when the teacher is near the student and makes eye contact with the student while giving the direction.
  3. Provide ***positive reinforcement*** when the student follows directions that are given to the whole class or group when the teacher is near the student but does not make eye contact with the student while giving the direction.
  4. Provide ***positive reinforcement*** when the student follows directions that are given to the whole class or group when the teacher is a few feet away from the student.
  5. Provide ***positive reinforcement*** when the student follows directions that are given to the whole class or group when the teacher is not near the student.
- Consider the following if the student is having trouble shifting attention to follow directions:
  - Use ***priming*** to let the student know ahead of time that a direction is going to be given that will require the student to stop what he or she is doing.
  - Use a visual timer (if it does not cause anxiety) to allow the student to see how much time is left to complete a task.
  - Create a special folder the student can use when an assignment is not finished and label it as "working folder" (see Figure 4.3). If helpful, attach a laminated card to the pocket of the folder and use a wet erase marker to indicate when the student will have an opportunity to finish the work (e.g., "I will finish this ____________________"). Don't just tell the student he or she can finish it later or at home.
  - Get at eye level and give the direction one to one when the student is heavily focused on something and must shift that focus to hear and respond to the direction you are about to give.

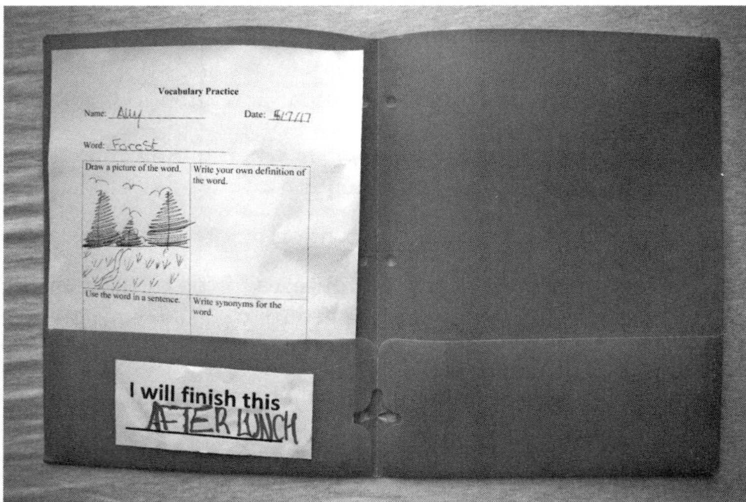

Figure 4.3. Working folder to help with shifting attention.

EXECUTIVE FUNCTIONING CHALLENGES

Impairments in executive functioning can significantly affect a student's ability to follow directions.

Understanding the Problem

Following directions will be difficult if the student with ASD lacks the ability to independently make a plan and execute the plan in sequential order. It will be especially difficult for students with executive functioning problems to comply with multistep directions because it requires a great deal of processing, planning, remembering, and follow-through.

Assessing the Problem

If you think executive functioning challenges may be affecting your student's ability to follow directions, then complete Section 7 of the FBA Checklist for Difficulty Following Directions in the appendix at the end of this chapter. Following are some tips for assessing each item:

7a: The Student Follows One-Step Directions and Simple Two-Step Directions but Cannot Follow Multistep Directions That Require Planning and Organizational Skills

Give the student directions ranging from one-step directions, to simple two-step directions that do not require great effort with planning, to more complex two-step directions, and finally to multistep directions. Note which directions the student can follow independently and which required prompting. If the student can follow one-step and simple two-step directions but has difficulty with directions requiring more complex processing, planning, remembering, and follow-through, then executive functioning problems are likely affecting compliance. The following is an example of a continuum of directions that increase in level of difficulty and level of executive functioning skills required:

- Throw away your scraps. (one step)
- Stand up and push in your chair. (simple two-step)

- Put your completed work in the basket and choose a book from the classroom library to read. (complex two-step)
- Take out a piece of paper, write your name and date at the top, number your paper 1–5, and write five facts you remember about volcanoes. (multistep)

7b: The Student Follows Multistep Directions Only When They Are Broken Down Into One-Step Directions or When They Are Given Visual Supports Such as a Task Analysis or Checklist

Provide ***visual supports***, such as a ***task analysis*** of the steps written in order or ***pictures*** of the steps sequenced, to determine if the student can comply with directions when those supports are provided. If so, then executive functioning problems are likely inhibiting a student's ability to follow multistep directions. Following is an example of a ***task analysis*** for the direction, "Go wash your hands."

1. Turn on the water.
2. Put soap in your hand.
3. Scrub your hands.
4. Rinse your hands in water.
5. Turn off the water.
6. Get a paper towel.
7. Dry your hands.
8. Throw away the paper towel.

Although it may be easy for teachers to identify the steps for a direction such as washing hands, academic directions may not be as simple to task analyze. Following is an example of a ***task analysis*** for the direction, "Write about what you did over the weekend."

1. Draw a picture about what you did over the weekend.
2. Write an introductory sentence using the following sentence frame, "I had a _____ weekend." (Fill in the blank with a word that describes your weekend, such as *great, awesome, terrible, exciting, memorable*).
3. Use your picture to write one sentence that describes what you did over the weekend.
4. Write another sentence to say more about what you wrote for Step 3.
5. Use your picture to write another sentence that describes what you did over the weekend.
6. Write another sentence to say more about what you wrote for Step 5.
7. Write a concluding sentence using the following sentence frame: "I hope I (have/do not have) another weekend like that again."

One thing to keep in mind when assessing if a ***task analysis*** will help a student follow multistep directions is that the student may not necessarily know how to use the ***task analysis*** to complete sequential steps of a direction. You may first need to teach a student how to use a ***task analysis*** before assessing if the ***task analysis*** will help the student comply with multistep directions.

Supporting the Student

Consider the following strategies and supports to increase a student's compliance with following directions when executive functioning difficulties are the problem:

- Use ***task analysis*** by breaking down multistep directions into sequential steps.
- Use ***visual supports*** to present the steps visually using ***pictures,*** words, phrases, or sentences.
- Use ***forward chaining*** to teach the student how to use the ***task analysis.***
- Create a ***self-monitoring*** tool the student can use to check off each step as it is completed and deliver self-reinforcement.
- Use ***video modeling, video self-modeling, point-of-view video modeling,*** or ***video prompting*** to help the student see and remember the parts of multistep directions or tasks.
- Have the student repeat back a multistep direction to make sure all parts were heard and processed. If any parts are missing when the student repeats the direction, then restate the direction, emphasizing the missing step, and have the student say the direction back to you.
- Teach the student how to use verbal rehearsal. This means the student will continue to state the multistep direction in his or her head as the direction is being followed to make sure no steps are left out.

ACADEMIC, COGNITIVE, OR MOTOR SKILLS DEFICITS

Students may not comply with directions in some instances because they lack the needed academic, cognitive, or motor skills.

Understanding the Problem

Whether the student has the skills necessary to comply is another factor that must be considered when determining why a student may have difficulty following directions. For example, if a student does not follow a direction to read a passage and answer the multiple-choice questions that follow, then it may be because the student does not have the needed reading comprehension skills. If you tell a student to cut out various shapes on a piece of paper, then the student may not comply due to fine motor skills weaknesses. If you ask a student to draw what he or she wants to be when he or she grows up, then he or she may not do so because he or she does not have the needed motor skills to draw or because he or she is not yet able to cognitively process and respond to abstract questions about the future.

Teachers often think it is not an academic, cognitive, or motor deficit that is affecting a student's ability to follow directions because they have seen the student demonstrate the skill before. There may be inconsistencies in the student's cognitive, academic, or motor performance until the student goes through the four stages of learning—skill acquisition, fluency, maintenance, and generalization (Alberto & Troutman, 2012). Students must first learn the skill (acquisition) and then demonstrate mastery of that skill with error-free automaticity (fluency), maintain use of the skill over time (maintenance), and ultimately apply that skill in various contexts and situations (generalization).

Assessing the Problem

If you think academic, cognitive, or motor skills deficits may be affecting your student's ability to follow directions, then complete Section 8 of the FBA Checklist for Difficulty Following

Directions in the appendix at the end of this chapter. Following are some tips for assessing each item:

8a: The Student Complies With Directions When They Are Academically Easy for the Student but Not When the Directions Require Skills the Student Has Not Fully Acquired or Mastered

Compare the student's responses to academic directions that are very easy for the student with more difficult academic directions. Academic deficits are likely the root of the problem if the student complies with directions that are easy but not when the directions are more challenging considering the student's present levels of performance.

8b: The Student Complies With Directions That Require Factual Responses at the Concrete Level but Does Not Comply When the Directions Require Abstract Thought and Reasoning

Many students with ASD have cognitive deficits when it comes to abstract thought. Thus, some students may not comply when teachers give directions that require thinking at the abstract level. Here is an example: A middle school English teacher reported that a student with Asperger syndrome was not following directions in class. When asked to give an example, the teacher explained that students were told to write a poem about love inside a cutout of a heart. The student refused to comply. It was recommended to give the student the same cutout of a heart but this time ask the student to write about the scientific workings of the heart. The student complied using words and graphics to explain in detail how the heart functions. This is a case in which cognitive differences were affecting compliance. The student did not comply because he did not have a strong understanding of the abstract concept of love. But he willingly complied when asked to write concrete information about the way the heart functions in the body.

8c: The Student Complies When the Fine or Gross Motor Skills Required Are Simple for the Student but Does Not Comply When the Fine or Gross Motor Skills Required Are Very Challenging for the Student

Give the student directions involving fine or gross motor skills that you are certain the student can easily perform. Record the student's compliance with these easy directions and then do the same with directions that require more difficult fine or gross motor skills. If the student refrains from following directions as the motor skills increase in difficulty, then motor deficits may be affecting the student's ability to follow directions.

Supporting the Student

Consider the following strategies and supports to increase a student's compliance with following directions when academic, cognitive, or motor skills deficits are the problem:

- Allow the student to use computer software or other ***AAC*** supports to respond to directions that require written responses.
- Provide word banks, multiple-choice responses, or picture choices for the student to use to respond to directions. See Figure 4.4 for a word bank example and Figure 4.5 for an example of multiple-choices responses and picture choices.
- Use ***AT*** to support the student's handwriting skills (e.g., pencil grips, large pencils, slant board). See Figure 4.6 for examples of AT for handwriting.
- Allow the student to draw to generate ideas; use ***graphic organizers,*** lists, or outlines; or put ***pictures*** or premade sentences in order instead of relying on written responses to

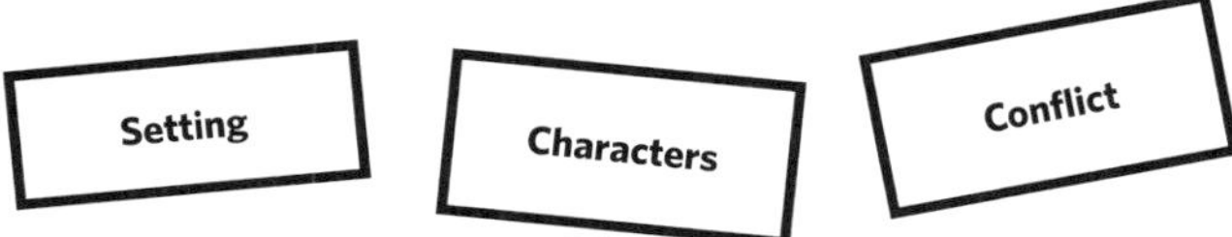

Directions: Paste the correct answer using the following words: setting, characters, conflict.

- The problem that must be solved in the story is called the ______________________.
- The location of the story is called the ______________________.
- The individuals the story is about are called ______________________.

Figure 4.4. Word bank example.

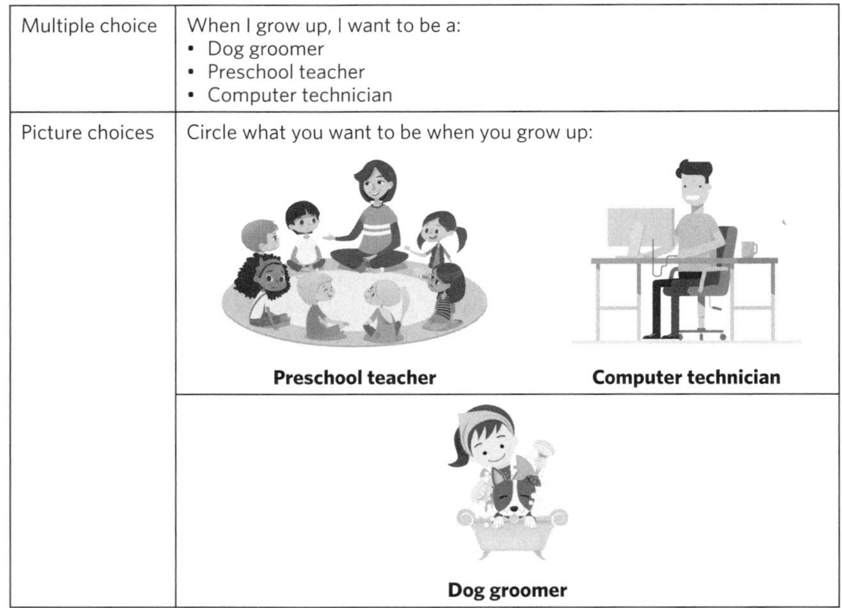

Multiple choice	When I grow up, I want to be a: • Dog groomer • Preschool teacher • Computer technician
Picture choices	Circle what you want to be when you grow up: **Preschool teacher** **Computer technician** **Dog groomer**

Figure 4.5. Multiple-choice and picture choices examples.

Pencil grips **Adapted pen**

Figure 4.6. Assistive technology for writing.

Directions: Paste the sentences in the correct order to show what happened in the beginning, middle, and end of the story.

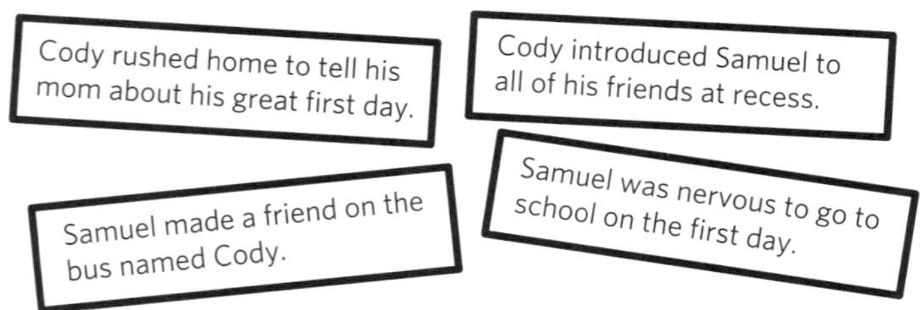

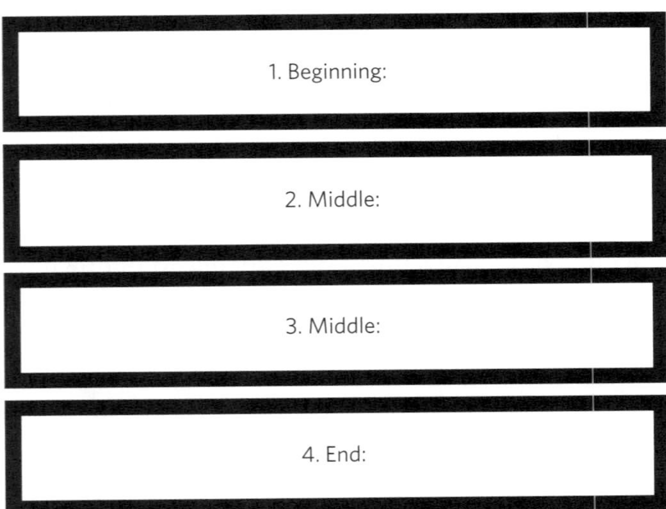

Figure 4.7. Graphic organizer with sentence strips example.

respond to academic directions. See Figure 4.7 for a ***graphic organizer*** with sentence strips that can be used for retelling a story in sequence.

- Allow the student to verbally express ideas prior to writing a response. The student can say what he or she is thinking about writing to a peer or teacher and receive ***positive reinforcement*** or corrective feedback prior to writing. If a sentence the student verbalizes is incomplete or has grammatical errors, then use ***modeling/request imitation*** to allow the student to have success with the language prior to writing.
- Provide a ***scribe*** for the student who will write down what the student says.
- Allow the student to audio record or video record what he or she wants to write. Either assess the content of the recording or have the student use the recording to transcribe the response in writing. Being able to start and pause the recording while writing or typing the response may be helpful.

MEDICAL CONDITIONS

Any one of numerous medical issues that are common to children in general or to children with ASD in particular may affect a student's ability to comply with directions.

Understanding the Problem

Students with ASD may struggle with various medical issues, including, but not limited to, gastrointestinal problems, seizures, sleeping problems, reactions to medications, and the typical illnesses that all children suffer with at one time or another. These medical conditions can cause feelings of pain, discomfort, distractibility, irritability, or lethargy that make it difficult for the student to consistently follow all teacher directions.

Assessing the Problem

It is important to know what medical issues your students with ASD are being treated for at all times. Thus, it is essential to maintain consistent communication with caregivers. Let them know that you want to understand all aspects of the child's treatment so you can provide appropriate supports in school. Ask for the caregivers or doctors to inform you about side effects of medications, symptoms of medical conditions, and what can be done to potentially ease the symptoms at school. If you think medical conditions may be affecting your student's ability to follow directions, then complete Section 9 of the FBA Checklist for Difficulty Following Directions in the appendix at the end of this chapter. Following are some tips for assessing each item:

9a: The Student Has Difficulty Following Directions That Require Sitting but Will Comply When Permitted to Stand (May Have Gastrointestinal Pain)

You may find out that a student does not like to sit down when feeling gastrointestinal pain. You can then assess if the student is better able to follow academic directions when permitted to stand instead of being forced to sit in a chair to comply.

9b: The Student Has Difficulty Following Directions When the Student Goes Untreated for Illness or Pain Due to the Inability to Expressively Communicate Symptoms

It is important to assess if noncompliance can be due to illnesses or pain for students who have limited expressive communication skills. For example, if a student is nonverbal and has severe tooth pain, then he or she may not be able to follow directions because he or she is suffering and is unable to communicate his or her needs.

9c: The Student Has Difficulties Following Directions Following Nights of Limited Sleep

You can use a daily communication log with caregivers for students who have sleep issues to document the child's sleep patterns to help determine if lack of sleep may be affecting the student's ability to follow directions.

9d: The Student Has Difficulty Following Directions Due to Reactions to New Medications or Reactions to Changes in Doses of Medications

If any new medications are being taken or doses are being changed to current medications, then it is important that you ask caregivers to keep you informed so you can determine if reactions to medication may be affecting compliance.

9e: The Student Has Difficulty Following Directions Following Periods of Seizure Activity

If the student is prone to having seizures, then you want to make sure you are kept informed of all seizure activity. A student may be unable to consistently follow directions when a seizure occurred earlier in the day, when red flags are present indicating that seizure activity will likely occur, or on the day(s) following a seizure.

Supporting the Student

Consider the following strategies and supports to increase a student's compliance with following directions when medical conditions are the issue:

- Allow the child to stand instead of sitting to increase compliance when the child is feeling gastrointestinal pain.
- If the child is tired, then give directions that are easy and enjoyable for the student, easing up on more challenging expectations. It may help to use ***behavioral momentum*** (also known as ***high-probability instructional sequences***) in which you use a repeated pattern of easy-easy-difficult-easy-easy-difficult when giving directions.
- Allow the child to have a brief rest period if doing so increases the student's ability to follow directions after the rest period is finished.
- Teach the child functional communication skills so the student can communicate if he or she is unable to follow a direction due to feeling sick or having pain or discomfort. When the child communicates such feelings, try to make the student more comfortable and ease up on the directions.
- Maintain regular communication with the student's caregivers to stay informed about medical conditions, side effects of medications, and so forth.

From Assessment to Successful Intervention

Case Study: Alex *Alex is a third-grade student with ASD who has been having great difficulty following directions throughout the school day. After reviewing the FBA Checklist for Difficulty Following Directions (see the appendix at the end of this chapter), Alex's teacher, Ms. Snow, begins to think that his problems may be due to his delayed language comprehension skills. Ms. Snow decides to test out different scenarios in Section 1 of the checklist because she is not completely sure. She first collects data to determine if he is better able to follow directions when she simplifies her language. Ms. Snow finds out that Alex follows 80% of directions that are given using very simple sentences and only 20% of directions that involve more complex language. Thus, she checks box 1a. She then discovers that Alex does follow directions that are given regularly throughout the school day, such as, "Stand up and push in your chair," or "Come sit on the carpet, and put your fingers on your lips." He is usually unable to follow unfamiliar directions without prompting, however. So, she checks box 1e. Finally, she predicts that Alex may be relying on environmental cues to understand behavioral, social, and academic expectations. She pays close attention to his behavior when cues are present and when they are not. Alex often needs several reminders to follow directions when environmental cues are not present. When Ms. Snow gives directions to get ready for a lesson, such as telling the students to get out their math folders, calculators, and colored pencils, Alex responds only after he sees the peers around him getting those materials as opposed to responding to the verbal directions as soon as they are given. She notices that this happens throughout the school day. Because of this, he is usually still attempting to gather the necessary materials when the teacher is ready to begin instruction. This impedes the learning in the classroom because Ms. Snow must then wait for Alex to finish getting his materials before beginning the lesson. Other students often begin to engage in disruptive behaviors while waiting for instruction to start. Ms. Snow checks box 1d.*

Figure 4.8 shows Section 1 of the FBA Checklist that Ms. Snow filled out, the hypothesis statement she formulated, and the intervention plan that was created based on the assessment.

Challenging Behavior: Difficulty Following Directions

1. Language Comprehension Difficulties

- ☑ 1a: The student can follow directions only when the directions are given using very simple sentences.
- ❒ 1b: The student often performs the incorrect behavior as an attempt to follow directions.
- ❒ 1c: The student can follow directions only when the teacher slows down the rate of speech when giving directions.
- ☑ 1d: The student relies on environmental cues to follow directions.
- ☑ 1e: The student can follow directions only when directions are familiar and given daily.
- ❒ 1f: The student follows directions only when they are given nonverbally or when oral directions are paired with visual supports.

Hypothesis Statement Alex has trouble following directions due to his language comprehension difficulties. He is usually able to comply when directions are given using very simple sentences or when they are very familiar. Alex is unable to comply or relies on environmental cues to follow directions when they are unfamiliar.

Intervention Plan

- Simplify language when giving directions to the whole class.
- If unable to simplify language for the whole class due to the nature of the direction, then give the direction to Alex one to one first, and make sure he understands what the teacher is going to tell the whole class.
- Use consistent language when giving directions.
- When feasible, write simplified directions on a note card before announcing them to the group, giving the note card to Alex when verbally stating the directions to the group. For example, hand Alex a note card that has the words *math folder, calculator,* and *colored pencils* written on it when stating, "Students, it is now time to get out your math folder, get a calculator from the back table, and get three different colored pencils from your pencil pouches." Having the simplified visual cue will allow Alex to read and process directions without getting confused by the teacher's verbal request. It also allows Alex to be ready for instruction at the same time as his classmates
- Deliver ***positive reinforcement*** when Alex follows directions.

Results

Ms. Snow sees tremendous gains in Alex's ability to follow directions after just a few days of using ***clear, consistent, and concise language*** and providing simplified written directions. Her next step will be to use ***shaping*** to gradually increase the complexity of the language she uses when giving directions to help Alex develop his language comprehension skills.

Figure 4.8. Functional Behavior Assessment Checklist and intervention plan for Alex.

From Assessment to Successful Intervention

Case Study: Julie *Ms. Anderson, a special education teacher providing inclusive services in a high school setting, is supporting Julie, a student with Asperger syndrome who is often noncompliant when given directions. Ms. Anderson has tried various behavioral interventions to attempt to increase her compliance. For example, she provided* ***positive reinforcement*** *every time directions were followed and* ***prompting/fading procedures*** *to help Julie follow the directions. Also, because Julie enjoys playing with young children, Ms. Anderson initiated the use of a behavioral contract related to following directions that would allow Julie to spend time in the child care setting on the school's campus if she followed at least 80% of teacher directions during the school day. Julie still struggles with following directions, however, even with these research-based strategies in place. Ms. Anderson decides to conduct an FBA to attempt to figure out why Julie is having so much trouble following directions. Julie takes medication to treat her anxiety, so Ms. Anderson decides to examine whether anxiety, fear, and emotional regulation difficulties may be affecting Julie's problems with following directions. She begins to observe Julie's behavioral responses when directions are given. She notices that Julie responds with a distressed facial expression and ignores the request each time directions are given to the whole class. Then the general education teacher or Ms. Anderson gives Julie the directions one to one. Julie typically avoids looking at the teacher and continues to ignore the request, looking worried and fidgeting with items on her table. Ms. Anderson then decides to test out if Julie will comply more often if she is given some time and space after a direction is given. During this observational period, Ms. Anderson also examines whether Julie responds better to directions that are given in writing instead of verbally because she noticed how distressed Julie gets every time she hears a direction.*

The assessment data indicate that Julie follows directions with 70% success when given written directions and time and space to comply; she follows with 30% success when given verbal directions and time and space to comply; and she follows with 10% success when given verbal directions without time and space to comply. After reflecting on this information and confirming her findings during an interview with Julie, Ms. Anderson realizes that the strategies she previously used with Julie were making the problems worse because they were anxiety producing. Using ***prompting/fading procedures*** *was problematic because it did not allow Julie time and space to comply. Julie did not need prompting to be successful because she does not struggle with language comprehension and has above-average academic skills. Also, the behavioral contract and heavy use of* ***positive reinforcement*** *were making Julie more anxious because it was an added stress for her to achieve the expected outcomes. When the teacher asked Julie why she does not like receiving praise and recognition when she follows directions, Julie said she feels worried that she would not be able to do it again and would let everyone down.*

Figure 4.9 includes the Section 3 of the FBA Checklist that Ms. Anderson checked off during the assessment, the hypothesis statement she formulated, and the intervention plan that was put in place.

Challenging Behavior: Difficulty Following Directions

3. Anxiety, Fear, and Emotional Regulation Difficulties

- ☑ 3a: The student follows directions when given time to comply and some personal space as opposed to when a teacher demands an immediate response.
- ☐ 3b: The student follows directions when someone uses a positive, supportive tone of voice and warm facial expressions as opposed to a stern, directive voice and flat or negative facial expressions.
- ☐ 3c: The student follows directions better on Thursdays and Fridays as the student gets more comfortable with the weekly routines.
- ☐ 3d: The student has difficulty following directions that do not follow the typical routine or schedule (need for sameness).

Hypothesis Statement Julie has difficulty following directions due to experiencing heightened levels of anxiety when directions are given. Julie has more success with following directions when she is given the direction only once and is allowed time and space to comply. She has even greater success when the directions are provided in writing only and she is given time and space to comply.

Intervention Plan

- Refrain from repeatedly giving verbal directions and waiting in close proximity for compliance.
- Whenever feasible, write her directions in a small black memo notebook and walk away to give her an opportunity to respond when she is comfortable.
- In situations when it is not feasible to write down the directions, state the direction once and walk away, giving Julie time and space to comply.
- To address Julie's increased anxiety when structured ***positive reinforcement*** systems are used, use an intermittent reinforcement schedule that involves simply giving Julie a pass to go the child care center for 20 minutes at times when it is permissible for her to miss class and she has been doing well with following directions.

Results

With this plan in place, Julie's compliance increases significantly when directions are given in writing in the memo notebook, allowing her to comply when she is ready. She complies 90% of the time when directions are given in that manner. She still has trouble following verbal directions, but her success rate has gone up to 50% when directions are given verbally one time and she is given time and space to comply.

Figure 4.9. Functional Behavior Assessment Checklist and intervention plan for Julie.

Challenging Behavior: Difficulty Following Directions

1. Language Comprehension Difficulties

- ❐ 1a: The student can follow directions only when the directions are given using very simple sentences.
- ❐ 1b: The student often performs the incorrect behavior as an attempt to follow directions.
- ❐ 1c: The student can follow directions only when the teacher slows down the rate of speech when giving directions.
- ❐ 1d: The student relies on environmental cues to follow directions.
- ❐ 1e: The student can follow directions only when directions are familiar and given daily.
- ❐ 1f: The student follows directions only when they are given nonverbally or when oral directions are paired with visual supports.

2. Deficits in Expressive Communication Skills

- ❐ 2a: The student does not follow certain directions because he or she is unable to ask for help or clarification when directions are not understood.
- ❐ 2b: The student does not follow directions because he or she does not have the expressive communication skills needed to negotiate and advocate for accommodations needed to comply.
- ❐ 2c: The student does not follow directions because he or she does not have the expressive communication skills needed to ask for a break when necessary.

3. Anxiety, Fear, and Emotional Regulation Difficulties

- ❐ 3a: The student follows directions when given time to comply and some personal space as opposed to when a teacher demands an immediate response.
- ❐ 3b: The student follows directions when someone uses a positive, supportive tone of voice and warm facial expressions as opposed to a stern, directive voice and flat or negative facial expressions.
- ❐ 3c: The student follows directions better on Thursdays and Fridays as the student gets more comfortable with the weekly routines.
- ❐ 3d: The student has difficulty following directions that do not follow the typical routine or schedule (need for sameness).

4. Social Skills Deficits

- ❐ 4a: Due to significant deficits in joint attention and social reciprocity, the student is often not engaged socially when directions are given, making it difficult to hear, process, or respond to the directions.
- ❐ 4b: The student has problems following directions that require the use of one or more social skills the student has not yet acquired.
- ❐ 4c: The student has problems following directions that require perspective taking.

5. Sensory Processing Problems

- ❐ 5a: The student has problems following directions that require facing increased levels of sensory input.
- ❐ 5b: The student has problems following directions that require the use of certain materials with specific textures or odors.
- ❐ 5c: The student has difficulty following directions that take away opportunities for the student to get the sensory input needed.

6. Problems With Focus and Attention

- ❐ 6a: The student follows directions that are given one to one and at eye level but has difficulty following directions given to the group.
- ❐ 6b: The student begins to follow the direction but gets distracted by something.
- ❐ 6c: The student has difficulty following directions when he or she is heavily focused on something and the direction requires the student to stop that activity and do something else (difficulty shifting attention).

Challenging Behavior: Difficulty Following Directions *(continued)*

7. Executive Functioning Challenges

- ❒ 7a: The student follows one-step directions and simple two-step directions but cannot follow multistep directions that require planning and organizational skills.
- ❒ 7b: The student follows multistep directions only when they are broken down into one-step directions or when they are given using visual supports such as a task analysis or checklist.

8. Academic, Cognitive, or Motor Skills Deficits

- ❒ 8a: The student complies with directions when they are academically easy for the student but not when the directions require skills the student has not fully acquired or mastered.
- ❒ 8b: The student complies with directions that require factual responses at the concrete level but does not comply when the directions require abstract thought and reasoning.
- ❒ 8c: The student complies when the fine or gross motor skills required are simple for the student but does not comply when the fine or gross motor skills required are very challenging for the student.

9. Medical Conditions

- ❒ 9a: The student has difficulty following directions that require sitting but will comply when permitted to stand (may have gastrointestinal pain).
- ❒ 9b: The student has difficulty following directions when the student goes untreated for illness or pain due to the inability to expressively communicate symptoms.
- ❒ 9c: The student has difficulties following directions following nights of limited sleep.
- ❒ 9d: The student has difficulty following directions due to reactions to new medications or reactions to changes in doses of medications.
- ❒ 9e: The student has difficulty following directions following periods of seizure activity.

Other ____

____

____

____

____

Hypothesis Statement ____

____

____

____

____

CHAPTER 5

Engaging During Group Instruction

Students with ASD often have difficulties engaging during group instruction. As a result, they may demonstrate challenging problems such as shouting out, using repetitive behaviors, getting out of their seat, walking around the room, talking to peers, exhibiting aggressive behaviors, and so forth. The reasons why students have difficulty participating during group instruction vary depending on each student's unique profile. This chapter discusses nine challenges faced by students with ASD that may explain why they do not regularly engage during group instruction:

1. Language comprehension difficulties
2. Deficits in expressive communication skills
3. Anxiety, fear, and emotional regulation difficulties
4. Restricted range of interests
5. Social skills deficits
6. Sensory processing problems
7. Problems with focus and attention
8. Academic, cognitive, or motor skills deficits
9. Medical conditions

LANGUAGE COMPREHENSION DIFFICULTIES

Some students may have difficulty engaging during group instruction due to language comprehension problems or deficits in receptive communication skills.

Understanding the Problem

Deficits in students' receptive communication skills mean that they may not understand the language that teachers use when delivering instruction, and, consequently, they are unable to actively engage during the lesson. Teachers often assume students innately understand the academic vocabulary, phrases, and sentences used during lessons. Students with ASD typically require explicit instruction to understand and apply the terminology of the academic lesson, however, due to their language impairments. For example, the teacher may use the following terms and phrases during a lesson related to measurement: *quadrilateral, length, width, area, perimeter, measure, distance, inches, feet, estimate, square feet, square inches,* and *educated guess.* The teacher may also use sentences such as the following: "Round your answer to the nearest whole number." "Explain why your answer makes sense." "Compare your answer with your partner's answer." Students with ASD may have difficulty engaging in the lesson if they do not comprehend all the terms, phrases, and sentences. Keep in mind that there is a difference between language impairments and cognitive impairments, and do not assume that the student is unable to meet the lesson's cognitive and academic demands simply because the student requires explicit instruction in the academic language of the lesson.

Some students with ASD may not only have difficulties comprehending the language used by teachers during group instruction, but they may also struggle with auditory processing problems. This means their difficulties engaging during group instruction may stem from the trouble they have with processing what they hear during the lesson. It is commonplace for teachers to do a lot of talking while delivering group instruction. A large amount of information is often given at one time without much consideration for processing issues students with ASD may face. Thus, students may disengage during instruction because they are unable to process the information quickly enough to stay meaningfully engaged.

Assessing the Problem

If you think language comprehension difficulties may be affecting your student's ability to meaningfully participate during group instruction, then complete Section 1 of the FBA Checklist for Difficulty Engaging During Group Instruction in the appendix at the end of this chapter. The following sections describe tips for assessing each item in Section 1 of the checklist.

1a: The Student Has Difficulty Engaging During Group Instruction When the Teacher Is Using a Lecture Format but Is Able to Engage When the Teacher Uses Various Strategies to Actively Involve the Student in the Lesson, Such as Hands-on Tasks and Visual Supports

Compare the student's engagement levels when the teacher is using a lecture format (the sit-and-get method of instruction) with situations in which the teacher uses various non–language-based strategies to actively involve the student in the lesson. If the student disengages when the format is primarily language based but engages much better when the lesson involves hands-on tasks; the use of ***guided notes, graphic organizers, pictures, video clips,*** and visual demonstrations; and so forth, then you can predict that a language impairment is affecting the student's ability to engage during group instruction.

1b: The Student Is Able to Engage During Group Instruction When the Teacher Uses Clear, Concise Language and Simple Sentence Structures but Has Difficulty Engaging When the Teacher Uses Complex Language and Long Verbal Elaborations to Explain Content

This will be difficult to assess if your lessons typically include complex sentence structures and long periods of talking to students, which is very common. You may want to test out what happens when you choose your words wisely, however, and observe how that affects the engagement of your student with ASD. For example, a teacher may typically say, "When you are rounding to the nearest whole number, round the number in the ones place up if the number in the tenths place is 5 or larger. If the number in the tenths place is less than 5, then keep the whole number the same." This is a lot of words to take in all at once, and the content is presented quite abstractly. Try this instead: Write "rounding to the nearest whole number" on a place on the board without any other distracting information around it. Point to it, and have the students read it using ***choral response.*** Then write "34.5" on the board. Say, "Here is the tenths place," and dramatically point to the 5. Then say, "It is 5 or higher. So…" Then draw an arrow from the 5 to the 4 and say, "This number rounds up." Put an arrow pointing up over the 4, and cross out the 5. Write "35" below "34.5."

Instead of using 45 words in long, complex sentences, this simplified version uses 15 words broken up into short, clear sentences with visual demonstration of the content between sentences to support comprehension of the language. There is a solution if you are concerned that the other students in the class need to hear all the academic language used in the original example. After instructing students using the simplified language, ask them to generate the rule using mathematics terminology. If the student with ASD is unable to engage during this time, then he or she can engage by completing some problems to practice the skill just learned.

1c: The Student Is Able to Engage During Group Instruction When the Information Is Presented in Manageable Chunks With Time Allotted for Processing but Is Unable to Engage When a Large Amount of Information Is Delivered at One Time Without Purposeful Pauses for Processing

Try delivering the information in manageable chunks with time allotted for processing to assess if the student's difficulties engaging during group instruction may be related to auditory processing problems and to see if the student is able to engage in more meaningful ways. For example, deliver a small amount of information and tell the students to think about what was just presented. If the student has difficulty staying focused, then you can have the student draw a picture about what was learned or write about it listing key words, phrases, or sentences. After providing time to think (approximately 1–2 minutes), instruct the students to share what they learned with a peer. If this time allotted for processing increases the student's engagement during group instruction, then you can predict that auditory processing problems are affecting the student's ability to engage. Most, if not all, other students in the classroom will also benefit from the added opportunities to think about what they learned and share their thoughts with a peer.

Supporting the Student

Consider the following strategies and supports if language comprehension difficulties are causing problems with a student's engagement during group instruction:

- ***Use clear, consistent, and concise language*** when delivering instruction.
- Keep sentence structures short and simple whenever possible.
- Pair verbal instruction with visual demonstration of the content being presented including ***pictures,*** charts, ***symbols, graphs,*** models, diagrams, ***cue cards*** with key words, physical demonstrations, video clips, and so forth (see Figure 5.1).
- Deliver small amounts of information and provide processing time before continuing with the verbal instruction. Students may engage in ***think-pair-share,*** think-write-pair-share, or think-draw-pair-share activities during the processing time in which they have time to process the information; summarize what they learned verbally, in writing, or through drawing; and share that summary with a peer.
- Use ***shaping*** by gradually increasing the complexity of the language used during group instruction to allow the student to improve language comprehension and processing skills at the appropriate instructional level. Continue using clear, concise language, however, even as the sentence structures become more complex.

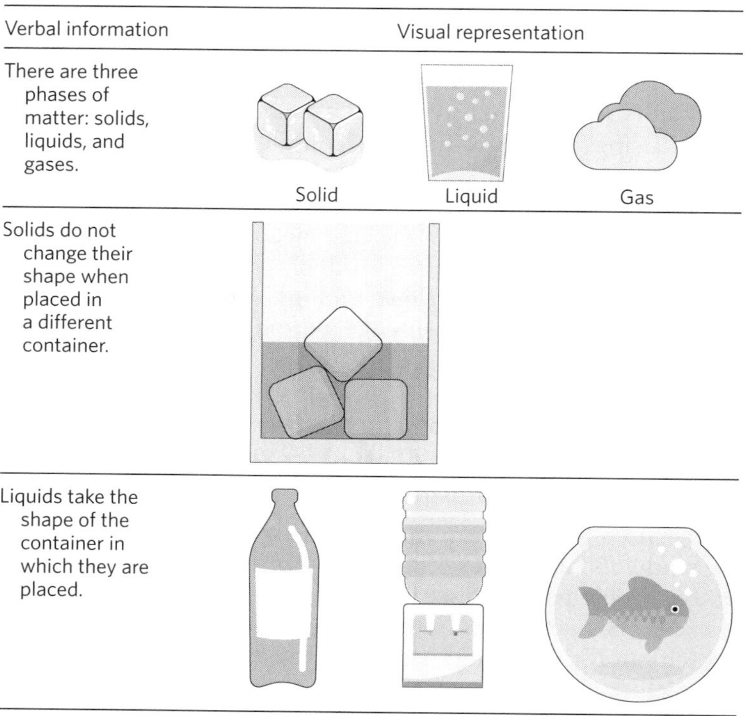

Figure 5.1. Examples for presenting information visually.

DEFICITS IN EXPRESSIVE COMMUNICATION SKILLS

Some students with ASD have deficits in expressive communication skills that may make it difficult for them to engage during group instruction in the ways students typically engage with content.

Understanding the Problem

Impairments in expressive communication skills can be a factor affecting a student's difficulty to engage during group instruction. Providing increased questioning is one of the most effective strategies to keep students actively engaged. Questioning will not promote the student's engagement, however, if the student does not have the expressive communication skills needed to answer teacher questions throughout the lesson or *AAC* supports in place. Asking questions related to the information presented is another way for students to stay actively engaged during lessons. Again, the student may disengage if he or she lacks the expressive communication skills to ask questions and cannot get clarification or additional information when needed. Also, the student will be unable to participate if he or she lacks the expressive communication skills to verbally interact with a peer or group of peers during a portion of the lesson that utilizes peer engagement.

Assessing the Problem

If you think deficits in expressive communication skills may be affecting your student's ability to meaningfully participate during group instruction, then complete Section 2 of the FBA Checklist for Difficulty Engaging During Group Instruction found in the appendix at the end of this chapter. Following are some tips for assessing each item:

2a: The Student Has Difficulty Engaging During Group Instruction Because He or She Does Not Have the Expressive Communication Skills Necessary to Respond, Initiate, and Interact

It is important to first assess how many opportunities students have to interact with the teacher and peers during group instruction that require expressive communication skills (e.g., asking questions, answering questions, making comments, responding to comments, sharing information and ideas verbally). This task may help you realize how much students must rely on expressive communication skills to participate during group instruction. You may ultimately predict that expressive communication deficits are a huge factor in your student's challenging behavior during lessons in which he or she cannot fully participate due to skill deficits in that area.

2b: The Student Engages During Group Instruction When Given Nonverbal Ways to Participate During the Lesson

Provide opportunities for the student to respond, initiate, or engage using nonverbal communication through the use of ***pictures, symbols,*** gestures, actions, ***response cards*** or ***AAC*** devices. For example, provide the student with three ***response cards*** that have the words *solid, liquid,* and *gas* written on them during a lesson on the three phases of matter, with corresponding ***pictures*** on each card to support the student's understanding of the terms if necessary. When questions are asked to the group to identify if something is a solid, liquid, or a gas, the student can respond by holding up the correct card. Also, give the student a voice output device that has SOLID, LIQUID and GAS prerecorded on the device. The student can then select the correct prerecorded response to actively participate in the questioning.

Actions or gestures can also help the student actively engage in lessons when expressive communication skills are deficient. For example, the teacher may teach the student different gestures to represent various weather terms, such as *tornado, hurricane,* and *tsunami.* The student can participate in the question-and-answer portions of the lesson by acting out the correct gesture when asked a question to demonstrate understanding of the different weather conditions. If the student is better able to engage when various nonverbal communication options are provided as opposed to relying only on verbal responses, then you can predict that expressive communication difficulties are affecting the student's ability to engage during group instruction.

Supporting the Student

Consider the following strategies and supports if deficits in expressive communication skills are causing problems with a student's engagement during group instruction:

- Provide opportunities for the student to respond using ***response cards.*** Give the student ***pictures, symbols,*** or ***cue cards*** with words or phrases printed on them to use to answer questions.
- Utilize ***AAC*** devices to allow the student to answer questions, ask questions, and make comments during group instruction. Content-specific ***symbols*** or words must be available during the lesson.
- Provide opportunities for the student to participate through movement, gestures, or role-play.
- Utilize instructional technology such as interactive apps on tablets or interactive digital whiteboard technology to provide opportunities for participation.
- Give the student ***graphic organizers*** or ***guided notes*** to complete during the lesson. The student can write, draw, or glue on words, ***pictures,*** or sentences in the appropriate places on the graphic or note-taking guide.

ANXIETY, FEAR, AND EMOTIONAL REGULATION DIFFICULTIES

Some students with ASD may have trouble engaging during group instruction if they feel anxiety or fear or other emotions that lead to emotional regulation difficulties.

Understanding the Problem

Group instruction may increase feelings of anxiety and fear for a variety of reasons. Students may have fears of getting called on and not knowing the answers, fears of speaking in front of larger groups, fears of not understanding the expectations for participation, and so forth. Challenging problems can certainly occur when students experience these heightened emotions and struggle with emotional regulation as they try to deal with their distress.

Assessing the Problem

If you think anxiety, fear, and emotional regulation difficulties may be affecting your student's ability to meaningfully participate during group instruction, then complete Section 3 of the FBA Checklist for Difficulty Engaging During Group Instruction in the appendix at the end of this chapter. Following are some tips for assessing each item:

3a: The Student Does Not Answer Questions or Participate During Group Instruction Even When the Teacher Is Certain the Student Knows the Answer and the Expectations for Participation

This could be a sign that the student is experiencing anxiety, fear, and emotional regulation difficulties. These emotions can cripple the student in a sense, making it very difficult for the student to answer questions and participate even when the student knows the answers or knows exactly what to do. When asked a question, the student may put his or her head down, look away from the teacher, say, "I don't know," or simply ignore the request. When asked to do something such as imitate gestures or movements, hold up ***response cards,*** write something, draw something, or talk with a peer, the student may be unable to do so because of heightened levels of anxiety and fear.

3b: The Student Demonstrates Self-Stimulatory Behaviors at an Increased Level During Group Instruction to Cope With Heightened Levels of Anxiety and Fear and to Deal With Emotional Regulation Difficulties

If you notice that the student increases use of self-stimulatory behavior (e.g., rocking, hand flapping, vocal stims, repetitive movements with objects) during group instruction specifically, then this can certainly be a response to heightened levels of anxiety and fear. If this is the case, then it is important to allow the child to use these coping behaviors if they are not causing significant distraction to peers. These behaviors are often used to help the child regulate emotions, and he or she may eventually be able to participate in the lesson once emotional regulation is established. Teachers often try to stop these behaviors immediately, and this does not allow the child to use them as coping strategies to calm down when stressed.

3c: The Student Attempts to Leave the Area During Group Instruction but Rarely Does So During Other Classroom Routines and Activities

The student may experience fight-or-flight tendencies when feeling extremely anxious and fearful. Thus, if you notice that the student often tries to run away or leave the area during group instruction, then this can be a response to anxiety and fear.

3d: The Student Has Difficulty Engaging During Group Instruction That Is New or Unfamiliar but Participates More Willingly and Actively During Group Instruction That Follows a Familiar, Predictable Format (Need for Sameness)

Some students are able to participate during group instruction when the lessons follow predictable formats and the expectations for participation are very clear. The student's anxiety and fear may increase, causing the student to disengage, however, when the format or content of the lessons are unfamiliar, which is often the case.

Supporting the Student

Consider the following strategies and supports if anxiety, fear, and emotional regulation difficulties are causing problems with a student's engagement during group instruction:

- Use a predictable format for lessons whenever possible.
- Use ***priming*** to prepare the student for a new lesson format or new content.
- Ensure high levels of success during question-and-answer periods of group instruction by doing any of the following:
  - Give the student the question(s) that will be asked in advance to give the student time to prepare an answer.
  - Use ***most-to-least prompting*** when asking questions to decrease student anxiety and fear that results from not being certain of the correct answer.
- Tell the student to raise his or hand to answer questions, and say you will not call on the student unless his or her hand is raised.
- Allow the student to use a quiet voice or whisper to answer or ask questions if that makes the student more comfortable responding, without saying things such as, "Say it louder," or "Say it so everyone can hear you."
- Allow the student to use repetitive behavior as a coping strategy to regulate anxiety and fear during group instruction as long as it does not cause significant disruption to others.
- Allow the student to choose where to sit and who to sit next to during group instruction if that helps ease anxiety and fear.
- Use ***positive reinforcement*** when the student participates and engages during group instruction.

RESTRICTED RANGE OF INTERESTS

Many students with ASD have a restricted range of interests due to the nature of their disability, which may make it difficult for them to engage with content unrelated to these interests.

Understanding the Problem

Although they may have fascinations related to very specific topics that can be tapped into to promote engagement and skill development, it may be very difficult for students with a restricted range of interests to engage during group instruction that is not connected to their special interests. Group instruction will likely cover content that is not of interest to all students because of the increased focus on standards-based lessons. Typically developing learners have a much wider range of interests than students with ASD, however. This promotes their motivation to engage during group instruction in more capacities than those students with ASD who have significantly limited interests.

Assessing the Problem

If you think your student's restricted range of interests may be affecting the child's ability to meaningfully participate during group instruction, then complete Section 4 of the FBA Checklist for Difficulty Engaging During Group Instruction in the appendix at the end of this chapter. Following are some tips for assessing each item:

4a: The Student Engages Well During Group Instruction Related to the Student's Interests

You need to make sure you are aware of the student's areas of special interest to assess if the student will engage during group instruction. You can get this information by observing the student or by interviewing the student, family members, or other professionals and paraprofessionals who may know more about the student's interests than you. Once you know the student's interests, plan group instruction lessons that tap into those interests. One obvious way is to directly connect the content of the lesson to the student's interests. For example, if the student loves trains, then the group lesson can pertain to the different trains and purposes they serve. More subtle ways that tap into the student's interests can be implemented, including selecting materials, providing various ways to participate during the lesson, and making comparisons related to special interest areas. A few scenarios follow:

- If a student is fascinated with NASCAR, then the teacher may use a visual of a speedway with cars in different locations to teach students how to use a scale to measure distances.
- If a student loves dinosaurs, then the student may use different dinosaur figurines to participate during the lesson—the student holds up a tyrannosaurus rex to ask for help, a brontosaurus to answer a question, or a pterodactyl to ask a question.
- If a student has a special interest in weather systems, then the teacher may compare feelings of characters in a story with weather conditions. The character feels as happy as a sunny day, as concerned as a dark sky before a rain storm, or as angry as a hurricane.

4b: The Student Does Not Engage During Group Instruction When the Topics Are Not Related to the Student's Interests

Once you are able to do what is described in 4a, you can then compare the student's level of engagement during group instructional activities that tap into the student's interest with those that do not.

Supporting the Student

If a restricted range of interests is causing problems with a student's engagement during group instruction, then tap into the student's interests as much as possible. Following are some examples:

- Connect lesson objectives to interests (e.g., if the student loves ocean animals, then students will learn about the food chain in ocean environments).
- Select learning materials and activities related to the student's interests (e.g. use Pokémon characters as puppets to act out a scene in a history lesson; if a student loves music, then play a tune on the piano to illustrate an ABBABB pattern in poetry stanzas).

- Expand on the student's interests (e.g., attempt to build interest in forest animals because the student already likes ocean animals).
- Make connections to special interests to teach new content (e.g., when a student interested in ocean animals is learning about the functions of organs in the human body, make the connection that fish use their gills to take oxygen out of the water and let water carry away carbon dioxide. Lungs in the human body take oxygen from the air and send carbon dioxide out through the air).

SOCIAL SKILL DEFICTS

Participating during group instruction requires social skills ranging from simple to complex; deficits in one or more of these skills can affect engagement during group instruction.

Understanding the Problem

First and foremost, students with ASD who have significant deficits in joint attention and social reciprocity will definitely have great challenges engaging during group instruction. Deficits in these areas make it extremely difficult for students to attend to what is being shared verbally or visually; listen to, process, and respond to questions posed by the teacher; actively listen to and process responses from peers; and engage in reciprocal interactions during the lesson. Difficulties understanding social expectations, such as raising one's hand and waiting to be called on, knowing how to follow along with the teacher's pace as opposed to going ahead or staying behind, having the conversational skills to participate in group discussion, and taking the perspective of others are additional social skills deficits that may negatively affect a student's ability to engage during group instruction.

Assessing the Problem

If you think social skills deficits may be affecting your student's ability to meaningfully participate during group instruction, then complete Section 5 of the FBA Checklist for Difficulty Engaging During Group Instruction in the appendix at the end of this chapter. Following are some tips for assessing each item:

5a: The Student Has Significant Deficits in Joint Attention Resulting in Difficulty Attending to the Teacher's Instruction, Peer Responses, or Learning Materials During Group Instruction

If you are unsure if joint attention deficits are the problem, then look for evidence of joint attention, including answering a question correctly, following a direction correctly, asking a question, making a relevant comment, completing an activity with a peer, completing an activity while following along with the teacher, following the point of the teacher to attend to something, or imitating the teacher or peers as requested during the lesson. Keep in mind that there are times when students with ASD do not look as if they are sharing attention because they do not make eye contact or use typical gestures. They may very well be taking it all in, however, even if they are not looking at the teacher and nodding their heads. That is why you want to look for evidence that joint attention was established, such as the previous examples.

5b: The Student Has Significant Deficits in Social Reciprocity Resulting in Difficulty Participating in Question-and-Answer Instructional Formats

It is often recommended that teachers ask a great deal of questions as opposed to delivering verbal instruction for extended periods of time without student participation to maintain active student engagement during group instruction. If a student has deficits in social reciprocity skills, then it will be very difficult to engage in the long chains of back-and-forth interactions required during student questioning. When a teacher asks a question and calls on a student, that interaction may require several reciprocal exchanges using scaffolding to support the student to fully answer the question. For example, suppose a teacher asks, "What is the capital of North Carolina?" and the student says, "Charlotte." The teacher may then say, "Charlotte is a city in North Carolina. But it is not the capital. Do you know what the capital is?" The student would then need to provide another response or say, "I don't know." The teacher would then continue the back-and-forth interaction until the student is able to say, "Raleigh." This may take as many as five or six back-and-forth interactions. This level of engagement during group instruction can be extremely challenging without fully established social reciprocity skills.

5c: The Student Does Not Understand the Various Social Expectations for Participating During Group Instruction

Students must follow a multitude of social expectations to actively participate during group instruction, including staying in one's seat; answering questions by raising one's hand or participating in ***choral response*** when the answer is known; following along with the teacher's pace; taking the perspective of another person such as the teacher, a peer, or characters in a story or lesson; accepting constructive feedback from a teacher after answering a question; using appropriate voice volume when participating in the lesson; and staying in the assigned area and maintaining appropriate space between oneself and peers. To assess these various social skills that are often not fully considered, it may be best to first observe the social skills typically developing peers use during group instruction. Create a list of those skills, and then observe the student with ASD, documenting which skills the student demonstrated and which skills needed prompting or support. If you see a discrepancy between the social skills demonstrated by peers and those demonstrated by the student with ASD, then you may decide that social skills deficits may be affecting the student's ability to engage during group instruction.

Supporting the Student

Consider the following strategies and supports if social skills deficits are causing problems with a student's engagement during group instruction:

- Use ***visual supports*** to increase joint attention (e.g., ***pictures,*** video clips, ***graphs,*** charts, ***graphic organizers, symbols,*** written words or phrases). See Figure 5.2 for an example of ***visual supports*** that can be used when teaching the concepts of area and perimeter.

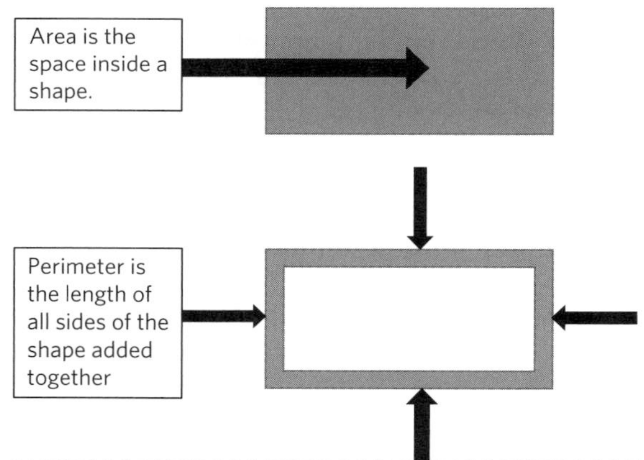

Figure 5.2. Visual supports for a geometry lesson.

Table 5.1. Examples of objects to use to support joint attention during lessons

Topic of lesson	Objects to support joint attention
Five food groups	Use various pretend or real foods (or packaging from real foods) to represent vegetables, fruits, protein, dairy, and grains. The student can hold up objects to respond to questions and sort the objects into the appropriate categories to demonstrate learning.
Using adjectives when writing	Use objects of interest to the student. The student can describe the objects using adjectives. For example, if the student loves dinosaurs, then provide different toy dinosaurs and have the student describe them. After describing a dinosaur using adjectives, the student can then write that description in a sentence.
Measuring perimeter	Use objects of interest that the student can measure to determine the perimeter (e.g. DVD cases, box tops from a favorite game, box from a favorite cereal).

- Point to ***visual supports*** to help the student attend to what you are referencing. If possible, have the student imitate pointing to what you are pointing to so you can be sure joint attention is established.
- Give the student personal copies of visuals being used during the lesson when appropriate to help the student attend to what the teacher is referencing. If the visuals are too far away, then the student may have difficulty establishing joint attention.
- Use real objects to support joint attention. Students with ASD are often object oriented, so having real objects to look at and engage with during the lesson can help establish and maintain joint attention (see Table 5.1).
- Give the student ***cue cards*** to read when asking questions to support social reciprocity. The ***cue cards*** can be faded as the student becomes more independent. See Table 5.2 for examples of ***cue cards*** that can be used during a group lesson on the five food groups.
- Set up opportunities for ***balanced turn-taking*** during group instruction whenever possible.

Table 5.2. Example of using cue cards to support social reciprocity during a group lesson

Questions asked by the teacher during a lesson about the five food groups	Cue cards the student can use to respond
What are the five food groups?	**Fruits, vegetables, grains, protein, dairy**
What are some examples of proteins?	**Chicken, beef, beans, fish**
What are some examples of vegetables?	**Broccoli, spinach, green beans, asparagus**
What are some examples of fruits?	**Apples, oranges, bananas, strawberries**
What are some examples of grains?	**Bread, rice, oatmeal, pasta**

- Use the following strategies if the student has not yet learned the social expectation of raising one's hand to participate during group instruction:
  - ***Video modeling/video self-modeling*** showing expectations for raising one's hand to answer questions.
  - ***Social narratives*** to teach expectations for raising one's hand to answer questions.
  - ***Self-monitoring*** (e.g., the student marks a tally every time he or she raises a hand to answer a question).
  - ***Least-to-most prompts hierarchy*** to teach a student how to raise his or her hand to answer questions:
    1. Visual prompt: picture of someone raising a hand or a ***cue card*** that has "raise hand" written on it.
    2. Minimal verbal prompt: "Do you know the answer?"
    3. Moderate verbal prompt: "You know the answer. Raise your hand."
    4. ***Modeling/request imitation***
- Deliver ***positive reinforcement*** when the student engages during group instruction.

SENSORY PROCESSING PROBLEMS

Sensory processing problems experienced by some students with ASD may result in sensory overload during group instruction or a need for additional sensory input during group instruction; either issue can make it harder for these students to engage.

Understanding the Problem

Group instruction can cause sensory overload for some students with ASD, making it very difficult for them to engage during the lesson. This can happen if there is a great deal of noise, chaotic movement, fluorescent lighting, use of materials that cause discomfort, and so forth. Yet, some students may be understimulated and require sensory input to engage during group instruction. For example, some students may need to be able to stand, sit on a balance ball, rock, or engage in some other form of movement activity to stimulate the senses and focus during the lesson.

Assessing the Problem

If you think sensory processing problems may be affecting your student's ability to meaningfully participate during group instruction, then complete Section 6 of the FBA Checklist for Difficulty Engaging During Group Instruction in the appendix at the end of this chapter. Following are some tips for assessing each item:

6a: The Student Has Problems Engaging During Group Instructional Activities That Require the Use of Certain Materials With Specific Textures or Odors

You can conduct observations or interview the student, family members, or other professionals or paraprofessionals who may know more about this issue to find out what materials make your student uncomfortable due to sensory processing problems. Occupational therapists typically are familiar with sensory processing problems and can help you understand your student's sensory profile. For example, students may have sensory aversions to materials such as finger paint, markers with strong scents, clay, playdough, sandpaper, pastels, and other items.

6b: The Student Has Difficulty Engaging in Group Instruction in Loud, Bright, Cluttered Environments but Is Better Able to Engage in Environments That Have Minimal Sensory Input

Note the child's level of engagement when group instruction is delivered in quiet settings, dim or dark settings, settings without a great deal of movement taking place, or environments without excessive materials to see and touch. Compare this with the child's level of engagement when group instruction is delivered in loud, bright, or cluttered environments.

6c: The Student Has Difficulty Engaging During Group Instruction That Limits Opportunities for the Student to Get the Sensory Input Needed

Permit the student to move during the lesson instead of requiring the student to sit still, be quiet, or put their hands in their lap to determine if your student may need sensory input to engage during group instruction. The student may be allowed to pace, stand and rock, bounce on a balance ball, manipulate fidget objects, and so forth. Compare the student's level of engagement during group instruction when sensory input it provided with engagement during lessons when the student must adhere to behavioral expectations that limit access to such input.

Supporting the Student

Consider the following strategies and supports if sensory processing problems are affecting a student's engagement during group instruction:

- Make the following environmental arrangements whenever possible:
  - Use small-group instructional arrangements instead of whole- or large-group instruction.
  - Limit the amount of materials present in front of the student to just the essentials.
  - Set clear behavioral expectations for all students to minimize loud noises caused by off-task behaviors or shouting while participating in the lesson.
  - Do not use fluorescent lighting.
  - Create sections of the classroom for group instruction, then cordon those areas off from large open spaces.
  - Use predictable and consistent routines to control movement during transitions during the lesson.
- Allow the student to do any of the following during group instruction:
  - Verbalize quietly
  - Rock back and forth
  - Stand
  - Play with fidget toys
  - Draw
  - Sit on a balance ball
- Allow the child to get some sensory input by doing any of the following before a group instruction:
  - Go for a walk
  - Perform physical exercises in the classroom

- Jump on a trampoline
- Swing
- Ride on a scooter
- Throw a ball back and forth

PROBLEMS WITH FOCUS AND ATTENTION

It is well documented that students with ASD often have trouble with focusing and paying attention. Group instruction is probably the most difficult time for students who have problems with focus and attention.

Understanding the Problem

The various activities in the classroom during group instruction, or even outside of the classroom, can easily distract some students with ASD. They may not focus on the right information (verbal or visual) at the right time. The movement, activity, and verbalizations of peers may be a distraction. Also, students with ASD often have trouble shifting their attention—meaning, if they are focused on something during the lesson, then they may not be able to easily switch their focus to the next part of the lesson. For example, if the student was working on filling in ***guided notes*** during the lecture part of the lesson and did not get a chance to finish, then he or she may not be able to switch gears and participate in a discussion activity with a group until the ***guided notes*** are finished.

Assessing the Problem

If you think problems with focus and attention may be affecting your student's ability to meaningfully participate during group instruction, then complete Section 7 of the FBA Checklist for Difficulty Engaging During Group Instruction in the appendix at the end of this chapter. Following are some tips for assessing each item:

7a: The Student Engages Well During One-to-One Instruction but Has Difficulty During Group Instructional Formats

The student loses focus and attention when the number of students in an instructional group is increased. Working one to one with a teacher is a permanent reminder to focus and attend. Also, teachers typically provide a great deal of prompting when working individually with a student to make sure the student is paying attention and complying as quickly as possible. Conversely, when the student then works in a small or large group, that level of support and prompting is no longer there to keep the student focused. This does not mean the student should always receive one-to-one instruction. It does mean the student needs intervention and supports to learn how to independently regulate focus and attention without needing a great deal of teacher prompting.

7b: The Student Participates During Group Instruction When the Teacher Makes Specific Efforts to Secure the Student's Attention but Gets Disengaged Without These Continuous Supports

If the student continually needs the teacher to give verbal, gestural, visual, or physical prompting to attend during the lesson, then focus and attention issues are impeding the student's ability to participate during group instruction.

7c: The Student Has Difficulty During Group Instruction When the Student's Attention Is Focused on Something Other Than the Topic of the Lesson

This means that the student struggles with shifting his or her attention. If there are instances when the student gets hyperfocused on something and cannot stop thinking about it or cannot stop working on a specific assignment to participate in the current group instruction activities, then you can predict that trouble with shifting attention is negatively affecting the student's ability to engage during group instruction.

7d: The Student Grasps Some Skills and Concepts During Group Lessons but Not All, Demonstrating Difficulty Knowing What to Focus on During the Lesson

If you notice that the student only grasps part of the content presented during group instruction on a regular bases, then the student may be losing focus quite often during the lessons. Your prediction may be even stronger if there is no pattern as far as the type of information the student is able to retain. The problem is probably not cognitive or academic if there is no rhyme or reason to the type of information the student is able to grasp during group instruction. More likely, the student's focus and attention comes and goes, resulting in missed learning opportunities.

Supporting the Student

Consider the following strategies and supports if problems with focus and attention are affecting a student's engagement during group instruction:

- Use preferential seating to limit distractions.
- Arrange furniture to limit visual and auditory distractions during group instruction.
- Use increased questioning to keep the student engaged.
- Provide various ***visual supports*** (e.g., ***symbols, pictures, graphs,*** diagrams, charts, video clips) to support the student's focus and attention skills.
- Provide natural cues to the whole group throughout the lesson (e.g., "Look right here to see …" "I am going to tell you something very important right now." "To summarize, the most important thing you need to know about …")
- Provide personal copies of materials the teacher is using during group instruction to the student. Sometimes the distance between the student and the learning materials is too far to allow the student to maintain focus and attention.
- Use ***peer-mediated interventions*** to teach peers how to redirect the student's attention when appropriate.
- Provide active engagement opportunities, such as using ***guided notes***, completing ***graphic organizers*** during the lesson, creating drawings that go along with the lesson, and role playing.
- Call on the student often to read small sections of the material to the class to keep the student engaged.
- Use the student as a helper during the lesson to keep the student engaged.

- Teach self-management skills:
  - Have the student set goals for attending during group instruction (e.g., "I will answer at least five questions." "I will read along in my book when the teacher is reading aloud").
  - Create a ***self-monitoring*** tool the student can use to record performance related to the goals that are set.
  - Have the student engage in self-evaluation after the lesson and use self-reinforcement to reward accomplishments.
- Deliver ***positive reinforcement*** when the student engages appropriately during group instruction.

ACADEMIC, COGNITIVE, OR MOTOR SKILLS DEFICITS

Although some students with ASD perform average or above average academically, others may struggle with academic and cognitive deficits that can greatly impede their ability to meaningfully engage during group instruction.

Understanding the Problem

Students may have weaknesses in academic skill areas such as reading, writing, or mathematics. They may have difficulty with abstract learning tasks due to their cognitive differences. Also, if a student has deficits in fine motor skills, then handwriting weaknesses can impede engagement during group instruction if other accommodations are not made. Likewise, if a student is required to use manipulatives during a group instruction lesson, thus requiring the student's use of fine motor skills that are deficient, then the student may disengage.

Assessing the Problem

If you think academic, cognitive, or motor skills deficits may be affecting your student's ability to meaningfully participate during group instruction, then complete Section 8 of the FBA Checklist for Difficulty Engaging During Group Instruction in the appendix at the end of this chapter. Following are some tips for assessing each item:

8a: The Student Engages Better During Group Instruction That Entails Concrete Learning Activities Versus the Presentation of Abstract Ideas and Concepts

If group instruction in your classroom is often presented at the abstract level without connecting the concepts to concrete ideas and experiences, then students with ASD may struggle with engagement due to their difficulties thinking at the abstract level without the necessary level of scaffolding. Consider a lesson on differences between living and nonliving things. A teacher may present this lesson relying on abstract ideas that are delivered primarily through oral language. For example, the teacher may instruct students that living things are able to grow and move, whereas nonliving things are not. The teacher may then give the students a worksheet containing ***pictures*** or words with directions to put the living and nonliving things into the correct categories. This is instruction at the abstract level.

To make this lesson more concrete to support students with ASD (and other learners), begin by presenting various living objects, such as a plant, the class pet, and a classmate. Tell students that all these things are living, and ask them to identify characteristics that prove this (e.g., they grow, they need water, they need food, they sleep, they move on their own). Then do the same for nonliving things, such as a pencil, chair, and ball. This can lead to students creating their own definitions of living versus nonliving things. After using concrete objects, the teacher can then move to representational learning activities (e.g., showing ***pictures*** and video clips of living and nonliving things). Once the students demonstrate understanding at the concrete and representational levels, the teacher can then move to the abstract.

Although this type of group instruction lesson may take more time than starting at the abstract level, the learning benefits are worth the extra time. It may be challenging to think of ways to present abstract ideas and concepts at the concrete and representational levels. It is helpful to think about how the student may have experiences related to the concepts, which will lead you to instruction at the concrete level. In some instances, connecting the concepts to everyday life is all students need to be able to learn the skills that can later be applied at the abstract level.

If you think this issue may be affecting your student's ability to participate during group instruction, then compare the student's level of engagement during instructional activities that are presented at the concrete and representational levels with engagement during those activities presented at the abstract level.

8b: The Student Engages Better During Group Instruction That Is Developmentally Appropriate for the Student as Opposed to Instruction That Requires Prerequisite Skills That the Student Has Not Yet Acquired

To assess if this may be the case for your student, you must understand the student's present levels of performance in reading, writing, and mathematics, obtained through informal and formal assessment, and understand the student's use of cognitive processes such as memory, sequencing, organizing ideas, and so forth. Once you understand your student's present abilities, determine if the group instruction typically requires the student to use academic or cognitive skills that have not been developed. If so, that is likely the reason why the student does not engage during group instruction. For example, a lesson on long division requires that the student already knows basic multiplication, addition, and subtraction concepts and can follow a sequence of steps in the appropriate order. If the student does not have any of those prerequisite skills, then engagement during the lesson will be quite difficult without the use of additional accommodations and supports.

8c: The Student Has Difficulties Engaging During Group Instruction Activities That Require the Use of Fine Motor Skills or Gross Motor Skills the Student Has Not Yet Acquired

If your student receives occupational or physical therapy, then it is important to collaborate with the related services providers to determine what fine or gross motor activities are appropriate for the student. For example, if the student has significant delays in fine motor skills, then a group instruction lesson that requires the student to use scissors to cut out small ***pictures*** and figures may be problematic. Likewise, a lesson that requires the student to fold paper in certain ways to create a flipbook that will be used to take notes during the lesson may be problematic for the student.

Supporting the Student

Consider the following strategies and supports if academic, cognitive, or motor skills deficits are causing problems with a student's engagement during group instruction:

- Adapt reading materials used during group instruction to the developmentally appropriate grade level when possible.
- Make accommodations when reading materials cannot be adapted, such as providing ***visual supports*** to aid in comprehension, reading the material aloud, using text-to-speech software, or having the student partner with a peer who can read the material aloud.
- Allow the student to use a word processor or other ***AAC*** supports for written responses during group instruction.

- Provide a ***scribe*** for the student when written responses are required during the lesson.
- Provide a calculator for the student when math lessons require computational skills the student has not yet acquired.
- Provide scaffolding during group instruction to help the student connect what is being learned to previously acquired skills and knowledge.
- Modify instructional objectives for the student so that they are developmentally appropriate.
- Plan for ***partial participation*** when necessary.
- Deliver ***positive reinforcement*** when the student engages appropriately during group instruction.

MEDICAL CONDITIONS

Medical conditions can potentially play a role in the behaviors students demonstrate during group instruction and their ability to engage.

Understanding the Problem

Aways consider if any medical conditions are affecting the student's behavior when challenging behaviors occur, especially when students do not have the communication skills needed to explain physical ailments, pain, or discomfort. Do not assume that students who are nonverbal are the only students with ASD who are unable to effectively communicate when they are not feeling well. Students who have advanced language skills may also have trouble with the social-communication skills required to share with others when they are sick or in pain.

Assessing the Problem

If you think medical conditions may be affecting your student's ability to meaningfully participate during group instruction, then complete Section 9 of the FBA Checklist for Difficulty Engaging During Group Instruction in the appendix at the end of this chapter. The items in Section 9 are explained in the Medical Conditions section of Chapter 4; review that section as needed as you continue reading this book.

Supporting the Student

The supports included in the Medical Conditions section of Chapter 4 are also appropriate for times when medical conditions are causing problems with a student's engagement during group instruction. Consider the following strategies and supports if the student has sleep problems and difficulty engaging during group instruction:

- Include movement in the lesson if doing so is enjoyable for the student.
- Place fewer demands on the student during group instruction.
- Ask questions and give directions that are easy for the student.
- Allow the child to have a brief rest period if doing so increases the student's ability to engage during group instruction after the rest period is finished.
- Teach the child functional communication skills so the student can ask for a break if he or she is unable to participate in the lesson.
- Use a sleep communication log with the caregivers so you are aware when the student had limited sleep and when the student should be well rested.

From Assessment to Successful Intervention

Case Study: Alondra *Alondra is a third-grade student with ASD who has trouble engaging during whole-group instruction. Her teacher, Mrs. Shore, reads through the FBA Checklist for Difficulty Engaging During Group Instruction and wants to conduct some assessments to determine if the problem could be related to Alondra's sensory processing problems. Mrs. Shore thinks this may be the problem because it is well documented that Alondra has sensory integration dysfunction. Group instruction is delivered with all the fluorescent lights turned on; the students are spread out in four rows of six desks, creating a great deal of visual information to process; and students are expected to sit still and be quiet for much of the time. Mrs. Shore realizes these conditions could be quite challenging for Alondra. Therefore, Mrs. Shore delivers the next few group lessons using only natural light. She asks the special education teacher to coteach using parallel teaching, breaking the whole group into two smaller groups of 12. Alondra is placed in a group that meets on the carpet in the front of the classroom, thereby limiting some of the visual distractions. Alondra is also permitted to sit on a balance ball, stand, or pace back and forth at the back edge of the carpet to get the sensory input she needs as long as she continues to participate in the lesson. Mrs. Shore notices significant increases in Alondra's engagement during group instruction under these conditions, so she checks of boxes 6b and 6c.*

Figure 5.3 shows Section 6 of the FBA Checklist that Mrs. Shore filled out, the hypothesis statement she formulated, and the intervention plan that was created based on the assessment.

Challenging Behavior: Difficulty Engaging During Group Instruction

6. Sensory Processing Problems

- ❐ 6a: The student has problems engaging during group instructional activities that require the use of certain materials with specific textures or odors.
- ☑ 6b: The student has difficulty engaging in group instruction in loud, bright, cluttered environments but is better able to engage in environments that have minimal sensory input.
- ☑ 6c: The student has difficulty engaging during group instruction that limits opportunities for the student to get the sensory input needed.

Hypothesis Statement Alondra has trouble participating during group instruction due to sensory processing problems. She gets overloaded with extensive amounts of visual stimuli, which may cause disengagement during group instruction. She may also have trouble engaging during group instruction when there is a lack of movement she needs for sensory input.

Intervention Plan

- Refrain from using fluorescent lighting during group instruction.
- Permit Alondra to sit on a balance ball, stand, or pace during group instruction.
- Use coteaching with the special education teacher to split the class into two groups to reduce sensory overload.
- Deliver group instruction in sectioned off parts of the classroom to reduce visual stimuli.
- Place Alondra in the front row on an end seat when the special education teacher is unable to be in the classroom to coteach and whole-group instruction is used to remove the visual distraction of rows of students in front of her.

Results

Using natural light as opposed to fluorescent lighting, allowing movement for sensory input purposes, and teaching in smaller groups result in significant improvements in Alondra's engagement during group instruction. Alondra continues to have problems with sensory overload, however, during whole-group instruction. Thus, other instructional support staff will be utilized, including the speech-language pathologist, a paraprofessional, and the guidance counselor, when the special education teacher is not able to coteach to ensure smaller groupings while providing instruction.

Figure 5.3. Functional Behavior Assessment Checklist and intervention plan for Alondra.

From Assessment to Successful Intervention

Case Study: Hunter *Hunter is a seventh-grade student with ASD who has difficulty engaging during whole-group instruction in his social studies class. The social studies teacher, Mr. Haddad, primarily uses a lecture format, using presentation software with slides to deliver his lessons. The slides contain lengthy sentences to explain information and textbook definitions for key vocabulary words. The students are expected to sit and listen to the lectures, take notes, and answer questions as they are posed. Mr. Haddad usually asks one question every 2–3 minutes, calls on one student who has his or her hand raised, and then continues on with the lecture. Hunter appears disengaged during these lessons. He does not raise his hand to answer questions, he fiddles with objects in his desk, and he draws* ***pictures*** *of dinosaurs when he can get away with it. Hunter performs poorly when it comes time to complete assignments and take tests due to his disengagement during instruction.*

Mr. Haddad asks Mrs. Rhodes, the autism specialist for the school district, to meet with him to offer support. They complete the FBA Checklist for Difficulty Engaging During Group Instruction together. After a lengthy discussion, they hypothesize that many functions contribute to Hunter's disengagement during group instruction. They think language comprehension is the main problem. The long lectures and lack of any ***visual supports*** *other than the slides filled with lengthy sentences are probably too much for Hunter to comprehend due to his language impairments. To assess if this may be part of the problem, Mr. Haddad and Mrs. Rhodes work together to plan a lecture with simplified language on the slides;* ***visual supports*** *through* ***pictures,*** *objects, and video clips to explain concepts; and frequent pauses in the delivery of instruction to allow students to process the new information presented. Students will engage in* ***think-pair-share*** *activities during the pause to briefly recap or summarize what they learned. Mr. Haddad observes a significant increase in Hunter's engagement and participation in the lesson. Thus, Mr. Haddad and Mrs. Rhodes check off boxes 1a, 1b, and 1c.*

They also predict that Hunter is having trouble engaging during group instruction due to his restricted range of interests. Mr. Haddad plans a geography lesson that incorporates Hunter's special interest in dinosaurs to assess if this may be true. Hunter is given dinosaur fossils during the lesson to paste on his map where they were discovered and the specific geographic regions being studied. This increases Hunter's engagement, participation, and knowledge of the different geographic regions because of the connection made to dinosaur fossils. Mr. Haddad reports this to Mrs. Rhodes, and they check off boxes 4a and 4b.

Mrs. Rhodes then explains that Hunter may also be having difficulties engaging during group instruction due to his social deficits in joint attention as well as his problems with focus and attention. Thus, Mrs. Rhodes suggests giving Hunter ***guided notes*** *for lectures to help him focus on the key information and tells Mr. Haddad that he will likely have to use proximity, visual prompts such as pointing to the* ***guided notes,*** *and verbal prompts such as telling Hunter when or what to write to establish and maintain joint attention. She helps Mr. Haddad develop a* ***guided notes*** *sheet for an upcoming lecture on different government systems with blanks provided for filling in key terms. Mr. Haddad reports that Hunter was successful with maintaining joint attention with just a minimal amount of prompting and redirection and was focused on filling in the* ***guided notes*** *throughout the lesson. They check off boxes 5a, 7a, 7b, and 7c.*

Figure 5.4 shows the sections of the FBA Checklist that Mr. Haddad filled out, the hypothesis statement that was formulated, and the intervention plan that was created based on the assessment.

Challenging Behavior: Difficulty Engaging During Group Instruction

1. Language Comprehension Difficulties

- ☑ 1a: The student has difficulty engaging during group instruction when the teacher is using a lecture format but is able to engage when the teacher uses various strategies to actively involve the student in the lesson, such as hands-on tasks and visual supports.
- ☑ 1b: The student is able to engage during group instruction when the teacher uses clear, concise language and simple sentence structures but has difficulty engaging when the teacher uses complex language and long verbal elaborations to explain content.
- ☑ 1c: The student is able to engage during group instruction when the information is presented in manageable chunks with time allotted for processing but is unable to engage when a large amount of information is delivered at one time without purposeful pauses for processing.

4. Restricted Range of Interests

- ☑ 4a: The student engages well during group instruction related to the student's interests.
- ☑ 4b: The student does not engage during group instruction when the topics are not related to the student's interests.

5. Social Skills Deficits

- ☑ 5a: The student has significant deficits in joint attention resulting in difficulty attending to the teacher's instruction, peer responses, or learning materials during group instruction.
- ☐ 5b: The student has significant deficits in social reciprocity resulting in difficulty participating in question-and-answer instructional formats.
- ☐ 5c: The student does not understand the various social expectations for participating during group instruction.

7. Problems With Focus and Attention

- ☑ 7a: The student engages well during one-to-one instruction but has difficulty during group instructional formats.
- ☑ 7b: The student participates during group instruction when the teacher makes specific efforts to secure the student's attention but gets disengaged without these continuous supports.
- ☑ 7c: The student has difficulty during group instruction when the student's attention is focused on something other than the topic of the lesson.
- ☐ 7d: The student grasps some skills and concepts during group lessons but not all, demonstrating difficulty knowing what to focus on during the lesson.

Hypothesis Statement Hunter has difficulties engaging during group instruction during social studies, primarily due to difficulties comprehending and processing the language during long lectures. He also does not actively participate during social studies lectures when the topics are not of interest, he is unable to establish and maintain joint attention, and he loses focus and attention while drawing dinosaurs.

Intervention Plan

- Simplify the language on presentation slides, making it more consistent and concise.
- Add ***pictures*** and video clips to the slide presentations to help Hunter understand the concepts being presented.
- Use ***choral responding*** with ***response cards*** when appropriate, use ***think-pair-share*** after a small segment of instruction to support processing and increase engagement, and call on Hunter more often for individual questions to maintain joint attention.
- Provide Hunter with ***guided notes*** so he has something to complete while participating in the lessons.
- Tap into Hunter's interests in science and math by looking for opportunities to integrate science and math concepts into the social studies lessons.

Results

Mr. Haddad and Mrs. Rhodes collaborated consistently to design lessons using the various supports included in the plan. Not only does Hunter actively participate much more during the lessons, but he also performs better on assignments and tests because of his increased engagement.

Figure 5.4. Functional Behavior Assessment Checklist and intervention plan for Hunter.

Challenging Behavior: Difficulty Engaging During Group Instruction

1. Language Comprehension Difficulties

- ❒ 1a: The student has difficulty engaging during group instruction when the teacher is using a lecture format but is able to engage when the teacher uses various strategies to actively involve the student in the lesson, such as hands-on tasks and visual supports.
- ❒ 1b: The student is able to engage during group instruction when the teacher uses clear, concise language and simple sentence structures but has difficulty engaging when the teacher uses complex language and long verbal elaborations to explain content.
- ❒ 1c: The student is able to engage during group instruction when the information is presented in manageable chunks with time allotted for processing but is unable to engage when a large amount of information is delivered at one time without purposeful pauses for processing.

2. Deficits in Expressive Communication Skills

- ❒ 2a: The student has difficulty engaging during group instruction because he or she does not have the expressive communication skills necessary to respond, initiate, and interact.
- ❒ 2b: The student engages during group instruction when given nonverbal ways to participate during the lesson.

3. Anxiety, Fear, and Emotional Regulation Difficulties

- ❒ 3a: The student does not answer questions during group instruction even when the teacher is certain the student knows the answer and the expectations for participation.
- ❒ 3b: The student demonstrates self-stimulatory behaviors at an increased level during group instruction to cope with heightened levels of anxiety and fear and to deal with emotional regulation difficulties.
- ❒ 3c: The student attempts to leave the area during group instruction but rarely does so during other classroom routines and activities.
- ❒ 3d: The student has difficulty engaging during group instruction that is new or unfamiliar but participates more willingly and actively during group instruction that follows a familiar, predictable format (need for sameness).

4. Restricted Range of Interests

- ❒ 4a: The student engages well during group instruction related to the student's interests.
- ❒ 4b: The student does not engage during group instruction when the topics are not related to the student's interests.

5. Social Skills Deficits

- ❒ 5a: The student has significant deficits in joint attention resulting in difficulty attending to the teacher's instruction, peer responses, or learning materials during group instruction.
- ❒ 5b: The student has significant deficits in social reciprocity resulting in difficulty participating in question-and-answer instructional formats.
- ❒ 5c: The student does not understand the various social expectations for participating during group instruction.

6. Sensory Processing Problems

- ❒ 6a: The student has problems engaging during group instructional activities that require the use of certain materials with specific textures or odors.
- ❒ 6b: The student has difficulty engaging in group instruction in loud, bright, cluttered environments but is better able to engage in environments that have minimal sensory input.
- ❒ 6c: The student has difficulty engaging during group instruction that limits opportunities for the student to get the sensory input needed.

Challenging Behavior: Difficulty Engaging During Group Instruction *(continued)*

7. Problems With Focus and Attention

- ❐ 7a: The student engages well during one-to-one instruction but has difficulty during group instructional formats.
- ❐ 7b: The student participates during group instruction when the teacher makes specific efforts to secure the student's attention but gets disengaged without these continuous supports.
- ❐ 7c: The student has difficulty during group instruction when the student's attention is focused on something other than the topic of the lesson.
- ❐ 7d: The student grasps some skills and concepts during group lessons but not all, demonstrating difficulty knowing what to focus on during the lesson.

8. Academic, Cognitive or Motor Skills Deficits

- ❐ 8a: The student engages better during group instruction that entails concrete learning activities versus the presentation of abstract ideas and concepts.
- ❐ 8b: The student engages better during group instruction that is developmentally appropriate for the student as opposed to instruction that requires prerequisite skills that the student has not yet acquired.
- ❐ 8c: The student has difficulties engaging during group instruction activities that require the use of fine motor skills or gross motor skills the student has not yet acquired.

9. Medical Conditions

- ❐ 9a: The student does not engage during group instruction lessons that require sitting, but will engage when permitted to stand (may have gastrointestinal pain).
- ❐ 9b: The student has difficulty engaging during group instruction when the student goes untreated for illness or pain due to the inability to expressively communicate symptoms.
- ❐ 9c: The student has difficulties engaging during group instruction following nights of limited sleep.
- ❐ 9d: The student has difficulty engaging during group instruction due to reactions to new medications or reactions to changes in doses of medications.
- ❐ 9e: The student has difficulty engaging during group instruction following periods of seizure activity.

Other ____

____

____

____

____

Hypothesis Statement ____

____

____

____

____

CHAPTER 6

Working Independently

Students with ASD often have difficulties working independently to complete tasks. As a result, they may engage in challenging behaviors such as getting out of their seat, walking around the room, talking to others, doing other activities they find entertaining, displaying repetitive or aggressive behaviors, and so forth. As with other challenges students with ASD face, the reasons why students have difficulty working independently vary depending on each student's unique profile. This chapter discusses nine challenges faced by students with ASD that may explain why they struggle with completing independent work:

1. Language comprehension difficulties
2. Deficits in expressive communication skills
3. Anxiety, fear, and emotional regulation difficulties
4. Sensory processing problems
5. Problems with focus and attention
6. Executive functioning challenges
7. Academic, cognitive, or motor skills deficits
8. Restricted range of interests
9. Medical conditions

LANGUAGE COMPREHENSION DIFFICULTIES

Difficulty in understanding or processing language can interfere with a student's ability to work independently.

Understanding the Problem

Students may have trouble starting and completing independent work if they do not understand the directions that are given. Most teachers give directions orally. If a student does not understand the language of the directions or is unable to effectively process all the language in order to comprehend what to do, then it may appear that the child is being noncompliant.

Asessing the Problem

If you think language comprehension problems may be affecting your student's ability to work independently, then complete Section 1 of the FBA Checklist for Difficulty Working Independently in the appendix at the end of this chapter. Following are some tips for assessing each item in Section 1 of the checklist:

1a: The Student Is Unable to Complete Independent Work That Requires Reading and Understanding Written Directions but Is Able to Complete Independent Work When the Directions Are Physically or Visually Demonstrated

Record the student's ability to start and complete independent work when the directions are provided in written format compared with directions that are physically or visually demonstrated. If the student complies with greater independence when directions are demonstrated physically or visually, then you can predict that language comprehension may be the problem.

1b: The Student Is Unable to Complete Independent Work That Requires Listening to Verbal Directions but Is Able to Complete Independent Work When the Directions Are Physically or Visually Demonstrated

Record the student's ability to start and complete independent work when the directions are provided orally compared with directions that are physically or visually demonstrated. If the student complies with greater independence in the latter circumstance, then you can predict that language comprehension issues may be the problem. If you think the problem may be due purely to auditory processing issues, and the student is able to read, then you can assess whether the student has more success when directions are given in written format instead of orally.

Supporting the Student

Consider the following strategies and supports if language comprehension difficulties are causing problems with a student's completion of independent work:

- Use ***explicit instruction*** to ensure the student understands expectations for independent practice.
- ***Use clear, consistent, and concise language*** when giving instructions for independent assignments.
- Keep sentence structures short and simple whenever possible when giving instructions for independent assignments.
- Pair verbal instruction with visual or physical demonstration of instructions.
- Have the student demonstrate understanding of independent assignments (verbally or physically) prior to expecting the student to begin working.
- Use ***prompting/fading procedures*** to support student success while completing independent work.
- Teach the student to ask for help when necessary.
- Use ***peer-mediated interventions*** to teach peers how to support the student during independent work activities.

DEFICITS IN EXPRESSIVE COMMUNICATION SKILLS

This area of skill deficit can interfere with a student's participation and engagement during group instruction, and it can also interfere in subtle ways with the ability to participate fully during independent work time.

Understanding the Problem

Although you may not think that deficits in expressive communication skills would affect a student's ability to work independently, communication skills do come into play when the student has to ask questions about the task, ask for help, or ask for materials. If the student does not have expressive communication skills or *AAC* supports in place, then it may cause the student to refrain from or stop working on independent assignments.

Assessing the Problem

If you think deficits in expressive communication skills may be affecting your student's ability to work independently, then complete Section 2 of the FBA Checklist for Difficulty Working Independently in the appendix at the end of this chapter. Following are some tips for assessing each item:

2a: The Student Is Unable to Complete Work Independently Because He or She Is Unable to Ask for Help or Clarification When Necessary

It is important to take note of how often typically developing students ask for help or clarification while completing independent work. This will help you see that expressive communication limitations may be preventing the student with ASD from getting the support needed to complete assignments. Keep in mind that students who are verbal may need communication supports, just like students who are nonverbal. Even when a student typically demonstrates expressive communication skills, the student may get frustrated and emotionally dysregulated during difficult tasks and lose the ability to use those expressive communication skills to ask for assistance.

2b: The Student Is Unable to Complete Work Independently Because He or She Is Unable to Ask for Needed Materials

It is important to take note of how often peers in the class need to ask for materials to complete independent work. If other students are doing so on a regular basis, and the student with ASD cannot ask for materials due to expressive communication deficits, then that may be affecting the student's ability to start and complete the work.

Supporting the Student

Consider the following strategies and supports if deficits in expressive communication skills are causing problems with a student's ability to complete work independently:

- Give the student ***visual supports*** that can be used to ask for help or clarification. For example, provide ***cue cards*** that say, "I need help," or "I have a question." Explicitly teach the student how to use the ***visual supports.***
- Utilize *AAC* devices to allow the student to ask for help or materials. Explicitly teach the student how to use the selected *AAC* device.

- Provide a checklist of materials needed or steps to complete that can be referenced when the student needs to ask for assistance or materials.
- Use ***priming*** before the student is expected to start the independent work task to remind the student that he or she can ask for help if needed.
- Deliver ***positive reinforcement*** when the student starts independent work, continues to work independently, and finishes independent work.

ANXIETY, FEAR, AND EMOTIONAL REGULATION DIFFICULTIES

The expectations for working independently cause anxiety and fear in many students with ASD for several reasons. These emotions can interfere with their ability to work independently, and their anxiety may increase because they are unable to do the work.

Understanding the Problem

Many factors can contribute to anxiety and fear when students with ASD are expected to work independently. Research has shown that individuals with ASD who have anxiety difficulties display more automatic negative thoughts than students who do not struggle with anxiety (Farrugia & Hudson, 2006). Thus, they may have immediate negative thoughts (e.g., "This is too hard." "I can't do this.") when presented with independent work that prevent them from starting and completing the task. In addition to these automatic negative thoughts, they may not feel secure enough to work without support and guidance from an adult, new tasks may be anxiety producing, they may be afraid of getting something wrong, or they may be experiencing emotional distress related to something other than the task at hand and thus be unable to begin independent work until after they have returned to a calm state. Students with ASD often have deficits in emotional regulation skills, so if they are feeling distressed about the tasks (or something else), then they may not be able to calm themselves down to start and complete independent work.

Assessing the Problem

If you think anxiety, fear, and emotional regulation difficulties may be affecting your student's ability to work independently, then complete Section 3 of the FBA Checklist for Difficulty Working Independently in the appendix at the end of this chapter. Following are some tips for assessing each item:

3a: The Student Is Able to Complete Independent Work Only When Prior Success With the Activity Has Previously and Consistently Been Demonstrated

If the student works well independently on some tasks but not others, then investigate factors that may be affecting the student's behavior. You may then determine that the student handles familiar tasks well, but the student engages in off-task behavior with unfamiliar or unsuccessful tasks. This can certainly be due to heightened levels of anxiety and emotional regulation difficulties.

3b: The Student Is Able to Work Independently When the Teacher Provides Reassuring Comments

If you think the student may be suffering from anxiety when independent work assignments are given, then try providing reassuring comments such as, "You can do this," "You are doing great," or "You got it" to the student throughout the task. If you notice that the student responds well to the reassurance emotionally and can start and continue working independently when this support is given, then you can predict anxiety is affecting the student's ability to work independently.

3c: The Student Is Able to Complete Work Independently When the Teacher Is in Close Proximity to Support Emotional Regulation

Students with ASD may be able to complete work without any prompting or assistance as long as the teacher is sitting with the student or is close by. Off-task behavior gets in the way of work completion, however, as soon as the teacher moves away because the student feels a sense of emotional security when the teacher is nearby, and anxiety builds up when that security is taken away. Also, teachers may not realize that they are providing more than ***proximity control*** when they are near the student during independent work tasks. They may also be providing specific praise, smiles, high fives, reassuring comments, smiles, gestures, and cues without even realizing it. Thus, a great deal of support is lost for the student when the teacher moves away, resulting in increased anxiety and failure to continue working.

3d: The Student Gets Upset When He or She Gets Something Wrong

It is not uncommon for students with ASD to get very upset when they get something wrong because of their strong desire to please others, or they do not understand that getting things wrong is a normal part of learning. They may think the expectation is to always get everything correct, and any errors are a sign of failure. Thus, they may avoid independent work tasks that may result in errors to prevent themselves from experiencing failure.

3e: The Student Gets Upset When the Teacher Provides Constructive Feedback During Independent Work Activities

Not only may getting something wrong cause emotional distress for students with ASD, but they may also get overly upset when the teacher provides corrective feedback while they are working independently. This may make them feel like they are not smart, causing emotional distress. Thus, they shut down and cease to continue working.

3f: The Student Is Able to Complete Independent Work When Calm and at Ease but Is Unable to Do So When Emotionally Distressed

If your student has emotional regulation difficulties, then you may notice that the student's ability to work independently is contingent on the student's emotional state and nothing else. The student can complete independent work without any problem when the he or she is feeling happy, calm, or content. Yet, working independently becomes impossible when the student is distressed and unable to regulate challenging emotions.

Supporting the Student

Consider the following strategies and supports if anxiety, fear, and emotional regulation difficulties are causing problems with a student's ability to complete work independently:

- Use ***social narratives*** to teach the student that getting things wrong is an important part of learning (see Figure 6.1).
- Engage in role-play activities to practice how to react when a teacher gives corrective feedback during pretend scenarios. Take video clips of the student responding appropriately during the role play, and use those clips for ***video-self modeling*** before actual independent work tasks are given.
- Use ***priming*** before the student is expected to start the independent work task to remind the student that getting something wrong and receiving support from the teacher are both important parts of learning.

Getting Corrections on My Work

My name is Damien, and I am in fifth grade in Ms. Summer's class. I am very smart, and I like for my work to be correct when my teacher checks it. There will be times, however, when I get answers wrong or need to improve my answers. This is expected, and Ms. Summer enjoys helping me fix my mistakes. I will do the following when Ms. Summer checks my work and finds something that I need to fix:

1. Take a deep breath and stay calm.
2. Say to myself, "I can fix it and get a good grade."
3. Make the correction.

I will feel good when my work is corrected, and Ms. Summer will be proud of me.

Figure 6.1. Sample social narrative for accepting academic corrective feedback.

- Deliver ***positive reinforcement*** when the student starts independent work, continues to work independently, and finishes independent work. Also, deliver ***positive reinforcement*** when the student responds appropriately after getting something wrong or receiving constructive feedback.
- Make sure independent work tasks are developmentally appropriate. Although it is important to teach the student that it is okay to get something wrong and get support from the teacher, the student should have the skills and knowledge necessary to be successful with most of the task and only need a small amount of correction or guidance.
- Use ***emotional regulation strategies*** to help the student identify feelings of anxiety and fear at the onset, choose calming activities to prevent further escalation, and return to the task at hand independently or with teacher support.
- Use ***shaping*** by gradually increasing the difficulty and length of independent work tasks.
- Support the student's emotional regulation by offering reassuring comments while the student is working. Fade out the frequency and intensity of the reassurance as the student's anxiety decreases.
- Embed the student's special interests into the independent work assignments to support the student in remaining calm and engaged.
- Allow the student to use natural coping strategies that you might normally prevent if these behaviors allow the student to continue working (e.g., brief verbal outbursts, standing up, jumping, hand flapping, rocking, humming, quiet self-talk).

SENSORY PROCESSING PROBLEMS

Difficulties that students with ASD have in working independently may be due to sensory processing problems—aversion to specific sensory stimuli, sensory overload, or insufficient sensory input.

Understanding the Problem

It is important to have a good understanding of your student's sensory profile, which is usually not something that has to be considered for typically developing students or even students with other disabilities. Many students with ASD suffer from sensory integration dysfunction, however, which can have a huge impact on behavior in the classroom and certainly can be a factor when determining why a student is having difficulty completing independent work. Refer to the examples provided in Chapters 4 and 5 to review specific examples of the ways in which sensory processing issues might affect a student; similar issues can interfere with completion of independent work.

Assessing the Problem

If you think sensory processing problems may be affecting the child's ability to work independently, then complete Section 4 of the FBA Checklist for Difficulty Working Independently in the appendix at the end of this chapter. Following are some tips for assessing each item:

4a: The Student Has Problems Completing Independent Work Activities That Require the Use of Certain Materials With Specific Textures or Odors

You may discover during your assessment that the student is unable to work independently when required to use finger paint, markers with strong scents, clay, sandpaper, or any other materials that cause sensory discomfort.

4b: The Student Has Difficulty Working Independently in Loud, Bright, Cluttered Environments but Is Better Able to Complete Independent Work in Environments That Have Minimal Sensory Input

You may find that the student is able to work independently in quiet settings, dim or dark settings, settings without a great deal of movement taking place, or environments without an excessive variety of materials to see and touch.

4c: The Student Has Difficulty Completing Independent Work When Restricted From Gaining Access to Needed Sensory Input

Behavioral expectations for independent work could be preventing students with ASD from regulating themselves by adjusting their sensory input that meets their sensory needs. They have trouble working because they cannot regulate themselves in this way. For example, students may be unable to work independently simply because they are expected to sit still and be quiet. Yet, they would be able to complete independent work activities if permitted to verbalize, stand, rock, or move during the activity.

Supporting the Student

If sensory processing issues are causing problems with a student's ability to complete work independently, then design independent work assignments with the student's sensory profile in mind by making adaptations such as the following:

- Avoid using materials with strong odors.
- Allow the student to choose materials.
- Use natural lighting in the classroom.
- Minimize noise during independent work.
- Have organized workspaces without clutter.
- Allow the child to work in a study carrel, at a personal desk, or in a modified grouping arrangement without a peer sitting directly next to the student.
- Ignore physical movements and brief verbal outbursts that the student displays before quickly getting back to work. The student may need to do these things to stay regulated.

PROBLEMS WITH FOCUS AND ATTENTION

Students may have difficulty completing independent work because of their challenges with focus and attention.

Understanding the Problem

Students may get easily distracted by all of the stimuli in the classroom. Their own thoughts and self-stimulatory behaviors can also distract them. It is important to refrain from excessive verbal prompting to redirect students because this will not help the student develop self-regulation strategies.

Assessing the Problem

If you think problems with focus and attention may be affecting your student's ability to work independently, then complete Section 5 of the FBA Checklist for Difficulty Working Independently in the appendix at the end of this chapter. Following are some tips for assessing each item:

5a: The Student Is Able to Complete Independent Work When an Adult Is in Close Proximity but Is Unable to Complete Independent Work Without an Adult Present

Although this could be an indication of anxiety, it is also possible that the presence of the adult helps the student remain focused. If this is the case, then it is important to document exactly what the adult is doing while in close proximity to the student. It is likely that the adult is doing much more than simply sitting nearby to keep the student focused. Specific behaviors the adult may be engaging in without realizing it (e.g., smiling to encourage the student, pointing to the student's paper) need to be determined so they can be systematically faded out.

5b: The Student Is Able to Compete Independent Work When Using a Self-Monitoring Tool to Focus His or Her Attention Throughout the Task but Is Unable to Complete Independent Work Without That Visual Support

If you are unsure if a ***self-monitoring*** tool will help a student remain focused during independent work, then start using one for various assignments and assess the affect it has on the student's ability to stay focused. Keep in mind that you cannot simply develop a tool and give it to the student. The student will require ***explicit instruction*** to learn how to use the tool while completing tasks. It is likely that the student will still require prompting to stay on task, even with this explicit instruction. Collect data to determine if the frequency of prompting is reduced when the ***self-monitoring*** tool is used, however, and if fewer verbal prompts are needed when the teacher can simply point to the ***self-monitoring*** tool to redirect the student.

5c: The Student Can Complete Short Independent Work Tasks but Is Unable to Stay Focused to Complete Lengthy Tasks

This is likely due to problems with focus and attention. If you are unsure if this is the case for your student because most independent work assignments are lengthy, then test this out by giving the student shorter assignments. If the student can complete independent assignments that take less time, then it may be that the student simply loses focus and attention as the length of time required to complete the task increases.

Supporting the Student

Consider the following strategies and supports if problems with focus and attention are affecting a student's ability to complete work independently:

- Use ***shaping*** to gradually increase the length of time required for completing independent work assignments.
- Minimize visual and auditory distractions in the environment.
- Use ***video modeling*** or ***social narratives*** to teach independent work expectations.
- Use ***self-management*** strategies to promote independent work behaviors (e.g., goal setting, ***self-monitoring,*** self-evaluation, self-reinforcement).

EXECUTIVE FUNCTIONING CHALLENGES

Difficulties with executive functioning can make independent work particularly challenging for students with ASD.

Understanding the Problem

If a student with ASD struggles with executive functioning challenges, then working independently is very difficult because most independent tasks require having good time management skills, following a sequence of steps, organizing, and planning. For example, even a brief, informal independent writing task involves executive functioning—thinking about what to write, jotting brief notes about it, writing one's name and the date at top of paper, allotting adequate time for generating and organizing ideas and physically writing them, and scanning one's completed writing for correctness and legibility. Those of us who do not have executive functioning challenges do not realize how much work our brains naturally do for us to help us meet the demands of our assigned work tasks and responsibilities.

Assessing the Problem

If you think executive functioning challenges may be affecting your student's ability to work independently, then complete Section 6 of the FBA Checklist for Difficulty Working Independently in the appendix at the end of this chapter. Following are some tips for assessing each item:

6a: The Student Can Complete Independent Work That Has One Simple Step but Is Unable to Complete Work That Has Multiple Steps or Requires Planning and Organization

If most of the independent work you assign requires multiple steps, planning, organization, or time management skills for successful completion, then you will have to alter assignments for your student with ASD to determine if executive functioning challenges may be the problem. Compare the student's ability to work independently when the task is simple and only has one step with the student's ability to work independently with more complex tasks.

6b: The Student Is Able to Complete Independent Work When a Visual Task Analysis Is Provided but Is Unable to Complete Independent Work That Requires Multiple Steps Without the Steps Broken Down Visually

Create a visual ***task analysis*** of the individual steps of an assignment to determine if this support helps the student complete independent work. The steps can be written in single words, short phrases, or sentences or represented in ***pictures*** or ***symbols.*** Keep in mind that you will also have to use ***forward chaining*** to teach the student how to go through each step of the task. It will help the student if you turn the ***task analysis*** into a ***self-monitoring*** tool so the student can check off each step as it is completed. After this systematic support and instruction is given, provide opportunities for the student to work independently using the ***task analysis.*** If the student can complete multistep tasks with no or minimal support beyond the ***task analysis,*** then you can predict that executive functioning challenges are preventing the student from being able to successfully work independently.

6c: The Student Can Complete Independent Work Tasks That Have a Clear Beginning, Middle, and End but Is Unable to Complete Open-Ended Assignments

If the expectations for the assignment are very clear to the student (i.e., the student knows exactly how to get started, what to do, and what it means to be finished) then a student who struggles with executive functioning challenges may have more success working independently. Unfortunately, many independent assignments are more open ended and abstract, making it quite difficult for students with ASD to know how to get started and complete the task. For example, students may be given the direction to write a persuasive letter to convince the principal to change a school rule. A student with ASD can get overwhelmed with the open endedness or abstractness of the assignment if a specific school rule is not already selected that has immediate relevance to the student and step-by-step procedures for starting the letter, writing the body of the letter, and ending the letter are not provided. Assess the student's success when assignments have a clear beginning, middle, and end. Compare this with the student's success with less structured, more open-ended assignments. (The difficulty level of the assignments should otherwise be similar; e.g., they should cover related topics and a similar amount of content.) If students can succeed with appropriately rigorous assignments that are highly structured but not with open-ended assignments that are otherwise comparable, then the open endedness of independent work assignments may be the cause of the problem.

Supporting the Student

Consider the following strategies and supports if executive functioning challenges are causing problems with a student's ability to complete work independently:

- Create assignments that have a clear beginning, middle, and end.
- Use ***task analysis*** and ***forward chaining.***
- Provide opportunities for the student to rehearse the steps of the task.
- Use ***self-management strategies*** (e.g., goal setting, ***self-monitoring,*** self-evaluation, self-reinforcement).
- Use ***shaping*** by gradually increasing the number of steps in independent assignments.
- Deliver ***positive reinforcement*** when the student begins work, continues working, and completes work. Be careful that the way ***positive reinforcement*** is delivered does not cause distraction or cause the student to discontinue work on the task. This may mean smiling, giving a thumbs-up gesture, and quickly moving on to other students as opposed to sitting with the student giving extended verbal praise or engaging in a lengthy interaction.
- Use visual timers to help the student regulate on-task behavior to complete work on time (unless the use of timers causes anxiety for the student).
- Create systems for organizing unfinished work, and provide explicit instruction to teach the student what to do with unfinished work when it is time to make the transition to another activity.

ACADEMIC, COGNITIVE, OR MOTOR SKILLS DEFICITS

Deficits in academic, cognitive, or motor skills may interfere with a student's ability to complete independent work activities.

Understanding the Problem

Students with ASD may struggle completing independent assignments if the tasks require academic skills, cognitive processes, or motor skills that are not developmentally appropriate for the student. Thus, it is important for teachers to be acutely aware of reading, writing, and math skills the student has mastered; skills that are developing; and skills the student is not yet ready to learn. It is essential to consider the four stages of learning when assigning independent work—skill acquisition, fluency, maintenance, and generalization. (To recap, *skill acquisition* means the student is currently learning the skill. *Fluency* means the student has learned the skills but is improving accuracy and speed with using the skill. *Maintenance* means the student can demonstrate fluency over long periods of time without losing the skill. *Generalization* means a mastered skill is being applied in various ways.) Independent work should focus on building fluency and maintenance. Students at the skill acquisition stage, the earliest stage of learning, need too much instructional support to be able to work independently. They also need support at the final stage of learning; students with ASD often require guidance to learn how to generalize mastered skills by completing application activities. Thus, in most instances, teachers should not expect students to work on generalization during independent work activities.

As previously noted, abstract thought can be challenging for some students with ASD. For example, independent work assignments that require students to write about prejudice and discrimination, draw a ***picture*** of what they want to be when they grow up, or solve word problems are very abstract and can result in a student disengaging from the task. Students with ASD can learn how to think and perform and the abstract level, but they may need scaffolding to understand the expectations of the assignment.

Fine motor skills are often an area of weakness for students with ASD, and deficits in fine motor skills can make the physical task of writing quite challenging. Most independent work tasks require written responses. Thus, students may not be able to complete independent work because it requires them to write. Also, if the student is expected to do other fine motor activities to complete the work, such as cutting, folding, or using materials that are difficult to manipulate, then the student may be unable to complete the task.

Assessing the Problem

If you think academic, cognitive, or motor skills deficits may be affecting your student's ability to work independently, then complete Section 7 of the Checklist for Difficulty Working Independently in the appendix at the end of this chapter. Following are some tips for assessing each item:

7a: The Student Is Able to Complete Independent Assignments That Consist of Concrete Learning Activities as Opposed to Those That Require Abstract Thought

Document the student's ability to complete independent activities when given abstract learning tasks and concrete learning tasks. For example, you can give the student an assignment during independent work time for a literacy block that requires drawing or sequencing ***pictures*** to tell a story about a recent trip to the beach. Compare the student's ability to complete a task such as that with the student's ability to write an essay about what job he or she wants to have as an adult.

7b: The Student Is Able to Complete Independent Assignments That Are Developmentally Appropriate or Easy for the Student as Opposed to Assignments That Are Too Difficult for the Student Based on Present Levels of Academic Performance

You will need to have a clear picture of the skills the student has mastered, is currently acquiring, and is not yet ready to learn to assess this item. Give the student assignments that only contain skills the student has mastered, and document how well the student was able to work independently. Do the same for tasks that require the student to use skills currently being acquired (i.e., skills at the student's instructional level). If the student is unable to work independently on tasks at the instructional level, then it is probably best to have the student work only on assignments that consist of mastered skills. It is never a good idea to give the student assignments that require skills the student has not yet begun to learn.

Keep in mind that students with ASD often have inconsistencies in their academic performance. One day they may be able to do something, and the next day they may not be able to perform the same skill. That is why it is often best to give assignments that only include fully mastered skills.

7c: The Student Has Difficulty Completing Independent Work Activities That Require the Use of Fine Motor Skills

Many independent work assignments require writing, so you may not realize that the physical task of writing is causing the student to have trouble working independently, not the actual academic task. Consult with the occupational therapist to learn the specifics about any possible motor deficits that may prevent the student from complying with independent work tasks. Then consider how to modify academic tasks so they are developmentally appropriate with the student's fine motor skill development. For example, a student may not be able to write a paragraph but may be able to record thoughts or share thoughts with a ***scribe.*** Assess the student's level of compliance and engagement when given tasks that do not require fine motor skills, or when fine motor tasks are adapted to the student's performance, and compare with compliance and engagement when given other writing or fine motor tasks.

Supporting the Student

Consider the following strategies and supports if deficits in academic, cognitive, or motor skills are causing problems with a student's ability to complete work independently:

- Assign alternative reading comprehension assignments that reduce or eliminate writing demands (e.g., draw a ***picture*** about the story, retell the story by creating a list of the things that happened, put sentence strips that list the events of the story in order, fill out a graphic organizer to demonstrate comprehension).
- Use ***behavioral momentum*** for independent math assignments by giving two or three easy problems before giving a more challenging problem, and continue the pattern.
- Allow the student to do a voice recording, have a ***scribe,*** or use a word processor to type for writing assignments.
- Use ***prompting/fading procedures*** to support the student as needed.
- Deliver ***positive reinforcement*** when the student completes work.

RESTRICTED RANGE OF INTERESTS

A restricted range of interests may interfere with a student's engagement in independent work activities.

Understanding the Problem

Some students with ASD may have trouble completing independent work that is not related to their special interests and passions. These students may not have a variety of interests to motivate them to complete various academic tasks due to the nature of their disability. If teachers can find ways to tap into the students' special interests and fascinations when giving independent assignments, however, then they may notice a significant increase in compliance, engagement, and completion.

There are many ways to tap into the student's special interests. It could be as simple as including ***pictures*** of the student's favorite characters on the assignment papers or in math word problems or having the student read stories that include these characters. If a student loves trains, then a reading comprehension activity might involve giving the student a ***graphic organizer*** using a ***picture*** of train to represent the beginning, middle, and end of a story. A student who loves NASCAR may analyze statistics about various race car drivers during an independent activity in a high school math class. A student's love of animals can be used in different subject areas (e.g., have the student create a map of a zoo to demonstrate how to use scale and then work on literacy skills by creating a pamphlet describing the different zoo attractions).

Assessing the Problem

You will first need to have a clear understanding of the student's interests, fascinations, and passions to assess if the student's restricted range of interests may be affecting his or her ability to complete independent work. You can find this out by giving preference assessments, observing the student, or interviewing the student, family members, and other professionals who may know the student very well. Compare the student's performance when given independent work tasks related to the student's special interests with performance when the tasks are not interest based. If you see more engagement and work completion when the assignment taps into the student's special interests, then you can check off the item listed for Section 8 of the FBA Checklist for Difficulty Working Independently in the appendix at the end of this chapter: The student is able to complete independent work related to the student's interests but disengages during non–interest-based activities.

Supporting the Student

Tap into the student's special interests, fascinations, and passions in any of the following ways if a restricted range of interests is causing problems with a student's ability to complete work independently:

- Connect the content to the student's interests (e.g., when learning specific research skills, have a student who loves dinosaurs research their extinction; when learning mapping skills, have a student who loves trains create a map of the state's railway system).
- Provide materials related to the student's interests that are only available during independent work time (e.g., if a student loves superheroes, sports, and trains, then provide Spider-Man pencils, football erasers, and paper with a border of trains during independent work activities).
- Create a ***self-monitoring*** checklist with the student's favorite character telling what to do for each step.
- Use a ***positive reinforcement*** system related to the student's special interests (e.g., have a student who loves football earn yards, first downs, field goals, and touchdowns for completing independent work).
- BLE:Use Power Cards (Gagnon, 2001) to teach expectations for working independently.

MEDICAL CONDITIONS

Medical conditions can potentially play a role in the behaviors students demonstrate while working independently.

Understanding the Problem

If your student is suffering from a medical issue, then it could certainly affect the child's ability to work independently. Consider how difficult it is for you to do your job when you are tired, sick, or in pain. Add the other challenges of ASD on top of that, and you can only imagine what it is like for your student to focus and comply with work tasks when ill, hurting, exhausted, or physically uncomfortable.

Assessing the Problem

If you think medical conditions may be affecting your student's ability to work independently, then complete Section 9 of the FBA Checklist for Difficulty Working Independently in the appendix at the end of this chapter. Refer to the Medical Conditions section in Chapter 4 if you need explanation for any of the items in that section.

Supporting the Student

Consider the following strategies and supports if medical conditions are causing problems with a student's ability to complete work independently:

- Allow the child to have a brief rest period if doing so increases the student's ability to complete independent work after the rest period is finished.
- Teach the child functional communication skills so the student can ask for help or for a break if he or she is unable to work independently.
- Alter independent assignments on days the student is not feeling well so they are very easy, short, or primarily interest based.
- Use a communication log with the caregivers so you are aware of the student's seizure activity, side effects of medications, and changes to medications.

From Assessment to Successful Intervention

Case Study: Robbie *Robbie is a first-grade student with ASD who needs excessive amounts of prompting to continue working during independent tasks. His teacher, Mrs. Gupta, met with the behavior specialist for the school district, Mr. Vincent, to get some ideas for improving Robbie's on-task behavior. They reviewed the FBA Checklist for Difficulty Working Independently together, and Mrs. Gupta reported the following: Robbie has the skills needed to complete the independent work assignments. He completes the tasks without any help when she sits with him. He gets easily distracted, however, when she leaves him by himself to complete work. He will often put his head down, chew on pencil erasers, tap his pencil, or look around the room. Although this does not cause disruption to other students, these behaviors are preventing him from getting his work done. Mrs. Gupta also shared that she tried having Robbie wear headphones to block out noise to see if it would help him focus. Although he wore the headphones willingly, it did not improve his ability to stay focused to complete his work. Mrs. Gupta also tried using only visual prompts (i.e., a* ***cue card*** *that says, "keep working") instead of verbal prompts to see if he would be successful without so much verbal prompting. This did not have any significant affect either.*

Mrs. Gupta also shared that Robbie will get upset and stop working when he receives corrective feedback from the teacher while working on an independent assignment. Robbie gets very upset if he gets something wrong. He also will not ask for help when he gets stuck on something. Instead, he will just put his head down and stop working.

Based on this information, Mr. Vincent hypothesizes that Robbie's problem with working independently is primarily a result of difficulty with focus and attention. They check off box 5a. He also shares that his inability to ask for help is affecting his successful completion of independent assignments, and they check off box 2a. Finally, Mr. Vincent shares that emotional regulation difficulties are also negatively affecting Robbie's independence because he gets overly upset when he gets something wrong and receives corrective feedback. Mrs. Gupta and Mr. Vincent check off boxes 3d and 3e.

Figure 6.2 shows the sections of the FBA Checklist that Mrs. Gupta filled out, the hypothesis statement that was formulated, and the intervention plan that was created based on the assessment.

Challenging Behavior: Difficulty Working Independently

2. Deficits in Expressive Communication Skills

- ☑ 2a: The student is unable to complete work independently because he or she is unable to ask for help or clarification when necessary.
- ☐ 2b: The student is unable to complete work independently because he or she is unable to ask for needed materials.

3. Anxiety, Fear, and Emotional Regulation Difficulties

- ☐ 3a: The student is able to complete independent work only when prior success with the activity has previously and consistently been demonstrated.
- ☐ 3b: The student is able to work independently when the teacher provides reassuring comments.
- ☐ 3c: The student is able to complete work independently when the teacher is in close proximity to support emotional regulation.
- ☑ 3d: The student gets upset when he or she gets something wrong.
- ☑ 3e: The student gets upset when the teacher provides constructive feedback during independent work activities.
- ☐ 3f: The student is able to complete independent work when calm and at ease but is unable to do so when emotionally distressed.

5. Problems With Focus and Attention

- ☑ 5a: The student is able to complete independent work when an adult is in close proximity but is unable to complete independent work without an adult present.
- ☐ 5b: The student is able to compete independent work when using a self-monitoring tool to focus his or her attention throughout the task but is unable to complete independent work without that visual support.
- ☐ 5c: The student can complete short independent work tasks but is unable to stay focused to complete lengthy tasks.

Hypothesis Statement Robbie has trouble working independently for a variety of reasons: 1) he has problems maintaining attention to his work when an adult is not close to keep him focused; 2) his deficits in expressive communication affect his ability to complete work when he is unable to ask for help when needed; and 3) emotional regulation difficulties negatively affect Robbie's independence because he gets overly upset and shuts down when he gets something wrong and receives corrective feedback.

Intervention Plan

- Use a ***social narrative*** to teach the expectations for completing work independently, the importance of asking for help when necessary, and how to respond when the teacher provides corrective feedback
- Create a ***self-monitoring*** tool that allows Robbie to check off whether he finished each independent work task throughout the school day
- Use an activity reinforcement system that allows Robbie to earn the privilege to be an assistant to the physical education (PE) teacher in another first-grade class following days that he completes all his independent work tasks. (Robbie chose that as his reward among a choice of various desired activities.)

Results

Robbie was able to complete all of his work and earn his privilege to be an assistant to the PE teacher after a few days of implementing these interventions. An unforeseen problem did arise, however. Robbie wanted to assist the PE teacher when his own class went to PE. He did not understand that he would only be permitted to do so with another first-grade class. A social narrative was developed to explain that Robbie needs to be a student with his class when he goes to PE so he can learn what to do to prepare him for helping students in another class. Robbie was then able to understand. On average, he now completes all of his work independently 4 out of 5 days each week.

Figure 6.2. Functional Behavior Assessment Checklist and intervention plan for Robbie.

From Assessment to Successful Intervention

Case Study: Emmanuel *Emmanuel is a fourth-grade student with ASD who engages in a variety of task-avoidance behaviors when expected to complete independent work. He is above average academically, so he certainly has the skills to complete the work. His teacher, Mr. Hamilton, feels that it is purely a problem with motivation and has become quite frustrated. Emmanuel gets up and walks around the room, engages in loud outbursts that disturb the other students in the class, or attempts to get on the computer to look up Spider-Man videos on YouTube every time he is given an independent assignment. These videos, or other materials related to Spider-Man, never fail to capture Emmanuel's attention, but he does not show nearly as much interest in other topics. After consulting with the special education teacher and reviewing the FBA Checklist for Difficulty Working Independently, Mr. Hamilton hypothesizes that Emmanuel's restricted range of interests is the main problem affecting his ability to complete assignments. He checks off the item for Section 8 on the checklist.*

Figure 6.3 shows the sections of the FBA Checklist that Mr. Hamilton filled out, the hypothesis statement that was formulated, and the intervention plan that was created based on the assessment.

Challenging Behavior: Difficulty Working Independently

8. Restricted Range of Interests

☑ The student is able to complete independent work related to the student's interests but disengages during non-interest-based activities.

Hypothesis Statement Emmanuel engages in task-avoidance behaviors such as getting up and walking around the room, making loud outbursts that disturb the other students in the class, or attempting to get on the computer to look up Spider-Man videos on YouTube when given independent work to complete. This is due to a significantly restricted range of interests. Although he is very fascinated with Spider-Man, Emmanuel does not have interests in any academic areas or recreational activities.

Intervention Plan

- Use a Power Card (Gagnon, 2001) intervention with Spider-Man teaching the importance of completing school work.
- Put a picture of Spider-Man on every assignment, allowing Emmanuel to color in the Spider-Man picture when his work is done.
- Allow Emmanuel to keep one of his Spider-Man figures on his desk as long as he is working on his assignment.

Results

Although this was a fairly simple plan, Emmanuel responded very enthusiastically to the Spider-Man Power Card and other Spider-Man motivators. He now shows increased success with completing his work.

Figure 6.3. Functional Behavior Assessment Checklist and intervention plan for Emmanuel.

Challenging Behavior: Difficulty Working Independently

1. Language Comprehension Difficulties

- ❒ 1a: The student is unable to complete independent work that requires reading and understanding written directions but is able to complete independent work when the directions are physically or visually demonstrated.
- ❒ 1b: The student is unable to complete independent work that requires listening to verbal directions but is able to complete independent work when the directions are physically or visually demonstrated.

2. Deficits in Expressive Communication Skills

- ❒ 2a: The student is unable to complete work independently because he or she is unable to ask for help or clarification when necessary.
- ❒ 2b: The student is unable to complete work independently because he or she is unable to ask for needed materials.

3. Anxiety, Fear, and Emotional Regulation Difficulties

- ❒ 3a: The student is able to complete independent work only when prior success with the activity has previously and consistently been demonstrated.
- ❒ 3b: The student is able to work independently when the teacher provides reassuring comments.
- ❒ 3c: The student is able to complete work independently when the teacher is in close proximity to support emotional regulation.
- ❒ 3d: The student gets upset when he or she gets something wrong.
- ❒ 3e: The student gets upset when the teacher provides constructive feedback during independent work activities.
- ❒ 3f: The student is able to complete independent work when calm and at ease but is unable to do so when emotionally distressed.

4. Sensory Processing Problems

- ❒ 4a: The student has problems completing independent work activities that require the use of certain materials with specific textures or odors.
- ❒ 4b: The student has difficulty working independently in loud, bright, cluttered environments but is better able to complete independent work in environments that have minimal sensory input.
- ❒ 4c: The student has difficulty completing independent work when restricted from gaining access to needed sensory input.

5. Problems With Focus and Attention

- ❒ 5a: The student is able to complete independent work when an adult is in close proximity but is unable to complete independent work without an adult present.
- ❒ 5b: The student is able to compete independent work when using a self-monitoring tool to focus his or her attention throughout the task but is unable to complete independent work without that visual support.
- ❒ 5c: The student can complete short independent work tasks but is unable to stay focused to complete lengthy tasks.

6. Executive Functioning Challenges

- ❒ 6a: The student can complete independent work that has one simple step but is unable to complete work that has multiple steps or requires planning and organization.
- ❒ 6b: The student is able to complete independent work when a visual task analysis is provided but is unable to complete independent work that requires multiple steps without the steps broken down visually.
- ❒ 6c: The student can complete independent wok tasks that have a clear beginning, middle, and end but is unable to complete open-ended assignments.

Challenging Behavior: Difficulty Working Independently *(continued)*

7. Academic, Cognitive, or Motor Skills Deficits

- ❒ 7a: The student is able to complete independent assignments that consist of concrete learning activities as opposed to those that require abstract thought.
- ❒ 7b: The student is able to complete independent assignments that are developmentally appropriate or easy for the student as opposed to assignments that are too difficult for the student based on present levels of academic performance.
- ❒ 7c: The student has difficulty completing independent work activities that require the use of fine motor skills.

8. Restricted Range of Interests

- ❒ The student is able to complete independent work related to the student's interests but disengages during non-interest-based activities.

9. Medical Conditions

- ❒ 9a: The student does not work independently if required to sit but will work when permitted to stand (may have gastrointestinal pain).
- ❒ 9b: The student has difficulty completing independent work when the student goes untreated for illness or pain due to the inability to expressively communicate symptoms.
- ❒ 9c: The student has difficulties working independently following nights of limited sleep.
- ❒ 9d: The student has difficulty working independently due to reactions to new medications or reactions to changes in doses of medications.
- ❒ 9e: The student has difficulty working independently following periods of seizure activity.

Other ____

____

____

____

____

Hypothesis Statement ____

____

____

____

____

CHAPTER 7

Repetitive Behaviors

Students with ASD may engage in repetitive behaviors that can be quite disruptive in classroom settings, including verbal self-stimulatory behaviors such as scripting or repeating certain sounds; repetitive motor movement such as hand flapping, rocking, or pacing back and forth; and nonfunctional ritualistic behaviors. Reasons for these behaviors vary among individual students. This chapter discusses 10 challenges faced by students with ASD that may explain why they demonstrate repetitive behaviors:

1. Language comprehension difficulties
2. Deficits in expressive communication skills
3. Anxiety, fear, and emotional regulation difficulties
4. Social skills deficits
5. Sensory processing problems
6. Problems with focus and attention
7. Executive functioning challenges
8. Academic, cognitive, or motor skills deficits
9. Restricted range of interests
10. Medical conditions

LANGUAGE COMPREHENSION DIFFICULTIES

If a student cannot understand directions or verbal instruction, then he or she may engage in repetitive behaviors as a means of coping with confusion, frustration, or disengagement.

Understanding the Problem

The student may be using the repetitive behavior to escape from instruction or avoid following directions when he or she is unable to comprehend due to language impairments. For example, suppose a teacher is delivering a 15-minute lecture with very little student participation and minimal to no visuals to support the verbal instruction. The student with ASD may begin engaging in vocal scripting, hand flapping, or repetitive sounds because he or she does not understand all of the language being used and has no time to process all of the information during the lecture.

Assessing the Problem

If you think language comprehension problems may be affecting your student's use of repetitive behaviors, then complete Section 1 of the FBA Checklist for Repetitive Behaviors found in the appendix at the end of this chapter. Following are some tips for assessing each item in Section 1 of the checklist:

1a: The Student Engages in Repetitive Behavior When Expected to Comply With Written Directions or Complex Verbal Directions but Does Not When the Directions Are Either Explained Using Simplified Language or Modeled

If you often give your students assignments that have written directions to follow, and you notice that your student with ASD engages in repetitive behavior instead of reading the directions and beginning the task, then the student may not understand the language in the direction. To assess if this may be the case, try other ways to explain the directions, such as verbally explaining them using simplified language, or model how to do the task and have the student imitate you. If the student does not engage in repetitive behavior when you explain the directions in one of these alternative ways, then language comprehension problems may be the cause of the behavior.

1b: The Student Engages in Repetitive Behavior When Expected to Comply With Verbal Directions or Listen to Lengthy Lectures but Does Not When Given Written Directions or When Given Material to Read to Learn New Information

The student may engage in repetitive behavior to cope with too much verbal instruction that the student is unable to process. To assess if this may be the case, provide directions in writing, or allow the student to read information instead of listening to extensive amounts of verbal instruction. If the student does not engage in repetitive behavior under those conditions (or if those behaviors dramatically decrease), then you can predict that problems processing oral language have been causing the repetitive behavior.

Supporting the Student

Consider the following strategies and supports if language comprehension difficulties are causing repetitive behaviors:

- Give a short amount of verbal instruction when using a lecture format, followed by time to process the information. Students can engage in ***think-pair-share*** activities, write notes, fill in ***graphic organizers,*** create illustrations, and so forth during this time to process the information received.
- Provide information for the student to read when learning new information instead of having the student listen to verbal instruction to allow for individualized processing at a developmentally appropriate pace. If the student cannot read, then visually represent new information when possible to support the student's understanding.
- Slow down your rate of speech when delivering verbal instruction to give the student more processing time. Then use ***shaping*** by gradually increasing your rate of speech to allow the student to improve auditory processing skills.
- ***Use clear, consistent, and concise language*** to support the student's ability to process the language.

DEFICITS IN EXPRESSIVE COMMUNICATION SKILLS

If a student with ASD has deficits in expressive communication skills, then he or she may engage in repetitive behavior as a means of communicating that something is wrong or that the he or she needs something.

Understanding the Problem

Suppose a student cannot ask for help, ask for a break, request to go to the bathroom or get a drink of water, ask when they are going to lunch, or tell the teacher that something hurts—all difficulties that might arise from expressive communication deficits. He or she may resort to engaging in repetitive behaviors to communicate. These behaviors are often reinforced because the teacher may approach the student and play a guessing game until the need is figured out and met. For example, if a student is engaging in loud verbal outbursts, then the teacher may come over and say, "What's the matter? Do you need a snack?" The student stops the verbal outbursts when the teacher asks about the snack, and the teacher assumes that was what the student was communicating and provides a snack.

Assessing the Problem

If you think deficits in expressive communication skills may be affecting your student's use of repetitive behaviors, then check off Section 2 of the FBA Checklist for Repetitive Behaviors found in the appendix at the end of this chapter: The student engages in repetitive behavior if he or is unable to verbally express wants and needs. If you are unsure if this is the case, then you can assess the situation by observing whether the repetitive behavior ceases when the student's apparent needs are met. Of course, you would have to be quite in tune with your student to know his or her needs for a true assessment. Refer to Chapter 2 for a discussion about assessing the student's strengths, interests, and needs.

Supporting the Student

Consider the following strategies and supports if deficits in expressive communication skills are causing the occurrence of repetitive behaviors:

- Use ***explicit instruction*** to teach the student how to ask for food, drinks, and preferred items using one-word utterances, ***pictures, symbols,*** sign language, or other ***AAC*** supports.
- Use ***video modeling*** to teach the student how to request desired items.
- Use ***incidental teaching*** and ***modeling/request imitation***: Model how the student should ask for the desired item when the student is about to or begins to engage in repetitive behavior, and have the student imitate.
- Use ***discrete trial*** training to teach the student how to ask for desired items with multiple learning opportunities each day.
- Deliver ***positive reinforcement*** by providing access to what was requested when the student requests desired items using functional communication skills.

ANXIETY, FEAR, AND EMOTIONAL REGULATION DIFFICULTIES

This may be one of the most common functions for repetitive behavior in students with ASD.

Understanding the Problem

Heightened levels of fear and anxiety are commonplace for these children, and to make matters worse, they usually lack emotional regulation skills needed to cope with and manage their feelings. Thus, many children will use repetitive behaviors as a coping strategy to help them deal with their intense fears and anxieties. Therefore, you should think carefully about whether to put interventions in place to stop the repetitive behaviors. You do run the risk of playing a game of whack-a-mole, which means that if you prevent the child from engaging in self-stimulatory or stereotyping behavior (the equivalent of hitting that mole with a hammer), then the student may be forced to choose another behavior to manage his or her feelings of fear and anxiety. Only this time, the behavior may be much more disruptive to the class. In this educational version of whack-a-mole, each time you hit one mole (target behavior) over the head with the hammer, a bigger mole pops up that is not as cute.

Therefore, before planning any interventions, ask yourself if the repetitive behavior the student currently displays is truly disruptive to the student's learning or to the learning of others in the class. For example, minimal rocking or whispered vocalization might be only mildly disruptive at most; hand flapping, pacing, or spoken vocalizations might be moderately disruptive; intense rocking and loud or lengthy vocalizations might be significantly disruptive to the student or peers. If the behavior is not very disruptive, then allow the student to self-regulate using those behaviors. If the behavior does cause a disruption, however, then proceed with the assessment and intervention process.

Assessing the Problem

If you think anxiety, fear, and emotional regulation difficulties may be affecting your student's use of repetitive behaviors, then complete Section 3 of the FBA Checklist for Repetitive Behaviors found in the appendix at the end of this chapter. Following are some tips for assessing each item:

3a: The Student Does Not Demonstrate Repetitive Behaviors When the Student Is Comfortable With the Routine or Activity but Does So During Certain Routines and Situations That Cause Anxiety and Fear

Examples of routines and activities that can cause anxiety and fear include, but are not limited to, new lesson formats; unfamiliar independent work tasks; an unfamiliar routine that is not a typical part of the school day; frequent inconsistency in routines; fear of failure for difficult tasks; or a new teacher, related services provider, support staff, or volunteer in the classroom.

3b: The Student Does Not Demonstrate Repetitive Behaviors When the Teacher Is in Close Proximity but Does When the Teacher Is Not Nearby

The teacher's proximity to the student may be supporting the student's emotional regulation. Thus, emotional dysregulation increases when the teacher walks away, and the student may engage in more repetitive behaviors.

3c: The Student Demonstrates Repetitive Behaviors When Emotionally Distressed

The student may experience emotional dysregulation for a variety of reasons in addition to 3a and 3b. For example, a student may be upset about getting in a fight with his or her brother on the way to school and begin the day with increased occurrence of repetitive behaviors as a result of that emotional distress. A student may get upset about what his or her mother packed for lunch, resulting in repetitive behaviors to manage that disappointment. Students with ASD generally are not equipped with a variety of coping strategies to manage and channel their feelings when they have emotional regulation difficulties, making it likely that repetitive behaviors will occur as a result of having few or no other means to calm themselves down.

Supporting the Student

Consider the following strategies and supports if anxiety, fear, and emotional regulation difficulties are causing increases in repetitive behaviors:

- If novelty is causing emotional distress, then use ***social narratives*** to provide detailed information about a new lesson format that will be used or a new type of assignment that will be given.
- Use ***priming*** before presenting the new lesson format or giving the new type of assignment to remind the student of what was learned from the ***social narrative.***
- Use ***explicit instruction*** to teach the student replacement behaviors that can be used to calm down instead of engaging in repetitive behavior (e.g., take deep breaths, play with a fidget toy, stand up and pace back and forth in a specified area, ask for help or a break, ask the teacher to stay nearby).
- Use ***differential reinforcement*** of zero rates of behavior by providing ***positive reinforcement*** when the student is not engaging in repetitive behavior. Use an interval system in which the student is reinforced after every minute of zero occurrences of repetitive behaviors.

SOCIAL SKILLS DEFICITS

The occurrence of repetitive behaviors can be a reaction to a student's social skills deficits in multiple ways.

Understanding the Problem

First, if the student is not interacting socially with others, then he or she may engage in these behaviors due to disengagement. The repetitive behaviors in this context keep the student entertained during periods of time when he or she is unable to meaningfully engage with others. Second, a student may engage in repetitive behaviors when expected to participate in social situations he or she is not yet equipped for, meaning the student does not yet have the social reciprocity capabilities and specific social skills needed to be successful. The student may use repetitive behaviors to cope and to manage his or her frustration when feeling ill-equipped.

Assessing the Problem

If you think social skills deficits may be affecting your student's use of repetitive behaviors, then complete Section 4 of the FBA Checklist for Repetitive Behaviors found in the appendix at the end of this chapter. Following are some tips for assessing each item:

4a: The Student Engages in Repetitive Behaviors During Periods of Social Disengagement; However, the Student Does Not Demonstrate These Behaviors When Joint Attention Is Established

You will first need to know ways to establish joint attention with the student so you can determine if the student refrains from using repetitive behaviors when socially connected with others. It is easy for teachers to assume that students with ASD prefer to be alone when they are not engaging with others. These students, however, may resort to being alone simply because they lack the social skills needed to engage with others. Not only do the repetitive behaviors cease, but the student's general mood and affect also become much more positive when you establish joint attention with him or her.

Following the student's lead is one way to establish joint attention. This means that you join the child's attentional focus and engage with the student during an activity in which the student is currently attending. For example, if the student is flipping through a book while engaging in physical and verbal self-stimulatory behavior, then you can join the student and look at the book with him or her, making positive comments, smiling, listening to what the student is saying as he or she looks through the book, and using those comments as a starting point for conversation. You may notice that the student's self-stimulatory behaviors decrease once you join the activity and establish joint attention. Presenting something related to the student's special interests for purposes of beginning a meaningful shared experience is another way to establish joint attention. You may notice that the student stops engaging in repetitive behaviors once joint attention is established with another person.

4b: The Student Engages in Repetitive Behavior When Activities Require Social Reciprocity Skills That Are Not Part of the Student's Repertoire

Countless expectations in school settings require social reciprocity skills, including answering questions, responding to comments, having conversations, playing games, interacting with cafeteria staff while going through the lunch line, participating in partner activities while learning academic subjects, and arrival and dismissal routines. If a student is unable to engage in the long chains of back-and forth-interactions required during these activities, then he or she may use repetitive behaviors to cope with failure or frustration.

4c: The Student Engages in Repetitive Behavior When Activities Require the Use of Specific Social Skills That the Student Has Not Yet Learned

When activities in the school and classroom require specific social skills that the student has not yet acquired, such as turn-taking, waiting, sharing, perspective taking, accepting feedback, protesting appropriately, and compromising, the student may engage in repetitive behaviors when unable to meet the social expectations. To assess if this may be the case, you first need to have a good understanding of the student's present level of social performance as far as which skills have been mastered, which are developing, and which skills the student has had limited or no instruction. Then you should document how often the student engages in repetitive behavior when there are not any social demands and when the social demands are feasible for the student. Compare this with the frequency of repetitive behavior in situations in which the social expectations are not appropriate for the student or situations in which no supports are in place to help the student manage the social components of the task at hand.

Supporting the Student

Consider the following strategies and supports if social skills deficits are causing problems with a student's ability to complete work independently:

- Use ***social narratives*** or ***video modeling*** to teach social expectations.
- Use ***priming*** before activities that require the use of newly learned social skills to remind the student what was learned from the ***social narrative*** or ***video modeling.***
- Use ***prompting/fading procedures*** to support the student with using the newly learned social skills in natural contexts.
- Use ***peer-mediated interventions*** to teach peers how to support the student's social success during structured and unstructured activities.
- Teach the student how to use ***self-management*** techniques (e.g., goal setting, ***self-monitoring,*** self-evaluation, self-reinforcement) to promote the development of social skills.

SENSORY PROCESSING PROBLEMS

Students with ASD may also display repetitive behaviors as a result of sensory overload or to obtain sensory input needed to regulate themselves.

Understanding the Problem

Those of us who do not suffer from sensory integration dysfunction have no idea what it feels like to be regularly put into environments and situations that literally cause pain and discomfort. In some cases, there is just too much to see, hear, smell, feel, and taste; too much personal movement to control; and too much surrounding movement in which to attend. In short, there is too much to process, so a student may have to engage in repetitive behaviors to prevent a full-blown loss of control or meltdown. Alternatively, the rules and behavioral expectations in the classroom may also prevent students with ASD from getting the sensory input they need. These students are often unable to remain in their seats, sit still, and be quiet due to sensory differences. If they are able to control their movement and verbal output to meet behavioral expectations, then the effort this requires may render them unable to fully engage in the learning activities. Movement and verbalizations may be what a student needs in order to listen, follow directions, and focus on work tasks.

Assessing the Problem

If you think processing problems may be affecting your student's use of repetitive behaviors, then complete Section 5 of the FBA Checklist for Repetitive Behaviors in the appendix at the end of this chapter. Following are some tips for assessing each item:

5a: The Student Engages in Repetitive Behavior When Activities Require the Use of Certain Materials With Specific Textures or Odors

If you think this may be an issue for your student, then the first thing you should do is ask the student about his or her preferences for learning materials and if there are certain things that the student would want to refrain from using. If the student is unable to answer those questions, then there are other ways to get that information. Provide different choices for materials and document what the student selects each time as well as what the student never selects, interview family members, or interview other professionals. You may find that the student has an aversion to using materials such as finger paint, markers with strong scents, clay, or sandpaper or that the student engages in repetitive behaviors to avoid engaging in tasks that will result in getting wet or dirty.

5b: The Student Engages in Repetitive Behavior When Environments Are Loud, Bright, Cluttered, and So Forth but Does Not in Environments That Have Minimal Sensory Input

If you think too much environmental stimuli may be the reason behind your student's repetitive behaviors, then alter the environment and examine if the behaviors decrease or stop. For example, create quiet settings, dim or dark settings, or settings without a great deal of movement taking place, and limit the variety of materials to see, touch, and smell. Record whether there is a change in the occurrence of the behaviors.

5c: The Student Engages in Repetitive Behavior When Prevented From Gaining Access to Needed Sensory Input

Document the presence of repetitive behaviors when the student is expected to stay seated, keep still, and be quiet. Create situations that allow for more sensory input, such as the following:

- Allowing the student to sit on a balance ball
- Placing bands on the front legs of the student's desk on which the student can bounce his or her feet
- Allowing the student to stand
- Allowing the student to move as long as the student stays in a specified area near or around his or her desk
- Planning more opportunities for movement and talking within the lesson through various active engagement strategies.

Document whether the repetitive behaviors decreased when the student was provided with more sensory input. Keep in mind that you should be looking for a decrease in the behaviors, not necessarily compete cessation. That may be unrealistic and not feasible for the student.

Supporting the Student

Consider the following strategies and supports if sensory processing problems are causing increases in repetitive behaviors:

- Make ***environmental modifications*** to support the student's sensory processing needs.
- Use ***shaping*** by gradually increasing sensory stimuli in controlled environments to allow the student to get more comfortable with the introduction of additional materials, noise levels, movement, or visuals.
- Use ***explicit instruction*** to teach the student how to ask for a break to a quiet space to get regulated in order to return to the task when calm.
- Consider altering the student's requirements for eating in the cafeteria or attending assemblies until the student learns to process that level of sensory input.

- Allow the student to use repetitive behaviors to get regulated if they serve that purpose, as long as they are not disturbing others. You can teach the student ways to alter his or her behavior so he or she is not disrupting others.

PROBLEMS WITH FOCUS AND ATTENTION

It is very difficult for some students with ASD to maintain focus and sustained attention during teacher-led instruction and independent work tasks. They may engage in repetitive behaviors when they lose their focus and attention as a natural consequence of not being engaged.

Understanding the Problem

The function of repetitive behavior in this context is not much different from how it functions in people who do not have ASD when they get bored or lose their focus. The main difference is the topography of the behaviors engaged in during periods of time when focus and attention is lost. For example, typically developing peers may lose focus and begin thinking about something else, doodling on their paper, biting their nails, twirling their hair, writing a note, reading a book, or sending text messages. Students with ASD may lose focus and begin engaging in verbal self-stimulatory behaviors or repetitive movements instead of those other more typical off-task behaviors.

Assessing the Problem

If you think problems with focus and attention may be affecting your student's use of repetitive behaviors, then complete Section 6 of the FBA Checklist for Repetitive Behaviors in the appendix at the end of this chapter. This item states the following: Repetitive behaviors do not occur when the student is focused and actively engaged during a learning activity; however, the behaviors do occur when the student loses focus and attention. Take note if the repetitive behaviors occur at the same level when the student is focused and actively attending to instruction or a work task compared with times when the student does not appear to be focused and engaged. If the student is focused and engaged and still using repetitive behaviors, then focus and attention problems are not the reason for the behaviors' occurrence. If the occurrence of repetitive behaviors increases when it appears that the student loses focus and attention, however, then check off the item listed in Section 6. It is also important to record information about what types of activities the student is most likely to be able to focus on and maintain attention for and what typically causes a student to lose focus and attention. This will help you select interventions and supports.

Supporting the Student

Consider using the following supports and strategies if problems with focus and attention are causing increases in repetitive behaviors:

- Provide ***increased opportunities for the student to respond*** during group instruction by increased questioning and use of ***response cards, choral response***, or ***think-pair-share.***
- Embed opportunities for movement during group instruction by playing games that involve moving around the room to learn or answer questions, using the imitation of gestures to teach concepts and engage learners, or rotating through stations.
- Provide ***guided notes*** for the student to complete during group instruction.

- Allow the student to draw or play with fidget toys to help the student focus and attend during instruction.
- Assign independent work tasks that include various engaging activities, such as creating models or drawings, participating in role-play activities with peers, developing multimedia presentations, and creating graphical representations of information.
- Provide ***positive reinforcement*** when the student is focused and attending to instruction or tasks.

EXECUTIVE FUNCTIONING CHALLENGES

Students with ASD who struggle with executive functioning challenges may engage in repetitive behaviors in certain circumstances that place a heavy demand on executive functioning skills.

Understanding the Problem

Students may engage in repetitive behaviors when their assigned tasks have multiple steps to follow, they have to use time management skills to regulate their work behaviors, or they have to use organizational skills to keep track of their assignments and materials. The repetitive behaviors in these instances can be a reaction to the frustration the student feels with being unable to successfully complete tasks, find needed materials, or adjust his or her behavior to meet time demands.

Assessing the Problem

If you think executive functioning challenges may be affecting your student's use of repetitive behaviors, then complete Section 7 of the FBA Checklist for Repetitive Behaviors in the appendix at the end of this chapter. This item states the following: The student does not demonstrate repetitive behaviors when learning tasks are simple but does when the tasks require multiple steps, organization, and time management. To assess if this may be the case for the student, determine whether the student refrains from the use of repetitive behaviors when assignments have one simple step that is easy for the student to follow in the given time period with all materials readily available. Then determine whether those behaviors increase when the tasks have two or more steps, the student must alter behavior to meet time constraints, the student has to gain access to and store materials, or the student has to locate and file assignments that have not yet been turned in to the teacher.

Supporting the Student

Consider the following strategies and supports if executive functioning challenges are causing the student to engage in repetitive behaviors:

- Use ***task analysis*** and ***forward chaining*** to break down multistep assignments into manageable steps.
- Provide ***self-monitoring*** tools and ***explicit instruction*** to teach the student how to use the ***self-monitoring*** tools to complete the steps of a task.
- Use ***video modeling*** to support the student in learning the expectations of multistep tasks.
- Use visual timers and self-management systems to help the student keep track of time and adjust behavior accordingly. The self-management system may include checkpoints

in which the student uses a visual cue to determine if the task can be completed at the current pace, if the student can finish if work is completed at a quicker pace, or if the student needs to ask for more time to complete the task.

- Provide ***positive reinforcement*** when the student uses the supports to complete assignments and refrains from excessive repetitive behaviors.

ACADEMIC, COGNITIVE, OR MOTOR SKILLS DEFICITS

Repetitive behaviors can occur as a result of deficits in academic understanding, cognitive skills, or motor skills that render the task at hand inappropriate for the student.

Understanding the Problem

Students with ASD are sometimes expected to participate in instructional activities and complete assignments that are too difficult based on their present levels of academic performance, cognitive development, and motor skills. If the teacher does not differentiate instruction and assessment to meet the unique needs of the learners in the classroom, then a student with ASD may engage in repetitive behaviors when the requirements for participation in group instruction or work tasks are not developmentally appropriate.

Assessing the Problem

If you think academic, cognitive, or motor skills deficits may be affecting your student's use of repetitive behaviors, then complete Section 8 of the FBA Checklist for Repetitive Behaviors. Following are some tips for assessing each item:

8a: The Student Does Not Demonstrate Repetitive Behaviors During Concrete Learning Activities but Does During Learning Activities Involving Abstract Thoughts and Ideas

This is an example of cognitive differences affecting a student's use of repetitive behaviors. If the instruction or assignment requires students to think and perform at the abstract level, but the student is unable to do so for that particular topic, then the student may begin to engage in repetitive behaviors to cope with his or her frustration with not understanding the expectations or being unable to complete an assignment. To assess if this is the case, take note of the student's use of repetitive behaviors during instruction and tasks that are more concrete in nature (e.g., watching a video clip of a volcano erupting, participating in a mock trial by reading lines of a script, using base 10 blocks to learn how to regroup, answering literal comprehension questions). Compare this with the occurrence of repetitive behaviors during more abstract lessons and assignments (e.g., listening to a lecture about what makes volcanos erupt, writing definitions to demonstrate understanding of legal concepts, completing addition problems involving three-digit numbers that require regrouping without having developed a concrete understanding of the regrouping process, answering inferential comprehension questions).

8b: The Student Does Not Demonstrate Repetitive Behaviors When the Learning Activities Are Developmentally Appropriate or Easy for the Student but Does When the Activities Are Too Difficult for the Student Based on Present Levels of Academic Performance

Give the student a variety of easy tasks, and document whether the student uses repetitive behaviors while completing the assignments. Then give assignments that are on the student's instructional level and do the same. Finally, give assignments that are quite difficult for the student, and document what you observe. You may notice that the repetitive behaviors occur when the student is given tasks that are on the instructional level or are more difficult than what is appropriate. Keep in mind that you can truly assess this only if you have a comprehensive understanding of the student's present level of academic performance. This should be part of formal and ongoing informal assessments (see Chapter 2).

8c: The Student Demonstrates Repetitive Behavior When Activities Require the Use of Fine Motor Skills

Students with ASD may engage in repetitive behaviors when expected to complete tasks or engage in activities that require fine motor skills beyond their capabilities, including writing tasks, drawing tasks, cutting/gluing activities, or tasks that require using small items that are difficult for the student to grasp and manipulate. To assess if this may be causing increases in repetitive behaviors for your student, make accommodations to activities and assignments to limit the use of fine motor skills, or provide the necessary adaptations for the student to be successful, and take note of whether the behaviors decrease or stop.

8d: The Student Demonstrates Repetitive Behavior When Activities Require the Use of Gross Motor Skills

You may notice that a student with ASD engages in more repetitive behaviors during structured outdoor play activities or physical education classes. This may be due to deficits in gross motor skills, such as throwing and catching a ball, playing team sports, running, skipping, or jumping. To assess if this may be causing increases in repetitive behaviors for your student, make the necessary adaptations to the gross motor tasks to allow the student to be successful, and take note of whether the behaviors decrease or stop.

Supporting the Student

Consider the following strategies and supports if academic, cognitive, or motor skills deficits are affecting the student's demonstration of repetitive behaviors:

- Use a ***CRA*** sequence to teach the student how to complete mathematical word problems. For example, first use manipulatives or role-play activities to show what is being stated in the problem. Then use drawings to do the same. The student be expected to complete problems at the abstract level only after the student is able to understand at these concrete and representational levels.
- Provide accommodations and AT for writing tasks (e.g., a computer for typing, a ***scribe,*** voice recording instead of writing).
- Allow the student to verbally state what will be written and get feedback to correct syntax and grammar before writing. Then have the student repeat the corrected sentence before writing or typing.
- Provide ***visual supports*** to facilitate written expression (e.g., ***graphic organizers,*** outlines, ***pictures***).
- Use scaffolding to help the student make connections between what he or she knows about literal information in a reading selection to draw conclusions and make inferences.

  Following is an example of a series of questions that provide the necessary scaffolding:

  - Literal question: What did the mother tell the boy to do when he got home from school? (clean his room)
  - Literal question: What did the boy do when he got home from school? (rode his bike)
  - Literal question: Did the boy clean his room after school like his mother asked? (no)

    - Inferential question: Why was the mother angry when the family was eating dinner? (because the boy did not clean his room like she had asked)
    - Adapt physical education activities to work on skill development instead of requiring the student to participate in actual team sports games. For example, teach the student how to throw and kick a ball back and forth with one peer instead of having the student play basketball or soccer.
- Deliver ***positive reinforcement*** when the student engages in learning tasks without the use of repetitive behaviors.

RESTRICTED RANGE OF INTERESTS

Your student with ASD may engage in repetitive behaviors when presented with instructional activities that are not interest based.

Understanding the Problem

Some students may need teachers to make increased efforts to tap into their special interests, fascinations, and passions to motivate them to engage in various learning tasks because of their restricted range of interests. This does not mean that every lesson and assignment has to be interest based to prevent repetitive behavior. Begin by simply increasing the opportunities students with ASD have to connect learning to their favorite topics.

Assessing the Problem

If you think your student's restricted range of interests may be affecting the child's use of repetitive behaviors, then complete Section 9 of the FBA Checklist for Repetitive Behaviors in the appendix at the end of this chapter. This item states the following: The student does not engage in repetitive behavior when activities are related to the student's interests but does so during non–interest-based activities. Examine the occurrence of repetitive behaviors during times when the student is engaged in learning activities that are related to special interests, fascinations, and passions in some way. Compare this with the occurrence of these behaviors at times when the student's interests are not considered when delivering instruction or giving assignments.

Supporting the Student

Consider the following strategies and supports if a student's restricted range of interests are causing the occurrence of repetitive behaviors:

- Use references to favorite characters to teach concepts during group lessons (e.g., if a student loves Star Wars, then ask the student to summarize the main events of one of the Star Wars movies when teaching about summarization).
- Give assignments that allow the student to demonstrate a learned skill while completing an activity related to the student's interests (e.g., write an essay about the three best attractions in Disney World, compare and contrast tornados and hurricanes, read nonfiction books about the weather and answer comprehension questions, write a time line of events of Darth Vader's life).
- Allow the student to use materials with his or her favorite characters to complete work (e.g., pencils, notebooks, markers, erasers, sticky notes).

- Increase the number of learning activities that tap into the student's interests so that at least half of the daily lessons and assignments have some connection to those things.
- Use a first-then ***visual support*** and schedule to let the student know that an interest-based activity will come next after the student completes a non–interest-based activity.
- Deliver ***positive reinforcement*** when the student engages in non–interest-based activities without the use of repetitive behaviors.

MEDICAL CONDITIONS

It is always important to rule out any possible medical conditions that may be affecting the occurrence of repetitive behaviors.

Understanding the Problem

The student may be using repetitive behaviors to cope with pain, discomfort, or lethargy that results from sickness, seizure activity, reactions to medications, or other medical issues. Students who are nonverbal or have limitations in expressive communication skills are often unable to report these problems to their teachers and engage in repetitive behavior when these issues go untreated.

Assessing the Problem

If you think medical conditions may be affecting your student's use of repetitive behaviors, then complete Section 9 of the FBA Checklist for Repetitive Behavior in the appendix at the end of this chapter. See Chapters 1 and 4 if additional explanation is needed for the items in that section.

Supporting the Student

Consider the following supports and strategies if medical conditions are causing an increase in repetitive behaviors:

- Keep a daily communication log with the student's family to stay informed of medication changes and potential side effects.
- Set clear expectations for when the repetitive behaviors are permitted (e.g., during earned or scheduled breaks).
- Reduce the academic and social demands and increase the use of interest-based activities when the student is having a difficult time refraining from using repetitive behaviors.
- Deliver ***positive reinforcement*** when the student engages in instructional activities without demonstrating repetitive behaviors.

From Assessment to Successful Intervention

Case Study: Pedro *Pedro is a first-grade student with ASD who receives small-group reading interventions to address his deficits using letter–sound correspondence to decode and spell unfamiliar words. Mr. O'Connor meets with Pedro and four other students 20 minutes each day to deliver specialized interventions to address these skills. Mr. O'Connor uses letter tiles to teach decoding and spelling skills to increase motivation and reduce the need for writing because most of the students struggle with the fine motor task of forming letters. Whereas the other students in the group enjoy using the letter tiles to decode words and spell words dictated by Mr. O'Connor, Pedro engages in excessive repetitive behaviors during this activity. He repeats "digga, digga, digga," throughout the activity, rocks back and forth in his seat, and often wiggles his fingers in front of his eyes.*

Mr. O'Connor reviews the FBA Checklist for Repetitive Behaviors to try to figure out why Pedro engages in these behaviors every time he leads the activity with the letter tiles. Although Mr. O'Connor knows that Pedro has fine motor deficits when it comes to writing, he never considered that manipulating the letter tiles would also be difficult for Pedro. Mr. O'Connor hypothesizes that Pedro's severe fine motor deficits cause him to increase his use of repetitive behaviors every time the letter tile activity is presented, and he checks off section 8c. To test his hypothesis, Mr. O'Connor creates adaptive materials for Pedro. He uses blocks instead of letter tiles, and he writes the letters on the blocks. This allows Pedro to easily manipulate the blocks to form words instead of struggling with grasping the letter tiles and placing them in order.

Figure 7.1 shows the section of the FBA Checklist that Mr. O'Connor filled out, the hypothesis statement that was formulated, and the intervention plan that created based on the assessment.

Challenging Behavior: Repetitive Behaviors

8. Academic, Cognitive, or Motor Skills Deficits

- ❒ 8a: The student does not demonstrate repetitive behaviors during concrete learning activities but does during learning activities involving abstract thoughts and ideas.
- ❒ 8b: The student does not demonstrate repetitive behaviors when the learning activities are developmentally appropriate or easy for the student but does when the activities are too difficult for the student based on present levels of academic performance.
- ☑ 8c: The student demonstrates repetitive behavior when activities require the use of fine motor skills.
- ❒ 8d: The student demonstrates repetitive behavior when activities require the use of gross motor skills.

Hypothesis Statement Pedro engages in repetitive behaviors during instructional activities (manipulation of letter tiles) that require the use of fine motor skills that he has not yet developed.

Intervention Plan

- Adapt learning materials so that they can be easily grasped and manipulated.
- Consult with the occupational therapist and assistive technology (AT) specialist as needed to create adapted materials.

Results

Mr. O'Connor contacted the physical therapist and AT specialist on a regular basis to determine what fine motor skills Pedro has mastered, what he is working on, and what is considered too difficult for him. Not only did he use the letter blocks as an adaptation to the letter tiles, but he also continued to develop and gain access to other materials that would help Pedro be successful during small-group lessons. Pedro's repetitive behaviors dramatically decreased as a result.

Figure 7.1. Functional Behavior Assessment Checklist and intervention plan for Pedro.

From Assessment to Successful Intervention

Case Study: Jordan *Jordan is a sixth-grade student with ASD who engages in repetitive behavior by repeating scripts from movies and television shows whenever he is expected to work with a small group of peers to complete science experiments. Mrs. Fowler, his science teacher, meets with Ms. Santiago, his special education teacher, to review the FBA Checklist for Repetitive Behaviors to come up with a hypothesis for why this is happening. They discuss the process of typical science experiments. The students have a list of materials to get, a worksheet that has step-by-step instructions for conducting the experiment, and a list of discussion questions they must answer following the experiment. The students figure out within their groups who will get the materials and who will conduct the different steps of the experiment. While answering the discussion questions, two or three students from the group usually take over the conversation. Jordan is completely disengaged during the entire process and repeats movie scripts throughout.*

Ms. Santiago shares her thoughts that Jordan's social skill deficits are causing his disengagement and use of scripting behavior. He does not have the joint attention and social reciprocity skills needed to independently participate in the experiments with the peers and converse about the findings without specialized supports. The teachers check off boxes 4a and 4b.

Figure 7.2 shows the section of the FBA Checklist that Mrs. Fowler filled out, the hypothesis statement that was formulated, and the intervention plan that was created based on the assessment.

Challenging Behavior: Repetitive Behaviors

4. Social Skills Deficits

- ☑ 4a: The student engages in repetitive behaviors during periods of social disengagement; however, the student does not demonstrate these behaviors when joint attention is established.
- ☑ 4b: The student engages in repetitive behavior when activities require social reciprocity skills that are not part of the student's repertoire.
- ☐ 4c: The student engages in repetitive behavior when activities require the use of specific social skills that the student has not yet learned.

Hypothesis Statement Jordan engages in excessive repetitive behaviors (repeating movie scripts) during science experiments performed with a peer group due to social skills deficits. Jordan does not have the joint attention and social reciprocity skills needed to independently meet the social expectations of the activities. Thus, he will engage in scripting behaviors because he is unable to engage with the peers as intended.

Intervention Plan

- Give Jordan specific roles to support his joint attention.
- Give Jordan a ***self-monitoring*** checklist of materials that he is expected to get for the group and bring back to the table.
- Use ***peer-mediated interventions*** to teach the peers how to prompt Jordan to use the checklist to gather the materials and how to positively reinforce him when he brings the materials to the table by saying, "Thank you, Jordan," "Thanks for getting the measuring cups, Jordan," "Looks like you got everything we need, Jordan!"
- Put Jordan's name next to the step(s) that he is responsible for completing on the worksheet that lists the steps for the experiment.
- When his peer group is answering the discussion questions, make Jordan responsible for reading the question aloud and writing the group's final answer because he has strengths in reading and writing. Teach the peers how to dictate the sentences to Jordan using clear, concise language so that he can successfully record the group's responses.

Results

Jordan's active participation in the science experiments increases significantly with these supports, and his verbal scripting behavior occurs less often. When it does occur, it is usually just one or two sentences instead of several minutes of scripting as was typical in the past.

Figure 7.2. Functional Behavior Assessment Checklist and intervention plan for Jordan.

Challenging Behavior: Repetitive Behaviors

1. Language Comprehension Difficulties

- ❒ 1a: The student engages in repetitive behavior when expected to comply with written directions or complex verbal directions but does not when the directions are either explained using simplified language or modeled.
- ❒ 1b: The student engages in repetitive behavior when expected to comply with verbal directions or listen to lengthy lectures but does not when given written directions or when given material to read to learn new information.

2. Deficits in Expressive Communication Skills

- ❒ The student engages in repetitive behavior if he or is unable to verbally express wants and needs.

3. Anxiety, Fear, and Emotional Regulation Difficulties

- ❒ 3a: The student does not demonstrate repetitive behaviors when the student is comfortable with the routine or activity but does so during certain situations that cause anxiety and fear.
- ❒ 3b: The student does not demonstrate repetitive behaviors when the teacher is in close proximity but does when the teacher is not nearby.
- ❒ 3c: The student demonstrates repetitive behaviors when emotionally distressed.

4. Social Skills Deficits

- ❒ 4a: The student engages in repetitive behaviors during periods of social disengagement; however, the student does not demonstrate these behaviors when joint attention is established.
- ❒ 4b: The student engages in repetitive behavior when activities require social reciprocity skills that are not part of the student's repertoire.
- ❒ 4c: The student engages in repetitive behavior when activities require the use of specific social skills that the student has not yet learned.

5. Sensory Processing Problems

- ❒ 5a: The student engages in repetitive behavior when activities require the use of certain materials with specific textures or odors.
- ❒ 5b: The student engages in repetitive behavior when environments are loud, bright, cluttered, and so forth but does not in environments that have minimal sensory input.
- ❒ 5c: The student engages in repetitive behavior when prevented from gaining access to needed sensory input.

6. Problems With Focus and Attention

- ❒ Repetitive behaviors do not occur when the student is focused and actively engaged during a learning activity; however, the behaviors do occur when the student loses focus and attention,.

7. Executive Functioning Challenges

- ❒ The student does not demonstrate repetitive behaviors when learning tasks are simple but does when the tasks require multiple steps, organization, and time management.

8. Academic, Cognitive, or Motor Skills Deficits

- ❒ 8a: The student does not demonstrate repetitive behaviors during concrete learning activities but does during learning activities involving abstract thoughts and ideas.
- ❒ 8b: The student does not demonstrate repetitive behaviors when the learning activities are developmentally appropriate or easy for the student but does when the activities are too difficult for the student based on present levels of academic performance.
- ❒ 8c: The student demonstrates repetitive behavior when activities require the use of fine motor skills.
- ❒ 8d: The student demonstrates repetitive behavior when activities require the use of gross motor skills.

Challenging Behavior: Repetitive Behaviors *(continued)*

9. Restricted Range of Interests

- ❒ The student does not engage in repetitive behavior when activities are related to the student's interests but does during non-interest-based activities.

10. Medical Conditions

- ❒ 10a: The student engages in repetitive behavior if required to sit, but these behaviors decrease when permitted to stand (may have gastrointestinal pain).
- ❒ 10b: The student engages in repetitive behavior when the student goes untreated for illness or pain due to the inability to expressively communicate symptoms.
- ❒ 10c: The student engages in repetitive behavior following nights of limited sleep.
- ❒ 10d: The student engages in repetitive behavior due to reactions to new medications or reactions to changes in doses of medications.
- ❒ 10e: The student engages in repetitive behavior following periods of seizure activity.

Other ____

____

____

____

____

Hypothesis Statement ____

____

____

____

____

CHAPTER 8

Aggressive Behaviors

Students with ASD may engage in aggressive behaviors that can be disruptive to the learning in the classroom (e.g., verbal aggression such as cursing, making threats, or ridiculing others; destruction of learning materials or school property), cause harm to themselves using self-injurious behaviors, or physically hurt others. Some teachers may assume that preventative and supportive strategies using MTSS structures should be skipped because the problem is so severe in nature, and the team should move the student to a more restrictive placement. Although these behaviors do require immediate attention, they can often be effectively addressed using the same thoughtful assessment and positive, child-centered intervention approaches that are described throughout this book.

Students exhibit aggression for different reasons, depending on the unique profile of each student. This chapter discusses nine challenges faced by students with ASD that may explain why they demonstrate aggressive behaviors:

1. Language comprehension difficulties
2. Deficits in expressive communication skills
3. Anxiety, fear, and emotional regulation difficulties
4. Social skills deficits
5. Problems with focus and attention
6. Sensory processing problems
7. Academic, cognitive, or motor skills deficits
8. Restricted range of interests
9. Medical conditions

LANGUAGE COMPREHENSION DIFFICULTIES

Students with ASD may have trouble following directions, completing work independently, or participating during group instruction due to language comprehension difficulties, or may use repetitive behaviors for this reason, and they may also demonstrate aggressive behaviors for the same reason. The function of the challenging behavior is the same, but the topography of the behavior changes.

Understanding the Problem

It can be very frustrating for students who are expected to follow directions, participate, and engage with others when they do not understand what is being told or explained to them. Although some students may deal with this frustration by disengaging, using repetitive behaviors, or regulating themselves in some other way, others may deal with it through aggressive behaviors.

Assessing the Problem

If you think language difficulties may be causing your student's physical aggression, then complete Section 1 of the FBA Checklist for Aggressive Behaviors in the appendix at the end of this chapter. Following are some tips for assessing each item in Section 1 of the checklist:

1a: The Student Demonstrates Aggressive Behavior When the Teacher Uses Complex Language, Lengthy Lectures, or Very Fast Speech When Giving Directions or Providing Instruction

Examine the student's presence of aggressive behaviors during the following conditions: 1) when the teacher uses simple sentence structures when giving directions or providing lessons; 2) when the teacher breaks long lessons down into smaller segments, allowing time to process the information learned; and 3) when the teacher talks more slowly when giving directions or providing instruction. If aggressive behaviors do not occur, or occur less frequently during those conditions, then you can predict that language comprehension problems are affecting the student's behavior.

1b: The Student Demonstrates Aggressive Behavior When Directions or Instruction Are Given Verbally or in Writing but Not When Expectations Are Physically Demonstrated or Information Is Explained Using Visuals

Observe the presence of aggressive behaviors when information is delivered visually as opposed to delivered solely through verbal instruction. If aggressive behaviors decrease during those conditions, then you can predict that language comprehension problems are causing the physical or verbal aggression.

1c: The Student Demonstrates Aggressive Behavior When Unfamiliar Directions Are Given Containing Language the Student Does Not Understand

Observe whether the student uses aggressive behavior when familiar directions are given and when familiar instructional formats are used that rely on using consistent language structures (e.g., direct instruction materials). If aggression is reduced in these contexts, then take note if aggression increases once unfamiliar is language is used when giving directions or delivering instruction. If so, then you can predict that language comprehension difficulties are the root of the problem.

Supporting the Student

If you determine that aggressive behaviors are a result of language comprehension issues, then the supports and strategies suggested in the Language Comprehension Difficulties section of Chapters 4–7 should be considered. In addition, it is important to immediately teach replacement behaviors for the aggression to prevent students from harming themselves or others. Teach functional communication skills that help the student share confusion and frustration in more appropriate ways because language comprehension difficulties are the root of the student's problem. You can teach the student to communicate any of the following: "I don't understand." "Can you repeat that?" "What do you mean?" "Can you slow down?" "Can I have some time to take notes?" "Can I read instead of listen?" Provide ***visual supports*** such as ***cue cards, symbols,*** or pictures to support the student in using the selected functional communication skills. ***AAC*** supports can also be used for functional communication skills. Even students who are verbal may need ***visual*** or ***AAC supports*** because engaging in aggressive behaviors shows that they are experiencing emotional regulation difficulties. Students with ASD who get emotionally dysregulated often are unable to use expressive communication skills in the same manner as when they are calm. Use ***explicit instruction, social narratives,*** or ***video modeling*** to teach students how to use the selected functional communication skills.

DEFICITS IN EXPRESSIVE COMMUNICATION SKILLS

The frustration of being unable to communicate can sometimes lead to aggressive behaviors by students with ASD who have expressive communication deficits.

Understanding the Problem

Those of us who are easily able to express ourselves verbally and in writing can only imagine what it would be like to have no means of communicating. It is amazing that more students with ASD who are nonverbal and do not have adequate ***AAC*** options do not exhibit aggressive behavior. For those who do, teachers must first understand that the aggressive behavior is certainly reasonable considering that the student has no other means of communication.

Assessing the Problem

If you think deficits in expressive communication skills may be affecting your student's aggressive behaviors, then complete Section 2 of the FBA Checklist for Aggressive Behaviors in the appendix at the end of this chapter. Following are some tips for assessing each item:

2a: The Student Lacks the Communication Skills Necessary to Express Wants and Needs and, Therefore, Communicates Wants and Needs by Demonstrating Aggressive Behavior

If a student is aggressive and nonverbal or has severe expressive communication impairments, then it is safe to assume that deficits in expressive communication skills are at least one reason for the aggressive behavior. The function of the aggressive behavior in this circumstance is to communicate because other modes of communication are unavailable to the student. The student has no other means of expressing day-to-day wants and basic needs such as feeling hungry, needing to use the bathroom, visiting the school nurse, or needing help with a task.

2b: The Student Demonstrates Aggressive Behavior When Having Difficulty Verbally Expressing His or Her Perspective to a Teacher or Peer, Resulting in Feeling as if His or Her Point of View Is Being Disregarded

Even students with ASD who are high functioning and have developed fairly good expressive communication skills can have great difficulty using language to effectively share their inner thoughts and feelings with others and engage in verbal negotiations when necessary. Typically developing students can ask questions, share their points of view, and present a rationale for why they think something should happen, and sometimes they do not let up until they get what they want. Students with ASD often do not have the advanced expressive communication skills needed to do these things. They may keep repeating the same phrases or sentences when others are not responding in the correct way. They ultimately end up getting either shut down or ignored and may engage in aggressive behaviors as a result.

Supporting the Student

Consider the following strategies and supports if deficits in expressive communication skills are causing the occurrence of aggressive behaviors:

- Teach functional communication skills using ***discrete trial training, incidental teaching, AAC*** supports, or ***video modeling.*** It is important to continually assess what the student may be trying to communicate through the aggressive behaviors so you can choose words and phrases to target for functional communication based on the student's individualized communication needs. This assessment is best done by collecting and analyzing A-B-C data (see Chapter 3).
- If a student keeps repeating the same words or phrases and appears agitated, then try to take the perspective of the student and figure out what the student is really trying to communicate. Think about the antecedents that just occurred and how what the student is repeating may be related to something that just happened. If the student is too frustrated to answer open-ended questions, then you can ask yes/no questions to assess your guesses to either rule them out or confirm them.

ANXIETY, FEAR, AND EMOTIONAL REGULATION DIFFICULTIES

Students with ASD who demonstrate aggressive behaviors as a result of severe levels of anxiety and fear may be described as going from 0 to 60 in .2 seconds. It may be difficult to prevent the aggression if you do not see it coming.

Understanding the Problem

It is important to conduct careful observations for these students, looking for red flags that may indicate aggressive behaviors are about to start. For example, some students who exhibit self-injurious behaviors may hit themselves lightly at the first signs of anxiety and fear and quickly progress to more forceful aggression. You may find that a student who hits others will first hit the table right before hitting another person. If you can determine what the red flags are for a student, then you will be able to redirect the student and prevent more severe aggression.

Students with ASD who have anxieties and intense fears usually struggle with emotional regulation problems, which is why anxiety and fear may lead to aggression. Difficulties with emotional regulation often lead to aggressive behaviors when students are not receiving intervention to learn how to identify when they are feeling heightened emotions and choose strategies to calm themselves down.

Assessing the Problem

If you think anxiety, fear, and emotional regulation difficulties may be affecting your student's aggressive behaviors, then complete Section 3 of the FBA Checklist for Aggressive Behaviors in the appendix at the end of this chapter. Following are some tips for assessing each item:

3a: The Student Demonstrates Aggressive Behavior When New Tasks or Activities Are Presented but Not When Familiar Tasks Are Presented

Students may become aggressive when they are presented with something unfamiliar without advanced preparation because of their intense need for sameness. This is easy to assess. Simply determine if the student has less or no aggression during familiar tasks and does demonstrate aggression when something new is presented.

3b: The Student Demonstrates Aggressive Behavior When There Is a Change in the Normal Routine or Schedule

Schedule changes or disruption to the normal routine may cause anxiety, fear, and emotional regulation problems that lead to physical aggression. This is best assessed using A-B-C data (see Chapter 3). Note the setting events and antecedent when physical aggression occurs to determine if there is a pattern of aggressive behavior when schedule changes take place.

3c: The Student Demonstrates Aggressive Behavior in Environments That Do Not Have a Consistent Schedule and Routine

A consistent schedule and routine in classroom settings often help reduce the anxiety and fear of students with ASD. They feel more at ease when they can predict what is coming next. If some of the student's classroom environments are very structured, consistent, and flexible and others are not, then you can collect data to determine if the aggressive behaviors occur less within the predictable environments and more in the classrooms that do not follow a set structure and routine. If the student is primarily in one class all day, and there is not a consistent schedule and predictable routine, then you can initiate more structure and assess if the aggressive behaviors lessen.

3d: The Student Exhibits Severe Anxiety When Teacher Directives Are Given but Is Not Aggressive When Allowed to Engage in Desirable Activities Without Teacher Involvement

Some students have a very strong aversion to directives from teachers. They may get very anxious when given academic directions to follow, expectations for participating during group instruction, or corrective feedback. Teacher directives can lead to aggressive behaviors for students with intense anxiety around these interactions. This is a great challenge in the school setting because a majority of the day involves receiving and responding to directives from teachers.

Supporting the Student

Consider the following strategies and supports if anxiety, fear, and emotional regulation difficulties are causing increases in aggressive behaviors:

- Interview the student to find out what the student worries about and whether the student has any intense fears. Interview family members if you are unable to interview the student due to expressive communication deficits. You may be surprised about what you find out and how you can make some simple accommodations to help the student become more comfortable in the classroom. For example, you may find out that the student worries intensely about getting the wrong answer when called on during small-group and whole-group instruction. To accommodate for this, you can give the student questions with the correct answers written below them to ease the worrying. After the student is comfortable with getting called on when the questions and answers are provided in advance, you can give the student only the questions in advance, allowing the student to select the question(s) that he or she will be comfortable answering during the lesson. The student may want to tell you the answer before the lesson starts to make sure it is correct to further reduce anxiety.
- Ensure there is a consistent schedule and routine in the classroom.
- Use ***priming*** to prepare the student in advance when any changes or disruptions to the routine are going to occur. Also use ***priming*** to prepare the student in advance for a new instructional activity.

- Teach the student ***emotional regulation strategies*** (e.g., breathing exercises; using rating scales to help the student identify how he or she is feeling; presenting choices of calming activities when the student is upset; allowing physical exercise such as swinging, jumping on a trampoline, or going for a walk).

SOCIAL SKILLS DEFICITS

Although social skills deficits may not be the most common cause of aggression for students with ASD, aggressive behavior can certainly be a result of specific social impairments.

Understanding the Problem

Certain social situations may interact with a student's social skills deficits in ways that result in aggressive behavior. Students may misinterpret situations due to difficulties understanding the social nuances, they may lack social problem-solving skills needed to handle stressful situations proactively, or they may demonstrate aggression through self-injurious behaviors during long periods of social disengagement.

Assessing the Problem

If you think social skills deficits may be affecting your student's aggressive behaviors, then complete Section 4 of the FBA Checklist for Aggressive Behaviors in the appendix at the end of this chapter. Following are some tips for assessing each item:

4a: The Student Demonstrates Aggressive Behavior During Periods of Social Disengagement From Teachers or Peers Due to Social Deprivation

If a student has severe joint attention, social reciprocity, and communication impairments, then there may be few opportunities for the student to meaningfully engage with others. Those severe deficits do not remove the human need for a sense of belonging and relationships with other people, however. Thus, a student may resort to using aggressive behaviors toward others or self-injurious behaviors to get attention and interaction from others.

4b: The Student Demonstrates Aggressive Behavior During Situations That Require Using Social Problem-Solving Skills the Student Has Not Yet Acquired

Sometimes students with ASD exhibit aggression because they do not know any other solutions to a problem they are facing. Consider a situation in which a student is working with a group of peers, and the peers are fooling around instead of doing the assigned task. The student wants to follow the teacher directions and gets frustrated with the peers. The student shouts "Stop it!" The peers continue fooling around. The student then hits one of the peers. The student in this situation does not have the social problem-solving skills needed to come up with alternative ways to handle the situation, such as trying to calmly redirect the peers to the task, privately explaining the problem to the teacher, or asking to switch groups.

Although ***social autopsies*** and the ***SOCCSS*** strategy are generally used for teaching social problem-solving skills, they can also be used to assess if the student has social problem-solving abilities. If the student is unable to generate positive alternatives to dealing with actual or hypothetical social problems, then you can make the prediction that deficits in social problem-solving skills may be increasing aggressive behavior.

4c: The Student Demonstrates Aggression Due to Errors With Perspective Taking

Students with ASD may have difficulty understanding the perspectives of other people (also referred to as *deficits in theory of mind*), so there may be instances in which aggression occurs due to the misinterpretation of situations. For example, if someone accidentally hits the student with a ball during recess, then the student may automatically think the peer did it on purpose and display aggression toward the peer.

Supporting the Student

Consider the following strategies and supports if social skills deficits are affecting the aggressive behaviors of your student:

- Teach perspective taking using ***social narratives*** and comic strip conversations.
- Teach social problem-solving skills using ***social autopsies*** or the ***SOCCSS*** strategy.
- Facilitate positive social interactions between the student with ASD and other peers as often as possible throughout the school day by ***following the student's lead,*** using ***balanced turn-taking,*** and ***peer-mediated interventions***.
- Deliver ***positive reinforcement*** when the student engages positively with peers, takes the perspective of others during social situations, or uses positive social problem-solving skills during naturally occurring contexts.

PROBLEMS WITH FOCUS AND ATTENTION

Problems with focus and attention usually do not cause aggressive behavior, but they may lead to this behavior during transitions.

Understanding the Problem

If a student with ASD has trouble shifting attention, then aggressive behaviors may occur when teachers force such a transition. For example, if a student is very focused on a specific task, and the teacher says to put the work away and line up to go to music, then the student may demonstrate aggressive behavior because of problems shifting focus from the task to something else. The student may feel the need to finish the task before shifting attention and may get emotionally dysregulated and demonstrate aggression if not permitted to do so.

Assessing the Problem

If you think problems with shifting attention may be affecting your student's aggressive behavior, then check the box in Section 5 of the FBA Checklist in the appendix at the end of this chapter: The student demonstrates aggressive behavior when asked to stop an activity that he or she is focused on due to difficulties shifting attention. If you are unsure if this is the case, then use some of the strategies and supports described next, and record the student's frequency and intensity of aggression. If the aggressive behavior decreases when supports are in place to help the student shift attention, then you can predict that problems with shifting attention causes aggressive behavior.

Supporting the Student

Consider the following strategies and supports if your student demonstrates aggressive behavior due to problems with shifting attention:

- Give warnings to let the student know when it will be time to make the transition to a new activity.

- Use a visual timer to allow the student to see how much time is left before the next transition.
- Create an unfinished work folder the student can use when it is time to make the transition and the current task is not complete. Make sure you let the student know exactly when there will be an opportunity to finish the work to support the transition.
- Give the student the direction to make the transition before you tell the rest of the class to provide necessary supports for the transition.
- Teach functional communication skills that will replace aggression, such as saying, "May I please finish this first?" "When will I be able to finish?" "I need just 5 more minutes please."

SENSORY PROCESSING PROBLEMS

Students with ASD who have severe sensory processing problems and are diagnosed with sensory integration dysfunction can demonstrate aggressive behaviors when they get over- or understimulated.

Understanding the Problem

Students with ASD may get overstimulated and demonstrate aggressive behavior toward others during physical activities because of their escalated state and sensory processing problems. They may also exhibit self-injurious behaviors as an attempt to make their pain go away because of the physical discomfort they feel as a result of sensory issues. Carly Fleischmann, the young adult with ASD who was mentioned in Chapter 1, explained another reason why she would engage in self-injurious behaviors. She reported that she would often do so to prevent herself from seeking sensory input in an inappropriate manner (Fleischmann & Fleischmann, 2012). For example, if a student has an urge to smell another student's hair but has been taught that the behavior is unacceptable, then the student may slap herself in the face to stop herself from smelling someone's hair.

Assessing the Problem

If you think sensory processing problems may be affecting a student's aggressive behaviors, then complete Section 6 of the FBA Checklist for Aggressive Behaviors in the appendix at the end of this chapter. Following are some tips for assessing each item:

6a: The Student Demonstrates Aggression When Experiencing Sensory Overload

The student may display aggression when overstimulated by visual, auditory, or olfactory stimuli. The student may also get overwhelmed by excessive clutter and chaotic movement in the classroom and become aggressive as a result.

6b: The Student Demonstrates Aggression When Denied Sensory Input

Teachers often try to restrict students with ASD from gaining access to necessary sensory input, which can lead to aggressive behavior. For example, teachers may say or signal, "Quiet hands" when a student is flapping his or her hands. If the student needs the sensory input gained from hand flapping and is restricted from doing so, then the student may become aggressive. Set aside a period when you do not restrict your student from getting sensory input, even if the manner of doing so is unusual. If the frequency and intensity of aggressive behaviors decrease when the student can gain access to sensory input, then you can predict that sensory needs are causing the aggression.

6c: The Student Demonstrates Aggression When Forced Into Sensory Experiences That Cause Pain or Discomfort

This happens quite often to students with ASD who suffer from sensory integration dysfunction because people who do not have this issue do not understand the physical pain and discomfort certain sensory experiences can cause. For example, students may be forced to wear certain clothing because of school uniform requirements or because a parent does not think the child should wear the same thing every day. Students with ASD do not have the expressive communication skills needed to effectively explain why they do not want to be exposed to certain stimuli. Thus, it appears that they are being noncompliant, so the adult puts his or her foot down to not give in to the student's controlling behaviors. Aggressive behaviors may be the result.

Supporting the Student

Consider the following strategies and supports if sensory processing problems are causing aggressive behaviors:

- Interview the student to find out what sensory experiences he or she finds uncomfortable or painful and what sensory stimuli he or she craves. Interview family members if you are unable to interview the student due to the child's expressive communication deficits.
- Collaborate with occupational therapists and speech-language pathologists (SLPs) to learn ways to address the student's sensory needs.
- Make ***environmental arrangements*** to reduce sensory stimuli or add sensory input based on the student's individualized sensory profile.
- Use ***priming*** to prepare the student for an upcoming event that may cause sensory overload. Discuss an exit strategy the student can use if he or she is not able to stay in the environment due to discomfort to prevent aggressive behavior from occurring.

ACADEMIC, COGNITIVE, OR MOTOR SKILLS DEFICITS

Aggressive behaviors can result from the challenges the student faces in situations that call for academic, cognitive, or motor skills beyond the student's present abilities.

Understanding the Problem

Students who have significant deficits in academic or motor skills may get extremely frustrated when they are continually presented with expectations that are too difficult for them. This can certainly result in aggressive behavior for some children, including verbal aggression, self-injurious behaviors, or physical aggression toward others.

Assessing the Problem

If you think academic, cognitive, or motor skills deficits may be affecting your student's aggressive behavior, then complete Section 7 of the FBA Checklist for Aggressive Behaviors in the appendix at the end of this chapter. Following are some tips for assessing each item:

7a: The Student Demonstrates Aggressive Behavior When Academic Tasks Are Too Difficult but Does Not When the Tasks Are Easy or Do Not Require Extensive Effort

Simply record the presence of aggressive behaviors from this student when tasks are easy, and compare that data with the occurrence of aggression when tasks are more difficult.

7b: The Student Demonstrates Aggression When Presented With Tasks That Require Using Fine Motor Skills

You may not realize how often fine motor skills are the problem behind the aggression because so many tasks in school require writing. Plan assignments that do not require writing or other fine motor skills that may be difficult for the student. Compare the student's aggressive behaviors during those tasks with the level of aggression during writing tasks to see if there is a difference.

7c: The Student Demonstrates Aggression When Presented With Tasks That Require Using Gross Motor Skills

You may find that the student exhibits aggressive behavior when expected to engage in gross motor tasks requiring skills that the student has not yet developed, especially in physical education classes, recess, and special events, such as field day.

Supporting the Student

Consider the strategies and supports that were included in this section in previous chapters as well as the following if academic, cognitive, or motor skills deficits are causing an increase in aggressive behaviors:

- Teach functional communication skills to serve as replacement behaviors for the aggressive behaviors. For example, the student may need to learn how to say or use ***AAC*** supports to say, "I need help" or "I don't know."
- Teach students with more advanced communication skills to say things such as, "May I type instead of write?" "Please show me how to do this." "Can you read this to me?" "What does this word mean?"

RESTRICTED RANGE OF INTERESTS

Students with ASD may also become aggressive when the majority of their day includes tasks that are not interest based, considering their restricted range of interests.

Understanding the Problem

Many professionals do not fully consider the importance of using ***strengths- and interests-based approaches.*** Yet, most education professionals enter the field due to their interest in teaching and the strengths they have in delivering instruction. If all teachers were told they would no longer be able to teach, and they would have to show up for jobs that they are not equipped for and hold no interest for them, then there would understandably be push back. Yet, we consider it a challenging behavior when students respond negatively because they do not have opportunities to do things they like.

Assessing the Problem

If you think your student's restricted range of interests may be affecting the child's aggressive behaviors, then check the box in Section 8 of the FBA Checklist for Aggressive Behaviors in the appendix at the end of this chapter: The student demonstrates aggressive behavior when given tasks that are not interest based but not when tasks are interest based. Compare the student's presence of aggressive behavior when working on interest-based activities with aggressive behavior when they are working on things outside of their areas of interest.

Supporting the Student

Provide more lessons and assignments that are connected to the student's interests to decrease aggressive behaviors. Keep in mind that you can work on expanding a student's limited range of interests by broadening the interests into similar or related topics and activities. For example, if a student is very interested in ocean animals, then try developing interest in animals that inhabit other environments. It takes creative thinking to continually come up with ideas that not only tap into or expand a student's passions and fascinations but also provide instruction related to the general education curriculum and IEP objectives.

MEDICAL CONDITIONS

It is imperative to consider the potential role of medical conditions in the occurrence of this particular type of challenging behavior sometimes displayed by students with ASD.

Understanding the Problem

You must first consider if medical conditions may be the problem any time a student demonstrates aggressive behaviors, especially for students who are nonverbal or have limited expressive communication skills who display self-injurious behaviors. For example, a fifth-grade student with ASD who was nonverbal was engaging in severe self-injurious behaviors by repeatedly hitting himself very hard in the jaw. As a behavior analyst, I was consulted about this student; my initial recommendation was to have him checked by a dentist. It turned out that the student needed a root canal in the area that he was hitting himself. If you have ever needed an emergency root canal, then you can understand the pain involved. It makes sense that self-injurious behaviors would occur when a student is unable to communicate that pain.

Assessing the Problem

If you think medical conditions may be affecting your student's aggressive behaviors, then complete Section 9 of the FBA Checklist for Aggressive Behaviors in the appendix at the end of this chapter. It is important to have ongoing communication with the student's family so that you know of any sleep issues, changes to medication, and any sicknesses or medical issues such as seizures, gastrointestinal problems, or allergies. If aggressive behaviors are not ordinary for a certain student, then undiagnosed medical problems may need to be addressed. Sometimes families do not automatically consider this, so be sure to recommend a doctor's visit if unexplained aggressive behaviors are occurring.

Supporting the Student

If a student's medical conditions are severe enough to bring the student to the point of exhibiting aggressive behaviors, then you should definitely ease up on academic and social demands. Find out what will make the student more comfortable, and make the necessary adjustments. Behavioral interventions cannot treat medical conditions, so it is important to consult with physicians to find out the specifics of the issues and to what extent the aggressive behaviors may continue.

From Assessment to Successful Intervention

Case Study: Christopher *Christopher is a fourth-grade student with ASD who is nonverbal and occasionally engages in aggressive behaviors at school and home. His aggression occurs most frequently on his bus ride to and from school. He often engages in self-injurious behaviors, such as banging his head, hitting himself, and picking at his skin during the bus ride. An aide on the bus will attempt to prevent him from doing those things by telling him to stop or physically prompting him to stop. He recently punched and shattered a window on the bus on the way home from school.*

The IEP team convened to discuss what the problem may be to prevent this type of dangerous aggression from happening again. They used the FBA Checklist for Aggressive Behaviors to guide their discussion. After taking a step back and reflecting, they realized many things could have led up to the incident on the bus. First, the team discussed how the bus is very hot in the afternoon and has no air conditioning. Christopher had been trying to get the window down on the day he punched through it, but it would not work. The aide directed him to sit down and opened several other windows on the bus. The team checked the box for 6c to indicate that the aggression can be caused by uncomfortable sensory experiences. The team also checked box 2a because Christopher is nonverbal. The aggression can certainly arise because Christopher has no means to communicate what he wants and needs on the bus. Although he likely has sensory needs to communicate, he also probably has social needs. He is on the bus for at least 45 minutes each way, and he is the only student on the bus. The aide only interacts with him to respond to his aggressive behaviors. Thus, the team checked box 4a.

Figure 8.1 includes the parts of the FBA Checklist that the team checked off, the hypothesis statement that was generated, and the intervention plan that was put in place.

Challenging Behavior: Aggressive Behaviors

2. Deficits in Expressive Communication Skills

☑ 2a: The student lacks the communication skills necessary to express wants and needs and, therefore, communicates wants and needs by demonstrating aggressive behavior.

☐ 2b: The student demonstrates aggressive behavior when having difficulty verbally expressing his or her perspective to a teacher or peer, resulting in feeling as if his or her point of view is being disregarded.

4. Social Skills Deficits

☑ 4a: The student demonstrates aggressive behavior during periods of social disengagement from teachers or peers due to social deprivation.

☐ 4b: The student demonstrates aggressive behavior during situations that require using social problem-solving skills the student has not yet acquired.

☐ 4c: The student demonstrates aggression due to errors with perspective taking.

6. Sensory Processing Problems

☐ 6a: The student demonstrates aggression when experiencing sensory overload.

☐ 6b: The student demonstrates aggression when denied sensory input.

☑ 6c: The student demonstrates aggression when forced into sensory experiences that cause pain or discomfort.

Hypothesis Statement Christopher may engage in self-injurious behaviors and physical aggression on the bus for multiple reasons. He may be engaging in self-injurious behaviors as a result of social deprivation because he has no peers to interact with and very limited interaction with the aide for the long bus rides. In addition, he is not given anything to do to occupy his time, so he can be extremely bored. Although Christopher uses an AAC app on his tablet device at school to communicate, he is not given this device on the bus. Thus, he has no means to communicate his wants and needs on the bus, which may be affecting his aggressive behaviors. Finally, the bus is very hot in the afternoon, and Christopher may be engaging in aggressive behaviors due to sensory discomfort.

Intervention Plan

- Give Christopher a water misting fan to keep him cool on the bus ride.
- Allow Christopher to use his tablet device on the bus to play games and have access to his ***AAC*** app.
- The aide should interact with Christopher in positive ways during the bus ride (e.g., watch him play games on the tablet and make comments related to what he is doing, create drawings together because Christopher likes to draw, show Christopher pictures of cars because he has a special fascination with different types of cars).

Results

Christopher's aggressive behaviors on the bus almost entirely ceased once this intervention plan was put in place. He never punched the windows again and only occasionally engages in mild self-injurious behaviors. At first signs of self-injury, the bus aide redirects by engaging in a drawing activity, showing pictures of cars, or offering a choice of a game on the tablet device.

Figure 8.1. Functional Behavior Assessment Checklist and intervention plan for Christopher.

From Assessment to Successful Intervention

Case Study: Charlotte *Charlotte is a middle-school student with ASD who has severe anxiety related to school expectations. She often demonstrates verbal aggression by cursing, making threats, and making negative comments to teachers when she is given directions related to academic assignments or expected to participate during group instruction. She will often escalate to physical aggression toward teachers and peers when the academic demands are not removed. In addition, Charlotte will become aggressive when she cannot get immediate access to desired items and activities (e.g., tablet device, candy). Her anxiety typically increases when presented with contingencies such as first-then or token reinforcement systems, and she will not complete the required tasks to earn her reinforcement, which often results in aggressive behaviors when she realizes she will not get what she wants if she does not do her work.*

Her teacher tried giving her only easy tasks to complete to get her reward, but this did not increase Charlotte's compliance or reduce her aggression. The IEP team gathered to discuss the problem and come up with a plan. They used the FBA Checklist for Aggressive Behaviors to guide their thought processes. The occupational therapist suggested eliminating writing tasks for a brief period to determine if that may affect the frequency and intensity of aggressive behavior. Charlotte has significant deficits in fine motor skills that makes writing very labor intensive for her. Many of her assignments require written responses because she can do many grade-level academic tasks. Her mother also informed the team that the doctor has been making dose changes to Charlotte's anxiety medications because no positive changes have been observed with the current dose.

Figure 8.2 shows the sections of the FBA Checklist that the team checked off, the hypothesis statement that was written, and the intervention plan that was put in place.

Challenging Behavior: Aggressive Behaviors

3. Anxiety, Fear, and Emotional Regulation Difficulties

- ☐ 3a: The student demonstrates aggressive behavior when new tasks or activities are presented but not when familiar tasks are presented.
- ☐ 3b: The student demonstrates aggressive behavior when there is a change in the normal routine or schedule.
- ☐ 3c: The student demonstrates aggressive behavior in environments that do not have a consistent schedule and routine.
- ☑ 3d: The student exhibits severe anxiety when teacher directives are given but is not aggressive when allowed to engage in desirable activities without teacher involvement.

7. Academic, Cognitive, or Motor Skills Deficits

- ☐ 7a: The student demonstrates aggressive behavior when academic tasks are too difficult but does not when the tasks are easy or do not require extensive effort.
- ☑ 7b: The student demonstrates aggression when presented with tasks that require using fine motor skills.
- ☐ 7c: The student demonstrates aggression when presented with tasks that require using gross motor skills.

9. Medical Conditions

- ☐ 9a: The student demonstrates aggression following nights of limited sleep.
- ☐ 9b: The student engages in self-injurious behaviors to respond to physical pain.
- ☑ 9c: The student's aggression is a side effect of medications being taken or a result of being weaned off a specific medication.

Figure 8.2. Functional Behavior Assessment Checklist and intervention plan for Charlotte.

Challenging Behavior: Aggressive Behaviors *(continued)*

Hypothesis Statement Charlotte demonstrates verbal and physical aggression due to severe anxiety she experiences when given teacher directives to complete tasks and when she is expected to participate during the delivery of a lesson. She does not exhibit aggression when she is permitted to engage in desirable activities without teacher demands being placed on her. Charlotte may have increases in aggression because many of the academic demands require written responses. Her significant impairments in fine motor skills may cause her increased frustration and anxiety when she is expected to write throughout the school day. Also, her anxiety medications have not had any positive impact on her, so the doctor has been making changes to the dosage, which may be affecting her aggression as well.

Intervention Plan

- Write directions for independent work on the board instead of giving repeated verbal directions that may be increasing anxiety.
- Create engaging, hands-on, interest-based activities that do not require written responses, and set them up as stations in the classroom. Give Charlotte the choice of going to one of the stations or completing the current assignment during independent work periods.
- Minimize directive interactions with Charlotte by using a more responsive interaction style. There should be fewer directives that must be followed immediately, and more opportunities are provided for interaction, participation, and engagement without getting into a power struggle. This does not mean that directives are not given. Begin using directives only when it is necessary, and then gradually increase the number of directives as Charlotte gets more comfortable and less anxious in the classroom and school environment.
- ***Follow Charlotte's lead*** as much as possible. For example, if she comments on something during a lesson or presentation, then go with that train of thought instead of following a strict set of procedures. Whenever Charlotte shows interest in something through her actions or words, use that as an opportunity to promote more social reciprocity and engagement in learning activities.
- Use ***differential reinforcement*** of other behaviors throughout the school day. Ignore verbal aggression, and ***positively reinforce*** all desirable behaviors that she presents throughout the day using various forms of positive reinforcement (e.g., natural, social, activity, tangible). Do not use token reinforcement during the initial stages of this plan because it is controlled by teachers. Token reinforcement may be reintroduced once Charlotte can effectively comply with more teacher directives.
- Provide as many choices as possible throughout the day. Have Charlotte create her own ***visual schedule.*** The teacher provides written options for instructional and noninstructional activities, and Charlotte selects them and puts them in the order she prefers. You can do this for small blocks of time at first and then eventually for the entire day if it works well.
- Provide a word processor or a ***scribe*** for all written responses.
- Use positive affect when interacting with Charlotte.
- If Charlotte uses verbal aggression, then consider that a red flag for impending physical aggression. Allow her to calm down before continuing any interaction.

Results

Although this plan did result in less physical aggression, the verbal aggression and noncompliance is still an issue for Charlotte. She allows teachers and peers to join her in activities, but she will use foul language, scream, or say mean things to others as soon as a directive is given. This may be because this behavior has essentially been reinforced. As is stated in the plan, the teacher ceases interacting with her when she uses verbal aggression. Although this does prevent physical aggression, this has maintained the use of verbal aggression. The next steps will be using functional communication training to teach replacement behaviors for the verbal aggression.

Challenging Behavior: Aggressive Behaviors

1. Language Comprehension Difficulties

- ❒ 1a: The student demonstrates aggressive behavior when the teacher uses complex language, lengthy lectures, or very fast speech when giving directions or providing instruction.
- ❒ 1b: The student demonstrates aggressive behavior when directions or instruction are given verbally or in writing but not when expectations are physically demonstrated or information is explained using visuals.
- ❒ 1c: The student demonstrates aggressive behavior when unfamiliar directions are given containing language the student does not understand.

2. Deficits in Expressive Communication Skills

- ❒ 2a: The student lacks the communication skills necessary to express wants and needs and, therefore, communicates wants and needs by demonstrating aggressive behavior.
- ❒ 2b: The student demonstrates aggressive behavior when having difficulty verbally expressing his or her perspective to a teacher or peer, resulting in feeling as if his or her point of view is being disregarded.

3. Anxiety, Fear, and Emotional Regulation Difficulties

- ❒ 3a: The student demonstrates aggressive behavior when new tasks or activities are presented but not when familiar tasks are presented.
- ❒ 3b: The student demonstrates aggressive behavior when there is a change in the normal routine or schedule.
- ❒ 3c: The student demonstrates aggressive behavior in environments that do not have a consistent schedule and routine.
- ❒ 3d: The student exhibits severe anxiety when teacher directives are given but is not aggressive when allowed to engage in desirable activities without teacher involvement.

4. Social Skills Deficits

- ❒ 4a: The student demonstrates aggressive behavior during periods of social disengagement from teachers or peers due to social deprivation.
- ❒ 4b: The student demonstrates aggressive behavior during situations that require using social problem-solving skills the student has not yet acquired.
- ❒ 4c: The student demonstrates aggression due to errors with perspective taking.

5. Problems With Focus and Attention

- ❒ The student demonstrates aggressive behavior when asked to stop an activity that he or she is focused on due to difficulties shifting attention.

6. Sensory Processing Problems

- ❒ 6a: The student demonstrates aggression when experiencing sensory overload.
- ❒ 6b: The student demonstrates aggression when denied sensory input.
- ❒ 6c: The student demonstrates aggression when forced into sensory experiences that cause pain or discomfort.

7. Academic, Cognitive, or Motor Skills Deficits

- ❒ 7a: The student demonstrates aggressive behavior when academic tasks are too difficult but does not when the tasks are easy or do not require extensive effort.
- ❒ 7b: The student demonstrates aggression when presented with tasks that require using fine motor skills.
- ❒ 7c: The student demonstrates aggression when presented with tasks that require using gross motor skills.

Challenging Behavior: Aggressive Behaviors *(continued)*

8. Restricted Range of Interests

- ❒ The student demonstrates aggressive behavior when given tasks that are not interest based but not when tasks are interest based.

9. Medical Conditions

- ❒ 9a: The student demonstrates aggression following nights of limited sleep.
- ❒ 9b: The student engages in self-injurious behaviors to respond to physical pain.
- ❒ 9c: The student's aggression is a side effect of medications being taken or a result of being weaned off a specific medication.

Other ____

____

____

____

____

Hypothesis Statement ____

____

____

____

____

CHAPTER 9

Working With Partners and Groups

Students with ASD often face great challenges working with partners or groups in classroom settings. Therefore, teachers often require or allow the student to work alone while other students are working in groups. Although that is an easy answer, it is not the recommended course of action. Students with ASD do not necessarily prefer to work alone; they just need supports in place to effectively work with peers. It is essential that they have as many opportunities as possible throughout the day to learn social-communication skills in natural contexts. Thus, they need more opportunities than typically developing students to work with partners and groups, not less. Social skills deficits are the most obvious characteristic that affects the ability of children with ASD to work with partners and groups. They may also have problems working with peers due other issues, however. Each of the following issues are addressed in this chapter:

1. Language comprehension difficulties
2. Deficits in expressive communication skills
3. Anxiety, fear, and emotional regulation difficulties
4. Social skills deficits
5. Problems with focus and attention
6. Executive functioning challenges
7. Sensory processing problems
8. Academic, cognitive, or motor skills deficits
9. Restricted range of interests

LANGUAGE COMPREHENSION DIFFICULTIES

Language comprehension difficulties can interfere with students' ability to work with partners and groups in several ways.

Understanding the Problem

Students with ASD who have language comprehension difficulties will likely have problems working with partners and groups because they may not always understand the directions given to the group, the comments the peers make during the activity, and the questions peers ask the student during the activity. The student may simply disengage or exhibit a challenging behavior, such as engaging in repetitive behaviors, leaving the work area, shouting out, or showing aggression, when this confusion occurs.

Assessing the Problem

If you think language difficulties may be affecting your student's ability to work with a partner or a group, then complete Section 1 of the FBA Checklist for Difficulty Working With Partners and Groups in the appendix at the end of this chapter. Following are some tips for assessing each item in Section 1 of the checklist:

1a: The Student Has Difficulty Working With Partners or Groups When the Directions and Expectations Are Not Clearly Understood by the Student but Is Able to Successfully Work With a Partner or Group When the Directions and Expectations Are Explicitly Taught in Ways the Student Can Understand

Take some extra time to ensure the student understands the expectations before placing the student with a partner or group. If the student is better able to work with a partner or group during those instances, then you can predict that language comprehension difficulties are negatively affecting the student's success with working with partners and groups.

1b: The Student Has Difficulty Working With Partners or Groups When the Activities Are Primarily Language Based but Is Able to Successfully Work With a Partner or Group When the Tasks Include Hands-on Activities

Plan partner or group activities that do not require much language at all (e.g., build a model, draw a picture, practice multiplication facts). If the student is successful when the activities have minimal language-based activities, then you can check off this section on the FBA Checklist for Difficulty Working With Partners and Groups.

Supporting the Student

Consider the following strategies and supports if your student has problems working with partners and groups due to language comprehension difficulties:

- ***Use clear, consistent, and concise language*** when giving directions for the partner or group activity, and ensure the student understands the directions prior to starting the activity.
- Use ***video modeling*** or other ***visual supports*** to support the student's understanding of the expectations for the activity.
- Use ***peer-meditated interventions*** to teach peers how to use simplified language when addressing the student to make comments or ask questions during the activity.
- Use ***priming*** by providing an opportunity for the student to do the activity with a teacher or teacher assistant prior to completing the activity with a partner or group to help the student understand expectations.

DEFICITS IN EXPRESSIVE COMMUNICATION SKILLS

Expressive communication deficits can affect the ability of students with ASD to work with partners or groups, particularly given that ***AAC*** supports may be less useful to students in this situation.

Understanding the Problem

It is rare that students who are nonverbal are equipped with ***AAC*** supports and devices needed to ensure they have opportunities to communicate with peers during academic activities using content and task-specific language. Their ***AAC*** supports typically only allow them to get their basic wants and needs met and answer simple questions (Iacono, Trembath, & Erickson, 2016). Therefore, they are unable to participate when they are expected to work with a partner or group due to deficits in expressive communication skills and supports.

Assessing the Problem

If you think deficits in expressive communication skills may be affecting your student's ability to work with partners and groups, then check the box in Section 2 of the FBA Checklist for Difficulty Working With Partners and Groups: The student has difficulty working with partners or groups when the activities require expressive communication skills that the student has not yet acquired. Although it is a no-brainer that you would check this for a student who is nonverbal or minimally verbal, be aware that even verbal students with ASD may not have the advanced expressive communication skills needed to participate in the partner or group activities. For example, a student may have no problem going around the table and taking turns answering simple, literal comprehension questions related to a reading selection. Problems may arise, however, if the student is expected to engage in more complex thinking during group work, such as making predictions, making inferences, or discussing similarities and differences between characters in two different book. If you are unsure if deficits in expressive communication skills may be affecting your student's ability to work with partners and groups, then plan activities that you are certain will require only those expressive communication skills the student has to actively participate. Compare the student's behavior during those situations with other situations in which you do not include modified language requirements.

Supporting the Student

Consider the following strategies and supports if deficits in expressive communication skills are affecting your student's ability to work with partners or groups:

- For students who are nonverbal
  - Use low- or high-tech ***AAC*** supports to allow full participation.
  - Use ***peer-mediated interventions*** to teach peers how to prompt the student's use of ***AAC*** to answer questions and make comments during the activity.
  - Plan activities that require minimal expressive communication skills to participate.
- For students who are verbal
  - Simplify the expressive communication requirements of the activity.
  - Assign specific roles to the student that are developmentally appropriate based on the student's present level of expressive communication skills.
  - Provide ***AAC*** supports.
  - Provide ***visual supports*** such as sentence starters, question words, sentence frames, and other ***cue cards*** that will support the student's expressive communication during the activity.

See Table 9.1 for some examples.

Table 9.1. Examples of visuals to support expressive communication during group activities

Group activity	Visual support	How visual is used for expressive communication
Small group is making a list of synonyms for the word *fun* to improve word choice during writing activities.	The student with ASD is given word cards that contain some synonyms for *fun* mixed in with other words (e.g., *thrilling, exciting, sad, fabulous, boring, super*).	The students take turns giving a synonym for the word *fun*. One student records the answers. The student with ASD gives an answer by selecting one of the cards that contains a synonym for *fun* and gives it to the recorder. The recorder gives positive or corrective feedback to the student with ASD (e.g., "Yes, *thrilling* means fun!" "*Boring* does not mean fun. Can you pick another card?")
Small group is completing a graphic organizer to list the sequence of events from a book chapter they read together.	The student with ASD is given sentence strips including various events from the story as well as sentences.	The peers take turns stating an event that happened. One peer records the responses. If a peer states an event that is included on the sentence strips, then the student with ASD holds up that sentence strip and gives it to the recorder. The recorder will paste the sentence strip on the graphic organizer. The student with ASD takes a turn by giving the recorder a sentence strip for an event from the story that another student has not already said. Peers can be trained to use prompts and positive reinforcement to support the student's participation.

ANXIETY, FEAR, AND EMOTIONAL REGULATION DIFFICULTIES

The expectations of partner and group activities can cause increases in anxiety and fear due to the social nature of the expectations that are directly related to the student's core social-communication deficits.

Understanding the Problem

Students with ASD usually know when they are ill-equipped for certain situations, and their anxiety and fear are heightened when they feel that way. This may result in disengagement or challenging behavior during the partner or group activity if their anxiety and fear leads to emotional dysregulation.

Assessing the Problem

If you think anxiety, fear, and emotional regulation difficulties may be affecting your student's ability to work with partners and groups, then complete Section 3 of the FBA Checklist for Difficulty Working With Partners and Groups in the appendix at the end of this chapter. Following are some tips for assessing each item:

3a: The Student Has Difficulty Working With a Partner or Group When the Tasks Are New or Unfamiliar but Is Able to Work With a Partner or Group During Established Routines and Activities

This is often difficult to assess when partner or group activities are not part of the established routines and activities in the classroom. If this is the case, then you need to create one or two partner or group activities that are conducted in the same manner at least once or twice a day. Once the routine is established, compare the student's behavior when working with a partner or group during that activity with the student's behavior during other activities that are new or unfamiliar.

3b: The Student Has Difficulty Working With a Partner or Group Due to Inflexibility

Students with ASD may have problems working with a partners and groups if they typically only see one way to do something. They may get anxious and emotionally distressed when their partner or group members suggest alternative ways, thinking they are going to do something the wrong way.

Supporting the Student

Consider the following strategies and supports if anxiety, fear, and emotional regulation problems are making it difficult for your student to work with partners or groups:

- Begin with partner activities before exposing the student to group activities.
- Have clearly defined roles for partner activities and group activities. It is helpful to use ***balanced turn-taking*** for partner activities, especially for students who have communication impairments paired with high levels of anxiety. Consider the student's strengths and interests when assigning roles in group activities. The student will likely be less anxious if the assigned role is related to something the student is interested in or good at doing.
- Make sure the requirements for the activity are very clear to the student and the student has the necessary skills to participate.
- Make partner and group activities part of your established instructional routines. For example, when teaching new information, consistently use ***think-pair-share*** to support student learning, use partner activities to practice rote memorization of math facts each day, or use partner reading each day to build fluency and comprehension skills.
- Use ***video modeling*** or ***priming*** to prepare the student for any new or unfamiliar partner or group activities that will be occurring.
- Develop a targeted intervention to teach the student how to understand that there is more than one way to do something or solve a problem. Create situations in which this is practiced each school day.

SOCIAL SKILLS DEFICITS

Social skills deficits are the main barrier to effective participation during partner and group activities for students with ASD. A variety of deficits in social skills can contribute to this difficulty.

Understanding the Problem

Significant deficits in joint attention and social reciprocity are the most problematic social skills deficits. Deficits in other specific social skills, however, can also make working with partners and groups very difficult. Challenging behaviors commonly occur during these situations due to an absence of explicit instruction in social expectations and an absence of repeated learning opportunities to develop the skills that other may students learn incidentally.

Assessing the Problem

If you think social skills deficits may be affecting your student's ability to work with partners and groups, then complete Section 4 of the FBA Checklist for Difficulty Working With Partners and Groups in the appendix at the end of this chapter. Following are some tips for assessing each item:

4a: The Student Has Difficulty Working With a Partner or Group Due to Deficits in Joint Attention and Social Reciprocity

Participating in partner or group activities can be challenging if the student has trouble establishing attention with others during shared activities, maintaining shared attention, responding to social initiations from others, making initiations during social situations, and engaging

Skill	Always or almost always	Sometimes	Only with prompting	Never
Responds to nonverbal cues (e.g., gestures, facial expressions, body language) from peers to attend to partner or group activities				
Responds to verbal prompts from peers to attend to partner or group activities				
Gives materials at the request of a peer				
Imitates the actions of peers when appropriate				
Appropriately responds to requests or directions from peers				
Appropriately responds to questions from peers				
Appropriately responds to comments from peers				
Asks appropriate questions to peers				
Asks for materials from peers when necessary				
Makes comments to peers to share information or enjoyment				
Engages in long chains of reciprocal interactions with peers during structured academic activities				
Engages in long chains of reciprocal interactions with peers during unstructured academic or social activities				

Figure 9.1. An example of a tool used to record overactions from a joint attention and social reciprocity with peers assessment.

in long chains of back-and-forth interactions. See Figure 9.1 for an assessment that can be used to gather information related to your student's joint attention and social reciprocity skills when working with partners or groups.

4b: The Student Has Difficulty Working With a Partner or Group When the Activities Require Specific Social Skills the Student Has Not Yet Acquired

Students with ASD may have problems with conversational skills, turn-taking, waiting, sharing, perspective taking, using appropriate voice volume, using and understanding nonverbal social communication, maintaining appropriate space between communication partners,

Skill	Always or almost always	Sometimes	Only with prompting	Never
Shares materials during joint tasks				
Shares materials during independent/parallel tasks				
Responds when others offer a turn				
Offers a turn to others				
Maintains attention while waiting for a turn				
Offers help to others				
Accepts help from others				
Empathizes with the feelings of others				
Uses appropriate voice volume				
Uses appropriate space with a social partner				
Responds to greetings				
Initiates greetings				
Uses appropriate eye contact when interacting with others				
Gives compliments to others				
Receives compliments positively				
Maintains personal hygiene				
Responds appropriately to facial expressions of others				
Responds appropriately to body language of others				
Appropriately responds when others are in the way				
Compromises during academic and social activities				

Figure 9.2. An example of a tool used to record observations from a social skills assessment. (From Leach, D. [2010]. *Bringing ABA into your inclusive classroom: A guide to improving outcomes for students with ASD*, p. 32–33. Baltimore, MD: Paul H. Brookes Publishing Co.; adapted by permission.)

delivering and accepting constructive criticism, and offering and accepting compliments. It is important to conduct a social skills assessment to determine which skills the student has and has not developed and plan instruction and supports accordingly during partner and group activities. See Figure 9.2 for an assessment that can be used to determine specific social skills the student has and has not yet acquired. It is best to use a team approach involving the general education teacher(s), special education teacher, and SLP to appropriately assess, select targeted skills, and plan and deliver interventions and supports.

Supporting the Student

Consider the following strategies and supports if social skills deficits are affecting your student's ability to work with partners or groups:

- Provide an adult facilitator for the partner or group work. The facilitator should primarily focus on supporting the peers' use of strategies and supports to encourage the student's participation so that facilitation can be systematically faded out. If the facilitator focuses primarily on the student, then it will be difficult to fade out support without the peer(s) knowing how to support the student.
- Create activities that consist of ***balanced turn-taking.***
- Use ***peer-mediated interventions*** to teach the peers how to ***follow the child's lead, use prompting/fading procedures,*** and give ***positive reinforcement.***
- Provide explicit instruction of social expectations for the partner or group activity prior to scheduling the actual activity, using ***social narratives, video modeling,*** or role play.
- Use script-fading procedures to support the student's joint attention and social reciprocity needs during partner or group activities.

PROBLEMS WITH FOCUS AND ATTENTION

Focus and attention difficulties may interfere with a student's ability to participate in partner or group activities, especially when these activities are unfamiliar.

Understanding the Problem

There may be a lot of confusion, noise, and challenging behavior when teachers initiate partner or group activities, especially when these activities are not fully established as part of the classroom routine or when new types of activities are introduced. If a student with ASD has problems with focus and attention, then it may be challenging for the student to meaningfully engage during partner and group activities that are chaotic in nature.

Assessing the Problem

If you think problems with focus and attention may be affecting your student's ability to work with partners and groups, then check the box in Section 5 of the FBA Checklist for Difficulty Working With Partners and Groups in the appendix at the end of this chapter: The student has difficulty working with a partner or group when there is a great deal of activity taking place, resulting in problems with focus and attention. If focus and attention problems are affecting the student's ability to participate in partner or group activities, then assess the student's performance when a partner or group activity is implemented in a separate, quiet area without extraneous distractions and activity. If the student does well when distractions are minimized, then you can predict that focus and attention problems are a factor in the student's performance.

Supporting the Student

Consider the following strategies and supports if your student has trouble working with partners and groups because of problems with focus and attention:

- Minimize distractions as much as possible.
- Allow the student with ASD to work with a partner or group in an alternative, quiet setting.

- Use ***prompting/fading procedures*** (through ***peer-mediated interventions*** when possible) to redirect the student to the task at hand. Try to use more ***visual supports*** and prompts than verbal prompts to decrease prompt dependency.
- Provide ***self-monitoring*** tools to set behavioral expectations and serve as reminders to stay focused.

EXECUTIVE FUNCTIONING CHALLENGES

The inherent challenges that partner and group activities pose for students with ASD can be compounded when these activities also call on students' executive functioning skills.

Understanding the Problem

Even though challenging behaviors often arise when teachers put students together to work in groups, the tasks that teachers typically assign for these activities can be quite complex. Thus, not only are students presented with the challenge of working with others, but the group tasks also often require more planning, organization, and sequential steps than many independent assignments. For example, a group of fifth-grade students may be given the task of figuring out the area and perimeter of the classroom for purposes of ordering new carpet and baseboards. This task requires effective social skills and communication skills for students to work together and well-developed executive functioning skills to plan and carry out the multitude of sequential steps that must be followed to meet the requirements (e.g., measure the classroom, determine the area and perimeter, find out how much carpet and baseboard cost, figure out how much it would cost to purchase carpet and baseboard, using the area and perimeter measurements previously determined). This type of group task will likely be difficult for many typically developing students. Students with ASD may have even greater problems, however, due to their impairments in social skills, communication skills, and executive functioning skills.

Assessing the Problem

If you think executive functioning challenges may be affecting your student's ability to work with partners and groups, then check the box in Section 6 of the FBA Checklist for Difficulty Working With Partners and Groups in the appendix at the end of this chapter: The student has trouble working with a partner or group when the task involves multiple steps, planning, and organizational skills. To assess if this is true for your student, create simple, one-step partner or group activities and compare your student's behavior during those activities with behavior during typical, more complex activities.

Supporting the Student

Consider the following supports and strategies if executive functioning challenges are affecting your student's ability to participate in partner or group activities:

- Use ***shaping*** by gradually increasing the complexities of partner and group activities, delivering ***positive reinforcement*** when the students are successful with sequentially increased demands.
- Create ***visual supports*** that can be used as planning tools for the students. See Figure 9.3 for an example that could be used with the fifth-grade group activity previously described.

Group project directions: Determine the area and perimeter of the classroom. Go to a web site for a home improvement store to figure out how much it will cost to purchase new carpet and baseboards using the area and perimeter measurements you determined in the first step.

Step 1: Measure the length and width of the classroom in feet.

Length = ______ feet

Width = _______feet

Step 2: Figure out the perimeter using this formula:

Perimeter = length + length + width + width

Perimeter = _____+ ______ + _____ + _____

Perimeter = ______feet

Step 3: Figure out the area of the classroom using this formula:

Area = length x width

Area = _______ x ________

Area = ________square feet

Step 4: Go to a home improvement store web site and get prices for carpet and baseboard.

Carpet price: ________ per square foot

Baseboard price: ________ per foot

Step 5: Determine the cost for the carpet for the classroom.

a. Area of classroom = ___________ square feet (see Step 3)

b. Carpet price per square foot = ________ per square foot (see Step 4)

c. Cost for classroom carpet = area of classroom x price per square foot (a x b)

__________ x ___________ = __________________

Step 6: Determine the cost for the baseboard for the classroom.

a. Perimeter of classroom = ___________ feet (see Step 2)

b. Baseboard price per foot = ________ per foot (see Step 4)

c. Cost for classroom baseboard = perimeter of classroom x price per foot (a x b)

__________ x ___________ = __________________

Step 7: Determine total cost for carpet and baseboard.

Cost of carpet (see Step 5) + Cost of baseboard (see Step 6)

_____________ + _______________ = __________________

Figure 9.3. Sample visual support for multistep group task.

- Explicitly teach organizational strategies related to the task at hand so students know how to manage the materials, manage their time, and store unfinished work.
- Use ***task analysis, chaining,*** and ***self-monitoring*** to support partner and group work.

SENSORY PROCESSING PROBLEMS

Sensory processing problems can be a significant factor for students with ASD during partner or group activities.

Understanding the Problem

There may be increased sensory stimuli to process (e.g., more conversational noise, proximity of other students, the visual distraction of other students' work materials) as well as limitations to gaining access to needed sensory input (e.g., the student may not be able to physically leave the group to gain access to this input, the student may feel uncomfortable engaging in behaviors that provide it) during these activities. Behavioral challenges may occur if a student experiences sensory overload or is understimulated.

Assessing the Problem

If you think sensory processing issues may be affecting your student's abilities to work with partners or groups, then complete Section 7 of the FBA Checklist for Difficulty Working With Partners and Groups in the appendix at the end of this chapter. Following are some tips for assessing each item:

7a: The Student Has Difficulty Working With a Partner or Group When Experiencing Sensory Overload

The student may be overstimulated by the sights, sounds, smells, clutter, and chaotic movement that is present during partner and group activities. If this is the case, then the student may cover his or her ears, shut his or her eyes, make loud noises, rock back and forth, or engage in other disruptive behaviors as a response to being overstimulated.

7b: The Student Has Difficulties Working With a Partner or Group When Denied Sensory Input

The teacher may attempt to restrict movement and noise levels while the students are working to ensure a sense of calm in the classroom during partner or group activities. A student with ASD may need movement or opportunities to vocalize, however, to get sensory input or to deal with overstimulation. As a result, a student may rock back and forth, jump up and down, engage in loud vocalizations, flap his or her arms, attempt to leave the group, or engage in other disruptive behaviors.

Supporting the Student

Consider the following strategies and supports if sensory processing issues are affecting your student's ability to work with partners and groups:

- Make environmental arrangements to respond to the student's sensory needs.
- Allow the student to engage in certain behavior to get the necessary sensory input (even if they choose repetitive behaviors to cope and regulate themselves).

ACADEMIC, COGNITIVE, OR MOTOR SKILLS DEFICITS

In addition to the social challenges that partner and group activities pose for students with ASD, these activities may also be more likely than other classroom activities to call on academic, cognitive, or motor skills beyond the student's present abilities. This can make it very difficult for them to participate in these activities.

Understanding the Problem

Because partner and group activities are typically designed to align with what is being taught within the general education curriculum, the requirements may include academic, cognitive, or motor skills that are not necessarily developmentally appropriate for the student with ASD. Disengagement and challenging behaviors may occur if the expectations are too difficult or impossible for the student.

Assessing the Problem

If you think academic, cognitive, or motor skills deficits may be affecting your student's ability to work with partners or groups, then it is important to have a clear understanding of the student's present level of academic, fine motor, and gross motor abilities. Complete Section 8 of the FBA Checklist for Difficulty Working With Partners and Groups in the appendix at the end of this chapter. Following are some tips for assessing each item:

8a: The Student Has Difficulty Working With a Partner or Group When Academic Tasks Are Too Difficult for the Student but Does Not Have Difficulty When the Academic Tasks Are Easy or Do Not Require Extensive Effort

Assign simple group tasks you are certain the student is able to do. If the student works with the group to complete these tasks but does not when the tasks are more challenging, then you can predict that the level of difficulty of the task is the issue.

8b: The Student Has Difficulty Working With a Partner or Group When Presented With Tasks That Require the Use of Fine Motor Skills

Provide group activities that do not require writing or other fine motor skills that are challenging for the student. If the student works with the group under these conditions but does not when fine motor tasks are required, then you can predict that fine motor impairments are negatively affecting the student's ability to participate in group activities.

8c: The Student Has Difficulty Working With a Partner or Group When Presented With Tasks That Require the Use of Gross Motor Skills

This will obviously only be an issue in classes in which group activities require gross motor skills, such as physical education, or academic activities that require students to run, jump, throw, or catch to participate in the activity. Assign group activities that do not require gross motor skills. If the student participates in the activities under those conditions but does not participate when gross motor skills are required, then you can predict the issue is related to gross motor impairments.

Supporting the Student

Consider the following strategies and supports if academic, cognitive, or motor skills deficits are causing problems with your student working with partners and groups:

- Use differentiation to set appropriate academic expectations for the student with ASD during the partner or group activity.
- Allow for ***partial participation*** when necessary to ensure expectations are developmentally appropriate.
- Use AT to make accommodations to the fine motor tasks when necessary.
- Provide ***visual supports*** that include the key terms and big ideas related to the content that is needed to participate in the partner or group activity.

RESTRICTED RANGE OF INTERESTS

Students with ASD who have very limited interests may find it difficult to stay engaged with partner or group activities that fall outside their narrow range of interests.

Understanding the Problem

Students with ASD who have a restricted range of interests may not be intrinsically motivated to engage in partner or group activities that are not related to their passions and fascinations. They may disengage or demonstrate challenging behaviors when expected to participate in an activity that they do not find interesting. This issue is compounded by the social challenges students with ASD have in general.

Assessing the Problem

If you think your student's restricted range of interests may be affecting the child's ability to work with partners and groups, then check the box in Section 9 of the FBA Checklist for Difficulty Working With Partners and Groups in the appendix at the end of this chapter: The student has difficulty working with a partner or group when given tasks that are not interest based but does not have difficulty when engaging in tasks that are interest based. Plan a few partner or group activities that are directly related to the student's special interests, and compare the student's behavior during those activities with behavior when the activities are not interest based.

Supporting the Student

Consider the following strategies and supports if your student's restricted range of interests is negatively affecting participation in partner or group activities:

- Tie the content of the activity into the student's special interests.
- Provide materials for completing the activity that are related to the student's interests.
- Teach expectations for the partner or group activities using Power Cards (Gagnon, 2001) if the student has interests in specific characters.

From Assessment to Successful Intervention

Case Study: Max *Max is a seventh-grade student with ASD who is on grade level academically and participates in all general education classes. His main problem is in social skills. The students in his science class are placed in groups to complete discussions and assignments and conduct experiments. His science teacher, Mr. Withers, has been allowing him to work alone for other types of work, but Max must complete science experiments with the group due to limited availability of materials. He makes negative comments about the activity and the students whenever he is working with a group of students to complete experiments, and he gets very frustrated when others do not do things the way he thinks they should be done. This may lead to yelling, destruction of materials, and, in some cases, aggression toward peers.*

Mr. Withers asked the special education teacher, Ms. Micucci, to help him address this problem. During their initial conversation, Ms. Micucci asked questions about the nature of the science experiments and found out that they do not follow a typical format or structure each week. She explained to Mr. Withers that Max may display challenging behaviors when he does not fully understand the expectations and his role in an activity. He always needs explicit instruction of expectations before completing an activity and sometimes needs repeated exposure to activities before he gains a level of comfort and confidence. Ms. Micucci also explained that Max may resist the ideas that other students suggest during group activities due to his rigidity in his thinking and difficulties with perspective taking. The expectation of listening to and valuing the input from all members of the group needs to be explicitly taught and practiced. Finally, Ms. Micucci discussed some additional social skills that Max needs to develop to better participate in group activities, including learning conversational skills, giving and taking turns, accepting constructive criticism, and using appropriate voice volume. She planned to provide instruction in the resource setting to teach those skills and work with Mr. Withers to generalize the learned skills in science.

Figure 9.4 shows the sections of the FBA Checklist for Difficulty Working with Partners and Groups that were checked off, the hypothesis statement that was generated, and the intervention plan that was put in place.

Challenging Behavior: Difficulties Working With Partners and Groups

3. Anxiety, Fear, and Emotional Regulation Difficulties

- ☑ 3a: The student has difficulty working with a partner or group when the tasks are new or unfamiliar but is able to work with a partner or group during established routines and activities.
- ☑ 3b: The student has difficulty working with a partner or group due to inflexibility.

4. Social Skills Deficits

- ☐ 4a: The student has difficulty working with a partner or group due to deficits in joint attention and social reciprocity.
- ☑ 4b: The student has difficulty working with a partner or group when the activities require specific social skills the student has not yet acquired.

Hypothesis Statement Max demonstrates verbal aggression, destruction of materials, and physical aggression when working with a group of peers to complete science experiments. He may be experiencing heightened levels of anxiety and fear when he is unsure about the expectations because the science experiments are different each week, which often leads to emotional dysregulation. He also is inflexible in his thought processes and gets extremely frustrated when other students want to do things differently than how he thinks the work should be done. In addition, Max has deficits in the following social skills that are needed to positively participate in group activities—conversational skills, perspective taking, turn-taking, giving and accepting constructive criticism, and using appropriate voice volume.

Intervention Plan

- Begin requiring Max to participate in partner and group activities to complete the discussions and assignments in the science class. Those activities are less complex than the science experiments, so he will be able to experience success with supports provided. Success during those activities will help him establish more positive relationships with peers, which can positively affect his success during the science experiments.
- Explicitly teach behavioral and social expectations for every partner or group activity.
- Provide a ***self-monitoring*** tool that allows Max to record his performance of the expectations that were set.
- Provide explicit instruction of the social skills included in the hypothesis statement during his resource period because he does not require the academic support that is usually provided at that time.
- Use ***social autopsies*** or the ***SOCCSS*** strategy to help Max learn social problem-solving skills.
- Use ***peer-mediated interventions*** to teach peers how to positively redirect Max when he makes negative comments. They should ignore the comments, ask him a specific question about the assignment or activity, and thank him for his help.
- Use adult facilitation as needed to maintain positive interactions between Max and his peers.
- Deliver ***positive reinforcement*** during and after partner and group activities when Max participates positively.

Results

This plan took several weeks to result in positive outcomes due to the nature of the challenging behavior and the comprehensive interventions required. Ms. Micucci arranged to coteach in his science class for a month to help put the plan in place. Max is now able to engage in a variety of partner and group activities in the science classroom with minimal challenging problems. He will still make some negative comments as a response to his anxiety, but his physical aggression and destructive behaviors have ceased.

Figure 9.4. Functional Behavior Assessment Checklist and intervention plan for Max.

From Assessment to Successful Intervention

Case Study: Shiro *Shiro is a third-grade student with ASD who has significant impairments in joint attention and social reciprocity. His teacher, Ms. Lyons, has established a daily routine in the classroom for peers to work together to practice multiplication facts. Shiro puts his head down each day when he is partnered with a peer, and he does not engage in the flash card practice activity. Ms. Lyons thought this would be an effective way to provide a daily opportunity for building social skills during an academic task, but it is not going as well as she expected. She asked the autism specialist for the district to come observe and offer any suggestions to help Shiro participate.*

Figure 9.5 shows the section of the FBA Checklist for Difficulty Working with Partners and Groups that was checked off after the observation and consultation, the hypothesis statement that was generated, and the intervention plan that was put in place.

Challenging Behavior: Difficulties Working With Partners and Groups

4. Social Skills Deficits

- ☑ 4a: The student has difficulty working with a partner or group due to deficits in joint attention and social reciprocity.
- ☐ 4b: The student has difficulty working with a partner or group when the activities require specific social skills the student has not yet acquired.

Hypothesis Statement Shiro does not participate in partner activities to practice multiplication facts due to deficits in joint attention and social reciprocity.

Intervention Plan

- Use ***peer-mediated interventions*** to teach Shiro's partner how to use ***discrete trials*** during the multiplication facts activity using the following format:
  - The partner and Shiro should sit face to face in chairs or on the carpet.
  - The peer should hold up a flash card and say, "What is ___ x ___?"
  - If Shiro answers, then the peer should smile and provide praise or a high-five.
  - If Shiro does not answer, then the peer should model the response and restate the question (e.g., "4 x 6 is 24. What is 4 x 6?").
  - The peer should praise Shiro for imitating the correct response.
- After the discrete trial format is used and successful, begin to use ***balanced turn-taking*** by giving Shiro flash cards to present to the peer. Shiro and the peer should take turns presenting a flash card to one another. The peer should continue to use the ***discrete trial*** procedures if Shiro does not respond. If Shiro does not initiate his turn to present a fact to the peer, then the peer should prompt Shiro to do so by saying something such as, "Show me a card, Shiro."
- Provide adult facilitation as necessary to ensure positive back-and-forth exchanges during the activity.
- Positively reinforce Shiro and the peer when they have successful exchanges.

Results

The autism specialist first trained three peers on the ***discrete trial*** procedures, which took just a few minutes and resulted in immediate success. Shiro remained engaged for at least 3 straight minutes when a peer used the ***discrete trial*** format. Peers were then trained on the ***balanced turn-taking*** procedures. Again, the peers learned this quickly, and there were immediate positive outcomes for Shiro. These approaches are now being used for other partner activities in the classroom.

Figure 9.5. Functional Behavior Assessment Checklist and intervention plan for Shiro.

Challenging Behavior: Difficulties Working With Partners and Groups

1. Language Comprehension Difficulties

- ❐ 1a: The student has difficulty working with partners or groups when the directions and expectations are not clearly understood by the student but is able to successfully work with a partner or group when the directions and expectations are explicitly taught in ways the student can understand.
- ❐ 1b: The student has difficulty working with partners or groups when the activities are primarily language based but is able to successfully work with a partner or group when the tasks include hands-on activities.

2. Deficits in Expressive Communication Skills

- ❐ The student has difficulty working with partners or groups when the activities require expressive communication skills that the student has not yet acquired.

3. Anxiety, Fear, and Emotional Regulation Difficulties

- ❐ 3a: The student has difficulty working with a partner or group when the tasks are new or unfamiliar but is able to work with a partner or group during established routines and activities.
- ❐ 3b: The student has difficulty working with a partner or group due to inflexibility.

4. Social Skills Deficits

- ❐ 4a: The student has difficulty working with a partner or group due to deficits in joint attention and social reciprocity.
- ❐ 4b: The student has difficulty working with a partner or group when the activities require specific social skills the student has not yet acquired.

5. Problems With Focus and Attention

- ❐ The student has difficulty working with a partner or group when there is a great deal of activity taking place, resulting in problems with focus and attention.

6. Executive Functioning Challenges

- ❐ The student has trouble working with a partner or group when the task involves multiple steps, planning, and organizational skills.

7. Sensory Processing Problems

- ❐ 7a: The student has difficulty working with a partner or group when experiencing sensory overload.
- ❐ 7b: The student has difficulties working with a partner or group when denied sensory input.

8. Academic, Cognitive, or Motor Skills Deficits

- ❐ 8a: The student has difficulty working with a partner or group when academic tasks are too difficult for the student but does not have difficulty when the academic tasks are easy or do not require extensive effort.
- ❐ 8b: The student has difficulty working with a partner or group when presented with tasks that require the use of fine motor skills.
- ❐ 8c: The student has difficulty working with a partner or group when presented with tasks that require the use of gross motor skills.

Challenging Behavior: Difficulties Working With Partners and Groups *(continued)*

9. Restricted Range of Interests

- ❒ The student has difficulty working with a partner or group when given tasks that are not interest based but does not have difficulty when engaging in tasks that are interest based.

Other ____

____

____

____

____

Hypothesis Statement ____

____

____

____

____

CHAPTER 10

Attempting Unfamiliar or Difficult Tasks

Many teachers report that students with ASD exhibit challenging behavior when presented with unfamiliar or difficult tasks. Students may simply be noncompliant or engage in challenging behaviors such as crying, yelling, attempting to leave the work area or classroom, repetitive behaviors, or aggressive behaviors, depending on their level of distress. Although the reasons why students with ASD demonstrate noncompliance with unfamiliar or difficult tasks varies depending on the child, some common characteristics associated with ASD explain why these students are challenged in this area. This chapter discusses eight challenges faced by students with ASD that may explain why they do not regularly attempt unfamiliar and difficult tasks:

1. Language comprehension difficulties
2. Deficits in expressive communication skills
3. Anxiety, fear, and emotional regulation difficulties
4. Social skills deficits
5. Sensory processing problems
6. Executive functioning challenges
7. Academic, cognitive, or motor skills deficits
8. Restricted range of interests

LANGUAGE COMPREHENSION DIFFICULTIES

Difficulty comprehending the language used within a new task can result in a student with ASD not attempting the task.

Understanding the Problem

Students with ASD who have language comprehension difficulties may not willingly attempt unfamiliar tasks because they do not understand the directions provided. Although they may understand directions for tasks given on a regular basis, new tasks will contain new language that the students may have trouble comprehending.

Assessing the Problem

If you think language difficulties may be affecting your student's ability to attempt unfamiliar tasks, then check the box in Section 1 of the FBA Checklist for Difficulty Attempting Unfamiliar or Difficult Tasks in appendix at the end of this chapter: The student avoids unfamiliar tasks due to difficulties understanding the language of the new directions. Give the directions using simplified language, ***modeling*** the expectations, using ***video modeling,*** or using ***visual supports*** when presenting unfamiliar tasks. If the student attempts the unfamiliar tasks when they are presented using simplified language or modes other than language, then you can predict that language comprehension difficulties are at the root of the problem.

Supporting the Student

Consider the following strategies and supports if your student is having trouble attempting unfamiliar tasks due to language comprehension problems:

- If the student can read, then provide written directions to allow the student time to read and process the directions for an unfamiliar task. If the student cannot read, then give visual representation of the directions when possible.
- Go over the directions multiple times using simplified language to ensure student understanding.
- Use any of the following strategies to support the student with understanding the unfamiliar task when directions cannot be given using simple sentences:
    - ***Modeling/request imitation***
    - ***Most-to-least prompting/fading procedures***
    - ***Visual supports***
    - ***Video modeling***

DEFICITS IN EXPRESSIVE COMMUNICATION SKILLS

Expressive communication skills are particularly necessary when students are attempting new or difficult tasks; students with deficits in this area may be unable to communicate in order to begin or complete the task.

Understanding the Problem

All students use expressive communication skills to cope and proceed when presented with unfamiliar or difficult tasks. They may need to ask for help or clarification if they are unsure how to complete the task. If they get frustrated, then they may say things such as, "I can't do this" or "It's too hard." Although it is not the most desirable behavior for students to say those things, having the ability helps them regulate their emotions and usually results in teacher support. Task avoidance and other challenging behaviors can occur if students with ASD do not have the expressive communication skills to ask for help or express their frustration.

Assessing the Problem

A student who is nonverbal or has a very limited vocabulary will generally find it harder to ask questions or express frustration and may not have the specific vocabulary needed to ask questions about unfamiliar tasks. If this is the case for your student, then deficits in expressive communication skills may be affecting your student's ability to attempt unfamiliar or difficult tasks. Check the box in Section 2 of the FBA Checklist for Difficulty Attempting Unfamiliar or Difficult Tasks in appendix at the end of this chapter: The student lacks the communication skills necessary to express frustration and ask for help, resulting in challenging behavior.

Supporting the Student

Consider the following strategies and supports if deficits in expressive communication skills are affecting your student's ability to attempt unfamiliar or difficult tasks:

- Explicitly teach functional communication skills to equip the student with the ability to ask for help. The student can be taught what to say; to raise his or her hand; or to use ***cue cards, pictures, symbols,*** or ***AAC*** supports.
- Have ***visual supports*** available that the student can use to request assistance (e.g., a green cup indicates the student is working well, a red cup indicates the student needs help).

ANXIETY, FEAR, AND EMOTIONAL REGULATION DIFFICULTIES

Unfamiliar tasks and difficult tasks are two things that easily trigger anxiety and fear in students with ASD, often leading to emotional dysregulation.

Understanding the Problem

Unfamiliar tasks may cause distress due to students' need for sameness and predictable routines. Some students rely on the opportunity for repetition to learn the expectations of assignments. Thus, when something unfamiliar is presented, they have not yet had the repeated exposure to help them feel comfortable. Their anxiety and fear may immediately escalate if they are not sure exactly what to do to get started with a new or difficult task.

Assessing the Problem

If you think anxiety, fear, and emotional regulation difficulties may be affecting your student's ability to attempt unfamiliar or difficult tasks, then complete Section 3 of the FBA Checklist for Difficulty Attempting Unfamiliar or Difficult Tasks in appendix at the end of this chapter. Following are some tips for assessing each item:

3a: The Student Generally Has a Strong Desire to Please Others and Gets Distressed When Unfamiliar or Difficult Tasks Are Presented Due to Intense Worries About Doing the Work Incorrectly

Use the explicit instruction model with several modeling examples during the "I Do It" phase of the lesson to assess if this is the case for your student. Do not move to guided practice until the student is fairly comfortable with the expectations. Then provide multiple examples during the "We Do It" phase, using ***most-to-least prompting*** to gradually include the student in the task, before moving to "You Do It," or independent practice. If the student can comply and participate when new or difficult tasks are presented this way, then it could be that anxiety and fear related to insecurity with the new or difficult work are the problem.

3b: The Student Is Able to Engage in Familiar Tasks That Are Repeated Daily, but the Student Is Unable to Get Started Due to Anxiety and Fear When Presented With Something That Is Out of the Ordinary or Does Not Follow a Familiar Pattern

Compare your student's behavior when given familiar tasks with behavior when given unfamiliar or difficult tasks. Observe whether the student's feelings of anxiety and fear immediately escalate when the tasks are not familiar to the student.

Supporting the Student

Consider the following strategies and supports if anxiety, fear, and ***emotional regulation strategies*** are affecting your student's ability to attempt unfamiliar or difficult tasks:

- Use explicit instruction with ***most-to-least prompting*** when unfamiliar or difficult tasks are presented.
- Use ***social narratives*** or Power Cards (Gagnon, 2001) to explain that doing things that are new or difficult is part of learning, and it is okay to feel anxious or afraid. Then include information about what to do when feeling anxious with new or difficult tasks and assure the student that the teacher is there to help.
- Use ***differential reinforcement*** by ignoring challenging behavior related to task avoidance and positively reinforcing the student when the student attempts or finishes an unfamiliar or difficult task.
- Use the ***behavioral momentum*** strategy (high-probability instructional sequences) by presenting at least two easy, familiar tasks with which it is easier for the student to succeed before presenting an unfamiliar or difficult task, and repeat this pattern.
- If the student's anxiety and fear are extremely severe, then use ***shaping*** by first presenting only one or two unfamiliar or difficult tasks per day. Once the student can comply with those tasks, deliver ***positive reinforcement*** and then add another unfamiliar or difficult task to the daily schedule.
- Use a first-then ***visual support*** that shows the student that there will be a highly desirable activity after the student completes the unfamiliar or difficult task.
- Teach ***emotional regulation strategies*** using breathing exercises, cognitive behavioral techniques (e.g., say encouraging phrases to oneself such as "I can do this"), or rating scales (e.g., The Incredible 5-Point Scale [Buron & Curtis, 2003]). Rating scales, or emotional thermometers, allow the student to go to a safe place, choose a calming activity, and then return to task when ready. Rating scales can also have just three levels. Students can be instructed to use the safe space and calming activity when they notice they are at a level 2. Following is an example of a three-point scale:
    - Level 1: I am happy, content, calm, okay.
    - Level 2: I am a little worried, anxious, afraid, upset, angry.
    - Level 3: I am very upset, and I need help.

SOCIAL SKILLS DEFICITS

Students with ASD may avoid new or difficult tasks if the tasks require social skills that have not yet been developed.

Understanding the Problem

Although these students may be able to work with a partner or group to complete tasks when they are part of the everyday routine in the classroom, if an unfamiliar partner or group task is given, then the student may feel uncomfortable with the social expectations of the activity, resulting in avoidance behaviors. Also, students may need to receive instructional support from the teacher that requires back-and-forth exchanges to get the guidance needed. If a student has deficits in social reciprocity, then the student will not have the ability to engage in reciprocal exchanges with the teacher to receive the necessary support.

Assessing the Problem

If you think social skills deficits may be affecting your student's ability to attempt unfamiliar or difficult tasks, then complete Section 4 of the FBA Checklist for Difficulty Attempting Unfamiliar or Difficult Tasks in appendix at the end of this chapter. Following are some tips for assessing each item:

4a: Some Unfamiliar Tasks Require Using Social Skills That the Student Has Not Yet Acquired

You will need to have a good understanding of the social skills the student has and has not mastered to assess if this may be the case for your student. Then assign unfamiliar or difficult tasks that require partner or group work, considering the student's skill set as you make decisions about the tasks. If the student can engage in the task when the social expectations are simplified but disengages when the expectations are beyond their mastery level, then you can predict that social skills deficits are affecting the student's compliance with attempting the new or difficult tasks that require peer interaction.

4b: Social Reciprocity Difficulties May Lead to Problems Interacting in the Long Chains of Back-and-Forth Exchanges With the Teacher That Are Often Required to Succeed With an Unfamiliar or Difficult Task

It is important to take note of the manner in which typically developing students receive support with unfamiliar or difficult tasks. You will probably recognize that they typically engage in quite a bit of back and forth with the teacher until they are comfortable to proceed independently. If your student with ASD is unable to do that because of social reciprocity difficulties, then you can predict that social skills deficits are affecting the student's ability to attempt unfamiliar or difficult tasks.

Supporting the Student

Consider the following strategies and supports if social skills deficits are affecting your student's ability to attempt unfamiliar or difficult tasks:

- Simplify social expectations during partner or group activities that are unfamiliar or difficult. For example, when a new partner activity is introduced that requires students to share their responses to a reading comprehension question, give feedback to one another, and adjust their answers based on peer feedback, the expectations may need to be modified if the student with ASD has difficulty giving and accepting constructive criticism. Instead, this student's partner activity may simply entail sharing responses with one another without giving feedback. The feedback piece can be introduced with facilitation from the teacher once this activity becomes familiar.
- Provide adult facilitation during new partner or group activities to ensure student success.

- If the student is unable to engage in long back-and-forth interactions to receive support to understand an unfamiliar or difficult task, then provide support by using visual methods of instruction, such as ***modeling,*** using ***pictures,*** or providing graphical representations.

SENSORY PROCESSING PROBLEMS

Sensory processing problems may interfere with a student attempting a task when a student has not had a chance to get accustomed to the sensory stimuli associated with a particular activity, which is more likely when tasks are unfamiliar or very complex.

Understanding the Problem

Students who have sensory processing problems often need repeated exposure to various environments and activities to get desensitized to the stimuli they are presented with to process what they are receiving. Students may need some time to adjust when unfamiliar tasks have new sensory stimuli. They may initially display avoidance behaviors as they struggle with processing the unfamiliar sensory stimuli.

Assessing the Problem

If you think sensory processing problems may be affecting your student's abilities to attempt unfamiliar or difficult tasks, then check the box in Section 5 of the FBA Checklist for Difficulty Attempting Unfamiliar or Difficult Tasks in appendix at the end of this chapter: The student has difficulties engaging in tasks that include unfamiliar sensory experiences. You need to be fully aware of the student's sensory profile as far as what things cause sensory overload and what the student needs in regard to sensory input to stay engaged. Present unfamiliar tasks while keeping this information in mind; adjust the environment or materials to ensure the student is as comfortable as possible and given the supports needed to engage when unfamiliar tasks are presented. Observe whether the student is more likely to attempt unfamiliar tasks when these adjustments are made as opposed to how often the student attempts unfamiliar tasks when these adjustments are not made.

Supporting the Student

Consider the following strategies and supports if sensory processing issues are causing problems with your student attempting unfamiliar or difficult tasks:

- Use environmental arrangements to make adjustments related to the student's sensory profile.
- Use ***priming*** to provide exposure to new materials that will be used during an upcoming unfamiliar task to allow the student to get comfortable using the materials before the actual task is presented.

EXECUTIVE FUNCTIONING CHALLENGES

Students with ASD may not attempt unfamiliar or difficult tasks because their executive functioning skills are limited, compared with what the task demands, or they have executive functioning skills but struggle to apply them to unfamiliar tasks.

Understanding the Problem

If unfamiliar or difficult tasks presented to the student typically require organizing, planning, and completing multiple steps, then this could be problematic if the student has executive functioning challenges. Although the student may be able to learn the executive functioning skills needed to complete tasks that are part of their everyday routines, support is needed when new activities are presented so the student can develop the executive functioning skills needed to attempt and complete the task.

Assessing the Problem

If you think executive functioning challenges may be affecting your student's ability to attempt unfamiliar or difficult tasks, then check the box in Section 6 of the FBA Checklist for Difficulty Attempting Unfamiliar or Difficult Tasks in appendix at the end of this chapter: The student has difficulty with unfamiliar tasks that require the student to plan and execute a sequence of steps. Provide support for unfamiliar or difficult tasks (e.g., checklists, ***visual schedules***) to help the student plan the steps of the task. Executive functioning challenges are likely a factor if the student can attempt or complete the tasks with this level of support but otherwise struggles to attempt or complete the tasks.

Supporting the Student

Consider the following strategies and supports if executive functioning challenges are affecting your student's ability to attempt unfamiliar or difficult tasks:

- Use ***task analysis*** by breaking down unfamiliar or difficult tasks that have multiple steps.
- Use ***visual supports*** to present the steps of the unfamiliar or difficult task visually (e.g., ***pictures,*** words, phrases, sentences).
- Use ***forward chaining*** to teach the student how to use the ***task analysis.***
- Create a ***self-monitoring*** tool the student can use to check off each step of the unfamiliar or difficult task as it is completed.
- Use ***video modeling, video self-modeling, point-of-view video modeling,*** or ***video prompting*** to help the student see and remember the different parts of unfamiliar or difficult multistep tasks.

ACADEMIC, COGNITIVE, OR MOTOR SKILLS DEFICITS

Lacking the academic or cognitive skills needed to complete tasks is the most obvious reason why students with ASD avoid difficult tasks.

Understanding the Problem

Although teachers attempt to provide learning activities that are not too easy and not too difficult, sometimes their expectations are beyond the student's present abilities. Sometimes the work is too difficult because it involves abstract thought and reasoning. Other times, the work involves reading, writing, or math skills that the student has not yet mastered. Also, students who have fine or gross motor skills deficits may have trouble attempting unfamiliar or difficult activities that include motor tasks that call on skills they have not been able to practice and develop.

Assessing the Problem

If you think academic, cognitive, or motor skills deficits may be affecting your student's ability to attempt unfamiliar or difficult tasks, then complete Section 7 of the FBA Checklist for Difficulty Attempting Unfamiliar or Difficult Tasks in appendix at the end of this chapter. Following are some tips for assessing each item:

7a: Difficult Work Causes Emotional Distress Due to Academic Frustration

Make sure tasks are developmentally appropriate for the student, which means the work must still be achievable for the student, even if it is difficult. Compare the student's behavior when you make these adjustments with behavior in other situations in which the tasks are not differentiated for the student to determine whether academic or cognitive deficits may be affecting the student's ability to comply with attempting difficult tasks.

7b: The Student Has Difficulty Attempting Unfamiliar Tasks That Require Using Fine Motor Skills

Consult with the student's occupational therapist to assess whether the unfamiliar or difficult tasks you are presenting may be beyond the appropriate level of challenge, considering the student's fine motor skills development.

7c: The Student Has Difficulty Attempting Unfamiliar Tasks That Require Using Gross Motor Skills

This will likely be an issue in physical education classes if the teacher is unaware of what gross motor skills the student has and has not yet developed. Thus, the special education teacher or physical therapist should consult with the physical education teacher to determine if the tasks being presented are too challenging for the student in terms of gross motor skills.

Supporting the Student

Consider the following strategies and supports if academic, cognitive, or motor skills deficits are causing problems with your student attempting unfamiliar or difficult tasks:

- Use differentiated instruction practices to adjust unfamiliar or difficult tasks to make sure they involve the appropriate level of challenge.
- Utilize AT to support the student's fine and gross motor needs.

RESTRICTED RANGE OF INTERESTS

Some students with ASD may be less likely to attempt new or difficult tasks that fall outside of a narrow range of interests.

Understanding the Problem

Problems with attempting unfamiliar or difficult tasks may arise for students who have a very restricted range of interests because most of those activities are not interest based. They may not have the internal motivation necessary to attempt and complete tasks they consider boring or irrelevant. Again, this lack of motivation is part of their ASD characteristics, not an isolated challenging behavior of being lazy or unmotivated.

Assessing the Problem

If you think your student's restricted range of interests may be affecting the child's ability to attempt unfamiliar or difficult tasks, then check the box in Section 8 of the FBA Checklist for Difficulty Attempting Unfamiliar or Difficult Tasks in appendix at the end of this chapter: Unfamiliar or difficult tasks are often not associated with the student's interests, which may cause avoidance behaviors due to the student's restricted range of interests. Present unfamiliar or difficult tasks that are somehow related to the student's special interests. If the student attempts those tasks but not assignments that are not interest based, then you can predict that the student's restricted range of interests is affecting compliance with attempting unfamiliar or difficult tasks.

Supporting the Student

Consider the following supports and strategies if the student's restricted range of interests is affecting compliance with attempting unfamiliar or difficult tasks:

- Increase the proportion of unfamiliar or difficult tasks that are based on the student's interests.
- Allow the student to use materials related to special interests while completing unfamiliar or difficult tasks.
- If the student has a favorite character, then use Power Cards (Gagnon, 2001) to teach expectations for attempting unfamiliar or difficult tasks.
- Try to expand the student's interests by exposing the student to activities and topics that are similar to things the student enjoys.

From Assessment to Successful Intervention

Case Study: Sharon *Sharon is a second-grade student with ASD who has very limited expressive communication skills. Although she can physically speak and read quite well, she does not have much spontaneous communication. She displays high levels of self-injurious behaviors when she is presented with academic tasks. She will complete tasks that are familiar and easy for her; however, she will almost immediately begin hitting herself or banging her head when presented with something new or slightly challenging.*

The behavior analyst met with Sharon's teacher to assess the situation. The behavior analyst observed Sharon in the classroom and noted that she does not seem to engage when verbal directions for unfamiliar or difficult tasks are being given. She engages in self-injurious behavior when given the task to complete because she is not receiving the instruction to learn how to do the task. It was also observed that the tasks being given to Sharon were the same exact tasks assigned to the rest of the students in the class, rather than appropriate differentiated tasks based on her academic present levels of performance.

Figure 10.1 shows the sections of the FBA Checklist for Difficulty Attempting Unfamiliar or Difficult Tasks that were checked off when the teacher and behavior analyst met after the observation, the hypothesis statement that was written, and the intervention plan they put together.

Challenging Behavior: Difficulties Attempting Unfamiliar or Difficult Tasks

1. **Language Comprehension Difficulties**
   - ☑ The student avoids unfamiliar tasks due to difficulties understanding the language of the new directions.

2. **Deficits in Expressive Communication Skills**
   - ☑ The student lacks the communication skills necessary to express frustration and ask for help, resulting in challenging behavior.

4. **Social Skills Deficits**
   - ☐ 4a: Some unfamiliar tasks require using social skills that the student has not yet acquired.
   - ☑ 4b: Social reciprocity difficulties may lead to problems interacting in the long chains of back-and-forth exchanges with the teacher that are often required to succeed with an unfamiliar or difficult task.

7. **Academic, Cognitive, or Motor Skills Deficits**
   - ☑ 7a: Difficult work causes emotional distress due to academic frustration.
   - ☐ 7b: The student has difficulty attempting unfamiliar tasks that require using fine motor skills.
   - ☐ 7c: The student has difficulty attempting unfamiliar tasks that require using gross motor skills.

Hypothesis Statement Sharon engages in self-injurious behaviors, such as hitting herself and banging her head, when presented with unfamiliar or difficult tasks. This is due to her language comprehension difficulties and inability to engage in reciprocal exchanges with the teacher to learn how to do the task. In addition, she does not know how to ask for help when necessary. Therefore, she immediately begins using self-injurious behaviors when she needs help with an unfamiliar or difficult task. The teacher responds very quickly by removing the student from the work area to prevent the student from harming herself, which is positively reinforcing the self-injurious behaviors.

Intervention Plan

- Provide directions for unfamiliar or difficult tasks visually by using simplified written directions, ***modeling/request imitation, visual supports,*** or ***video modeling.***
- Teach Sharon how to ask for help using a ***cue card*** that says, "I need help." Use the following **least-to-most prompts** hierarchy:
  1. Have a cue card available for independent use that says, "I need ____."
  2. Have a cue card available for independent use that says, "I need help."
  3. Point to the cue card to prompt the student to read, "I need help."
  4. Tell the student to read the cue card that says, "I need help."
  5. Use ***modeling/request imitation*** (read the cue card and have Sharon imitate)
- Embed mastered skills within the task using ***behavioral momentum*** (repeated pattern of easy-easy-difficult tasks or problems) when giving her unfamiliar or difficult tasks. Encourage use of the ***cue card*** to ask for help when she gets to the difficult task or problem.
- Use blocking if Sharon begins to engage in self-injurious behaviors, but do not remove her from the work area. Positively redirect her to the task at hand, offering the necessary levels of support. Deliver ***positive reinforcement*** when she attempts the task.

Results

When this plan was initiated, the teacher found it difficult to think of ways to present directions for new tasks visually. Therefore, the behavior analyst met with her on a weekly basis to discuss the upcoming tasks planned for the student. They created ***visual supports*** together to show the student how to do the task. Sometimes this included ***graphic organizers*** that made it clear what the student was supposed to do, or they created ***point-of-view video modeling*** clips that the student could view before doing the task. The teacher began to automatically think of ways to present tasks visually after a few weeks of this collaboration, and she needed less support from the behavior analyst. Sharon responded immediately when the teacher implemented the ***cue card*** and ***behavioral momentum*** strategies to teach her to ask for help, resulting in a dramatic decrease in her self-injurious behaviors when she got to a difficult task or problem.

Figure 10.1. Functional Behavior Assessment Checklist and intervention plan for Sharon.

From Assessment to Successful Intervention

Case Study: Terrell *Terrell is a high-functioning eighth-grade student with ASD who is above average academically and included in all general education classes. His main areas of difficulty include social interaction with peers, severe anxiety and fear, and emotional regulation challenges. His general education teachers have requested support from the special education teacher because he often has meltdowns in class when he is expected to complete assignments independently. If the assignments are easy, then he does not display any challenging behavior and completes the tasks. Terrell immediately escalates into yelling, crying, and lying on the floor kicking his feet, however, if the assignments are challenging. The team reviewed the FBA Checklist for Difficulty Attempting Unfamiliar or Difficult Tasks to determine why Terrell may be having trouble attempting difficult tasks. They came to a consensus that they believe his anxiety, fear, and emotional regulation difficulties are impeding his compliance with attempting difficult tasks. In addition, he loses the ability to use communication skills to express his frustration when he gets distressed.*

Figure 10.2 shows what items they checked off, the hypothesis statement they agreed on, and the intervention plan they devised.

Challenging Behavior: Difficulties Attempting Unfamiliar or Difficult Tasks

2. Deficits in Expressive Communication Skills

- ☑ The student lacks the communication skills necessary to express frustration and ask for help, resulting in challenging behavior.

3. Anxiety, Fear, and Emotional Regulation Difficulties

- ☑ 3a: The student generally has a strong desire to please others and gets distressed when unfamiliar or difficult tasks are presented due to intense worries about doing the work incorrectly.
- ☑ 3b: The student is able to engage in familiar tasks that are repeated daily, but the student is unable to get started due to anxiety and fear when presented with something that is out of the ordinary or does not follow a familiar pattern.

Hypothesis Statement Terrell experiences meltdowns (e.g., yells, cries, lies on the floor, kicks his feet), when given difficult assignments to complete. Although the assignments are appropriately challenging, considering his academic performance, he gets extremely anxious and fearful when he is not 100% sure how to complete the task. He is rarely able to attempt the task to try to figure it out because he gets emotionally dysregulated right away. Therefore, he is unable to communicate to get assistance or request a break before he has a meltdown.

Intervention Plan

- Use ***social narratives*** to teach Terrell that it is okay to get anxious and fearful when difficult tasks are given, and provide strategies he can use to manage those feelings. He may like comic strip conversations (Gray, 1994) instead of Social Stories (Gray, 2010) because he likes superhero movies.
- Use the following emotional regulation scale to teach Terrell how to ask for help or a break when he is at a level 2 instead of going into a meltdown:
  1. I can do the work.
  2. I am worried that I cannot do the work.
     - I can ask for help.
     - I can ask for a break.
  3. I am extremely upset that I cannot do the work.
- Provide a visual cue that says, "I need help" on one side and "I need a break" on the other. Terrell should give the card to the teacher when he gets to a level 2 to request help or a break. He does not need to make a verbal request if unable to do so.
- Use ***priming*** before assigning a difficult task to remind Terrell how to ask for help or a break if he gets to a level 2.
- Remain in close proximity to Terrell when first implementing this plan, and prompt him (if necessary) when he gets to a level 2 by pointing to the ***cue card.*** Avoid verbal prompting because that may escalate his emotions.
- If Terrell asks for a break, then allow him to go to a safe space to calm down. He can select an activity to distract him from the frustration. He should then return to task when calm. If he needs to yell or scream to get out his frustration, then allow him to do so in a designated, supervised area that is not disruptive to other students.

Results

Terrell was able to learn how to prevent his meltdowns when given difficult tasks when all of his teachers consistently used ***emotional regulation strategies.*** He was involved in developing comic strip conversations, and these scenarios helped him understand that it is acceptable to get anxious and fearful when difficult tasks are assigned, but he can use strategies to calm down instead of having a meltdown. He can either ask for help or take a quick break and return to task on most days. There are times, however, when he needs to leave the room and have his meltdown. The meltdowns are shorter than before because teachers do not intervene. They simply allow him to get his frustration out, and then he returns to the classroom. The tasks themselves never need to be adjusted because he can actually do the work if he just remains calm.

Figure 10.2. Functional Behavior Assessment Checklist and intervention plan for Terrell.

Challenging Behavior: Difficulties Attempting Unfamiliar or Difficult Tasks

1. **Language Comprehension Difficulties**
   - ❒ The student avoids unfamiliar tasks due to difficulties understanding the language of the new directions.
2. **Deficits in Expressive Communication Skills**
   - ❒ The student lacks the communication skills necessary to express frustration and ask for help, resulting in challenging behavior.
3. **Anxiety, Fear, and Emotional Regulation Difficulties**
   - ❒ 3a: The student generally has a strong desire to please others and gets distressed when unfamiliar or difficult tasks are presented due to intense worries about doing the work incorrectly.
   - ❒ 3b: The student is able to engage in familiar tasks that are repeated daily, but the student is unable to get started due to anxiety and fear when presented with something that is out of the ordinary or does not follow a familiar pattern.
4. **Social Skills Deficits**
   - ❒ 4a: Some unfamiliar tasks require using social skills that the student has not yet acquired.
   - ❒ 4b: Social reciprocity difficulties may lead to problems interacting in the long chains of back-and-forth exchanges with the teacher that are often required to succeed with an unfamiliar or difficult task.
5. **Sensory Processing Problems**
   - ❒ The student has difficulties engaging in tasks that include unfamiliar sensory experiences.
6. **Executive Functioning Challenges**
   - ❒ The student has difficulty with unfamiliar tasks that require the student to plan and execute a sequence of steps.
7. **Academic, Cognitive, or Motor Skills Deficits**
   - ❒ 7a: Difficult work causes emotional distress due to academic frustration.
   - ❒ 7b: The student has difficulty attempting unfamiliar tasks that require using fine motor skills.
   - ❒ 7c: The student has difficulty attempting unfamiliar tasks that require using gross motor skills.
8. **Restricted Range of Interests**
   - ❒ Unfamiliar or difficult tasks are often not associated with the student's interests, which may cause avoidance behaviors due to the student's restricted range of interests.

Other ____

____

____

____

Hypothesis Statement ____

____

____

____

CHAPTER 11

Engaging in Nonpreferred Tasks

Motivating students with ASD to complete nonpreferred tasks is a common challenge that teachers face. Although typically developing students do not enjoy everything their teachers ask them to do, they will generally do what is required. It is important to think about what actually makes nonpreferred tasks nonpreferred for students with ASD. Instead of just viewing this problem as a compliance issue, consider figuring out why certain activities are nonpreferred and address it from that angle. The following characteristics may have an impact on which tasks are preferred and which are nonpreferred:

1. Anxiety, fear, and emotional regulation difficulties
2. Social skills deficits
3. Sensory processing problems
4. Executive functioning challenges
5. Restricted range of interests
6. Academic, cognitive, or motor skills deficits

ANXIETY, FEAR, AND EMOTIONAL REGULATION DIFFICULTIES

If a task is nonpreferred for a particular student, then something about it could produce anxiety.

Understanding the Problem

A student may get overly anxious and fearful when the assignments are out of the ordinary and disrupt the typical classroom routine. The student may get worried that he or she does not know how to do certain tasks, and those tasks become nonpreferred. Of course, a student who experiences extreme anxiety may have difficulty regulating his or her emotions and ultimately refuse to do the nonpreferred tasks.

Assessing the Problem

If you think your student does not prefer specific tasks because they cause anxiety, fear, and emotional regulation difficulties, then check the box in Section 1 of the FBA Checklist for

Difficulties Engaging in Nonpreferred Tasks in the appendix at the end of this chapter: The student primarily prefers tasks that follow a familiar pattern due to a need for sameness. Nonpreferred tasks are typically assignments that are unfamiliar or disrupt the typical routine. If you are unsure whether this is the case for your student, then write down all the tasks that you can think of that you would consider nonpreferred tasks for the student. Put a star next to any that do not follow a familiar pattern. If many tasks have stars next to them, then you can predict that the student gets anxious when unfamiliar tasks are presented, making those tasks nonpreferred.

Supporting the Student

Consider the following supports and strategies if you determine that unfamiliar tasks are nonpreferred because they cause anxiety, fear, and emotional regulation difficulties:

- The majority of the student's assignments should be familiar, with only one or two unfamiliar tasks presented each day.
- The first time an unfamiliar task is given, simply complete the task or have a peer complete the task, allowing the student to watch how it is done. Do this up to three more times until the student feels comfortable with the task and is ready to complete it independently. Remain close to the student the first time the task is being attempted to provide the necessary supports to ensure success.
- Use ***video modeling*** for unfamiliar tasks. Allow the student to watch the video model as many times as necessary before attempting the task.
- Deliver ***positive reinforcement*** when the student attempts or completes a task that was once considered nonpreferred.

SOCIAL SKILLS DEFICITS

Some tasks may be considered nonpreferred for your student because they require using specific social skills that are challenging for the student.

Understanding the Problem

Tasks that may be nonpreferred for this reason include tasks that involve question-and-answer activities with a teacher, circle time activities, or activities that require long periods of waiting, turn-taking, sharing, reciprocal conversation skills, and so forth. Students may not have acquired the social skills they need to complete these tasks or activities or engage in them for extended periods of time.

Assessing the Problem

If you think your student does not prefer specific tasks because the student has deficits in the social skills needed to participate, then check the box in Section 2 of the FBA Checklist for Difficulties Engaging in Nonpreferred Tasks in the appendix at the end of this chapter: Tasks are considered nonpreferred when they require using social skills the student has not yet acquired. If you are unsure whether this is the case for your student, then write down all the tasks that you can think of that you would consider nonpreferred tasks for the student. Put a star next to any that involve social skills that the student may be lacking. If many tasks have stars next to them, then you can predict that tasks that involve social skills and interacting with others are considered nonpreferred.

Supporting the Student

Consider the following supports and strategies if you determine that tasks are nonpreferred because they require using social skills that are difficult for your student:

- Assess the student's social skills and set goals to target that will support the student when assigned tasks that require interaction with others. Teach the targeted social skills using explicit instruction, ***social narratives, video modeling***, or role play.
- Use ***peer-mediated interventions*** to teach peers how to make initiations with the student, encourage responses from the student, and respond to the student's initiations in a positive manner during tasks that require back-and-forth interaction.
- Use ***script-fading procedures*** for tasks that require peer interaction to complete.
- Modify the social expectations for tasks to address the student's present abilities. For example, if a kindergarten student has difficulty during circle time due to deficits in joint attention skills, then the teacher can give the student an interactive flip book related to the circle time activities. This way, the student can complete the flip book activities that go along with the teacher's instruction instead of sitting still with hands in his or her lap, attending to the teacher without talking other than the few times the student may be called on to answer a question. The student may just need prompts to stay on the appropriate page of the book to follow the teacher's pacing. The teacher can still call on the student to participate with the class, but having the flip book allows the student to stay engaged even when not being directly called on by the teacher. The flip book also helps the student attend to the appropriate material at the appropriate time as opposed to being distracted by other stimuli in the environment.
- If the student does not prefer verbal question-and-answer activities, then provide the questions in written form and allow the student to respond verbally or in writing.

SENSORY PROCESSING PROBLEMS

Consider whether a nonpreferred task presents too much or too little sensory input because it is common for students with ASD to have sensory processing problems.

Understanding the Problem

Tasks may be considered nonpreferred due to a student's sensory processing problems. The tasks may cause sensory overload or limit the sensory input the student needs to engage in learning tasks.

Assessing the Problem

If you think tasks are nonpreferred for the student due to sensory processing problems, then complete Section 3 of the FBA Checklist for Difficulties Engaging in Nonpreferred Tasks in the appendix at the end of this chapter. Following are some tips for assessing each item:

3a. Tasks That Are Considered Nonpreferred Do Not Provide the Sensory Input the Student Needs to Stay Engaged

If you are unsure whether this is the case for your student, then write down all of the tasks that you can think of that you would consider nonpreferred tasks for the student. Put a star next to any that require the student to sit still, be quiet, and write with pencil and paper. If many tasks have stars next to them, then you can predict that tasks that limit sensory input are considered nonpreferred.

3b. Tasks That Are Considered Nonpreferred Cause Sensory Overload and Discomfort

If you are unsure if this is the case for your student, then write down all of the tasks that you can think of that you would consider nonpreferred tasks for the student. Based on your knowledge of what situations or materials cause sensory discomfort or overload for this student, put a star next to any of the tasks that include using materials the student finds aversive, excessive movement, loud noise, many students working close to one another, and so forth. If many tasks have stars next to them, then you can predict that tasks that result in sensory overload for the student are considered nonpreferred.

Supporting the Student

Consider the following supports and strategies if you determine that tasks are nonpreferred because they cause sensory overload or limit sensory input:

- Allow the student to get the necessary sensory input during tasks that are considered nonpreferred (e.g., allow the student to stand while working, sit on a balance ball instead of a chair, listen to music while working, make verbalizations as long it is not disturbing others).
- Make environmental modifications when giving nonpreferred tasks, considering the student's sensory profile to address the aversion to the tasks.

EXECUTIVE FUNCTIONING CHALLENGES

Tasks that require planning, organization, and multiple steps to complete may be nonpreferred for students with ASD.

Understanding the Problem

Students with ASD may prefer simple, one-step tasks due to executive functioning challenges. They may not know how to begin complex tasks, have a clear plan for completing each step of the task, and successfully manage their time to complete the task because of problems with executive functioning. Thus, complex tasks become nonpreferred.

Assessing the Problem

If you think tasks are nonpreferred for the student due to executive functioning challenges, then check the box in Section 4 of the FBA Checklist for Difficulties Engaging in Nonpreferred Tasks in the appendix at the end of this chapter: Tasks that are considered nonpreferred require multiple steps to plan out and complete. If you are unsure whether this is the case for your student, then write down all the tasks you can think of that you would consider nonpreferred tasks for the student. Put a star next to any that are complex in nature and require planning, organization, time management, or multiple steps to complete. If many tasks have stars next to them, then you can predict that tasks that require strengths with executive functioning skills are considered nonpreferred.

Supporting the Student

Consider the following supports and strategies if you determine that unfamiliar tasks are nonpreferred because they call on a student's executive functioning skills:

- Break down the nonpreferred tasks into simple, one-step assignments and present each step one at a time. Although it is important to teach executive functioning skills, it is best to first focus on task completion if the student is extremely noncompliant.
- Once the student succeeds with the individual steps of a complex task several times, use ***shaping*** by giving the student two steps to complete, delivering ***positive reinforcement*** after the student complies. Then move on to three steps and so forth.
- Break down the task into sequential steps using ***task analysis,*** and use ***chaining*** (forward, backward, or total task presentation) to gradually increase the student's independence.
- Once the student can do each step of the task, provide a ***self-monitoring*** tool that allows the student to check off each step as it is completed.
- Use ***video modeling, video self-modeling, point-of-view video modeling,*** or ***video prompting*** to teach the student how to complete the nonpreferred task.

RESTRICTED RANGE OF INTERESTS

Many students with ASD have a restricted range of interests, which is a common reason why they have so many nonpreferred tasks.

Understanding the Problem

Typically developing students are usually interested in a diverse list of topics and activities and are open to exploring new interests. Students with ASD, however, often have an extremely narrow focus of interest, with one or two intense passions or fascinations. Sometimes their areas of interest are seamlessly connected to at least one topic of study at school (e.g., interests related to historical events, math, animals). The student's interests, however, are quite difficult (but not impossible) to connect to learning activities at school (e.g., Star Wars, Disney World, Dr. Seuss books, video games). If a student is hyperfocused on specific special interests, then this may result in severe noncompliance with tasks unrelated to these topics.

Assessing the Problem

If you think tasks are nonpreferred due to the student's restricted range of interests, then check the box in Section 5 of the FBA Checklist for Difficulties Engaging in Nonpreferred Tasks in the appendix at the end of this chapter: Nonpreferred tasks include those that are not related to the student's special interests. You must first know what the student's special interests include. Then examine if any of the nonpreferred tasks tap into the student's interests. If none of them do, then you can predict that the student's restricted range of interests may be the reason why so many tasks are considered nonpreferred.

Supporting the Student

Consider the following supports and strategies if you determine that tasks are nonpreferred because they are not related to the student's special interests:

Table 11.1. Examples of using special interests to motivate students to complete nonpreferred tasks

Special interest	Nonpreferred task	Options for making the task interest based
Dinosaurs	Reading and answering comprehension questions	Have the student read fiction or nonfiction books about dinosaurs when feasible and answer comprehension questions about those books. Engage the student in a characterization activity that involves assigning character traits to different dinosaurs. Each set of comprehension questions given after an assigned reading can include one question that asks the student to compare and contrast a character in the story to one of the dinosaurs, using the character traits listed. Use a first-then visual: First the student completes the reading assignment, then time is given to play with dinosaur figurines.
New York Giants, football	Math word problems	Relate math word problems to the New York Giants (e.g., 75% of the attendees at last Sunday's Giants game were male. What percentage were female?). Give the student New York Giants pencils to use only while solving math word problems. Create a ***positive reinforcement*** system that involves scoring field goals and touchdowns. Problems solved with teacher support are worth a field goal (3 points). Problems solved independently are worth a touchdown (6 points). The student needs to explain why the answer makes sense to get the extra point.
NASCAR	Written expression activities	Allow the student to write about topics related to NASCAR when feasible. Here are some sample writing prompts: "If you could ride with one of the race car drivers during a race, who would it be and why?" "Why is NASCAR a very entertaining sport to watch?" "One day you wake up and realize you have switched bodies with your favorite NASCAR driver. Describe what happens that day." Use a picture of a speedway as a prewriting graphic organizer for any writing topic. Teach the student to write about sensory experiences by having the student write about what you see, hear, smell, touch, and taste at a NASCAR race. Teach the student about using adjectives by having the student listen to a NASCAR announcer and record all of the adjectives the announcer used while describing the event.

- Use an interest-based approach as often as possible by assigning tasks that are connected to the student's special interests in some way. Table 11.1 includes examples of ways to use a student's interests for motivation with nonpreferred tasks.
- Allow the student to use materials related to their special interest(s) when completing nonpreferred tasks.
- Use a first-then ***visual support*** that shows how the student will first complete a nonpreferred task, then have access to an item or activity related to the student's special interests that is not typically available to the student.

ACADEMIC, COGNITIVE, OR MOTOR SKILLS DEFICITS

Students with ASD may have significant academic, cognitive, or motor skills deficits that make a variety of tasks extremely challenging and, therefore, nonpreferred.

Understanding the Problem

Many tasks presented in school call on one or more areas of academic, cognitive, or motor skill that may be challenging for students with ASD. Written expression tasks are often nonpreferred due to a combination of fine motor deficits and language deficits that directly affect written expression. Math word problems are often nonpreferred by students with ASD because their language impairments and reading comprehension deficits cause great challenges with solving the problems. Tasks that require abstract thought and reasoning may be nonpreferred tasks due to challenges in that area.

Assessing the Problem

If you think tasks are nonpreferred for the student due to academic, cognitive, or motor skills deficits, then complete Section 6 of the FBA Checklist for Difficulties Engaging in Nonpreferred Tasks in the appendix at the end of this chapter. Following are some tips for assessing each item:

6a: Tasks That Are Academically Difficult Are Considered Nonpreferred Tasks

Create a list of all the student's nonpreferred tasks. Compare that list with the student's present level of academic performance in different subject areas. If there is a discrepancy between what the student is currently able to do and what the nonpreferred tasks require, then you can predict that tasks are considered nonpreferred due to academic or cognitive deficits.

6b: Tasks That Involve Fine or Gross Motor Skills That Are Challenging for the Student Are Considered Nonpreferred Tasks

Create a list of all of the student's nonpreferred tasks. Compare that list with the student's present level of fine and gross motor skills (consult with the occupational or physical therapist). If there is a discrepancy between what the student is currently able to do and what the nonpreferred tasks require in terms of motor skills, then you can predict that tasks are considered nonpreferred due to fine or gross motor skills deficits.

Supporting the Student

Consider the following supports and strategies if you determine that tasks are nonpreferred because they are too difficult based on the student's present levels of academic, cognitive, or motor skills:

- Use differentiated instruction practices to adjust nonpreferred tasks to make sure they involve the appropriate level of challenge.
- Utilize AT to support the student's fine and gross motor needs during nonpreferred tasks.

From Assessment to Successful Intervention

Case Study: Grace *Grace is a third-grade student with ASD who demonstrates challenging behavior whenever she is presented with nonpreferred tasks. Her preferred tasks include drawing, coloring, and reading her favorite book series. The tasks that she finds the most aversive include writing tasks, answering reading comprehension questions, and completing math worksheets. Grace will usually indicate that she does not want to complete the nonpreferred tasks assigned to her. Grace may begin yelling, crying, or lying on the floor and kicking if her teacher, Ms. Sullivan, tells her that she must get started or tries to redirect her with a verbal direction. Ms. Sullivan requests a meeting with the special education teacher, SLP, and behavior specialist to get some ideas for helping Grace complete nonpreferred tasks. After a lengthy discussion and a review of the FBA Checklist for Difficulties Engaging in Nonpreferred Tasks, the team hypothesizes that Grace's restricted range of interests is the main reason she avoids nonpreferred tasks. She performs on or above grade level in all areas, has begun to socialize fairly well with peers, and is able to understand and use language quite effectively. She does have executive functioning challenges, however, that could also be involved in her aversion to writing tasks that require planning and multiple steps to complete.*

Figure 11.1 includes the sections of the FBA Checklist that the team checked off, the hypothesis statement that was written, and the intervention plan that was put in place.

Challenging Behavior: Difficulties Engaging in Nonpreferred Tasks

4. **Executive Functioning Challenges**
   ☑ Tasks that are considered nonpreferred require multiple steps to plan out and complete.

5. **Restricted Range of Interests**
   ☑ Nonpreferred tasks include those that are not related to the student's special interests.

Hypothesis Statement Grace will not engage in nonpreferred tasks such as writing activities, reading comprehension assignments, and math worksheets due to her restricted range of interests and executive functioning challenges.

Intervention Plan

- Allow Grace to demonstrate comprehension of reading selections by drawing ***pictures*** to show what happened in a story or what she learned from a nonfiction text.
- Make the math worksheets coloring pages with the math problems inside the coloring page. She can color the picture after she solves the math problems.
- Break down the steps of writing assignments into simple, one-step activities instead of expecting her to do her prewriting, first draft, and revisions at her own pace. Her prewriting activity can include drawing about what she is going to write because she loves drawing.
- Assign written expression activities that are related to her favorite book series.
- Use a first-then visual that lets Grace know that she will have 5 minutes to read her favorite book or color after she completes a nonpreferred activity.

Results

This plan created positive changes almost immediately. Grace enjoyed drawing to demonstrate her comprehension of reading materials as opposed to answering multiple-choice questions. Ms. Sullivan would ask her comprehension questions after she drew her ***pictures,*** allowing her to use her drawing as a ***visual support.*** Grace was successful with responding and quite accurate in her responses. The next step is for Ms. Sullivan to give written questions for Grace to answer, allowing her to use her drawing as a support. Ms. Sullivan also came up with the idea of telling Grace to add to her drawing if a question refers to something that she did not draw about. Grace breezes through the math worksheets now because she is highly motivated to color when she is finished, and her accuracy is strong. Grace willingly complies when she is permitted to write about topics related to her favorite book series, but she still needs to work on writing more lengthy and detailed responses.

Figure 11.1. Functional Behavior Assessment Checklist and intervention plan for Grace.

From Assessment to Successful Intervention

Case Study: Roberto *Roberto is a high school student with ASD who participates in a community-based instruction program to learn job skills. He goes to a thrift store three times a week and is assigned tasks such as folding clothes, ringing customers up on the register, bagging items, and vacuuming the carpets. All but one of these tasks are nonpreferred. He will comply only when asked to bag items that another person rings up for the customer. Roberto will refuse to do the other tasks, and he becomes aggressive by engaging in self-injurious behaviors or hitting others if the job coach attempts to prompt him to work on those things. After receiving complaints from the thrift store manager about Roberto's disruptive behaviors, the transition specialist schedules a meeting with the job coach and special education teacher to put some interventions in place in the hopes that Roberto could continue with his job placement. The team uses the FBA Checklist for Difficulties Engaging in Nonpreferred Tasks during their discussion and makes the following predictions: Roberto does not want to vacuum the carpets due to his sensory processing problems. The noise of the vacuum cleaner may be causing discomfort. Roberto needs excessive verbal prompting from the job coach when using the register to ring up customers because of his executive functioning challenges, which makes the task quite aversive for Roberto. Finally, Roberto does have problems with fine motor skills that make it difficult for him to fold shirts. Thus, he avoids that task when it is assigned.*

Figure 11.2 includes the sections of the FBA Checklist that were checked off, the hypothesis that was written, and the intervention plan that was developed.

Challenging Behavior: Difficulties Engaging in Nonpreferred Tasks

3. Sensory Processing Problems

- ❒ 3a: Tasks that are considered nonpreferred do not provide the sensory input the student needs to stay engaged.
- ☑ 3b: Tasks that are considered nonpreferred cause sensory overload and discomfort.

4. Executive Functioning Challenges

- ☑ Tasks that are considered nonpreferred require multiple steps to plan out and complete.

6. Academic, Cognitive, or Motor Skills Deficits

- ❒ 6a: Tasks that are academically difficult are considered nonpreferred tasks.
- ☑ 6b: Tasks that involve fine or gross motor skills that are challenging for the student are considered nonpreferred tasks.

Hypothesis Statement Roberto engages in self-injurious behaviors and hits others when assigned non-preferred tasks at his job training placement at the thrift store. He does not prefer vacuuming the carpet due to the sensory discomfort he feels when hearing the loud noise. He gets upset and avoids folding shirts because he does not have the fine motor skills needed to be successful with the task. Finally, he will not comply when asked to ring up customers because he has executive functioning challenges that make it difficult for him to know what steps to complete. The excessive verbal prompting from the job coach during that task causes distress and self-injurious behaviors.

Intervention Plan

- Provide noise-cancelling headphones for Roberto to wear when he vacuums.
- Replace the folding shirts task with washing the window sills with a damp sponge (a task that is easier, considering this fine motor weakness).
- Use ***video prompting*** to teach Roberto how to follow the steps for ringing up a customer. Provide practice when customers are not in the store to avoid rushing him through the task and providing excessive verbal prompting. Post a visual ***task analysis*** that Roberto can follow as he rings up a customer. If he needs prompting, then the job coach should simply point to the next step and avoid giving verbal prompts.

Results

Roberto willingly wears the noise-cancelling headphones while vacuuming and completes the task with no challenging behaviors. He is able to comply with washing the window sills because it is a fairly easy motor task for him. He needed 5 days of training using the ***video prompting*** and ***task analysis*** intervention to learn how to ring up customers, and he is now able to do so without any prompting from the job coach.

Figure 11.2. Functional Behavior Assessment Checklist and intervention plan for Roberto.

Challenging Behavior: Difficulties Engaging in Nonpreferred Tasks

1. **Anxiety, Fear, and Emotional Regulation Difficulties**
   - ❐ The student primarily prefers tasks that follow a familiar pattern due to a need for sameness. Nonpreferred tasks are typically assignments that are unfamiliar or disrupt the typical routine.
2. **Social Skills Deficits**
   - ❐ Tasks are considered nonpreferred when they require using social skills the student has not yet acquired.
3. **Sensory Processing Problems**
   - ❐ 3a: Tasks that are considered nonpreferred do not provide the sensory input the student needs to stay engaged.
   - ❐ 3b: Tasks that are considered nonpreferred cause sensory overload and discomfort.
4. **Executive Functioning Challenges**
   - ❐ Tasks that are considered nonpreferred require multiple steps to plan out and complete.
5. **Restricted Range of Interests**
   - ❐ Nonpreferred tasks include those that are not related to the student's special interests.
6. **Academic, Cognitive, or Motor Skills Deficits**
   - ❐ 6a: Tasks that are academically difficult are considered nonpreferred tasks.
   - ❐ 6b: Tasks that involve fine or gross motor skills that are challenging for the student are considered nonpreferred tasks.

Other ____________________

____

____

____

____

Hypothesis Statement ____________________

____

____

____

____

CHAPTER 12

Transitions

Making the transition from one activity to another within the classroom or making the transition from one environment to another within the school can be an area of difficulty for students with ASD. Although the reasons why students with ASD demonstrate problems with transitions vary depending on each child's unique profile, some common characteristics associated with ASD explain why these students are challenged in this area. This chapter discusses eight challenges faced by students with ASD that may explain why they may struggle with transitions:

1. Language comprehension difficulties
2. Anxiety, fear, and emotional regulation difficulties
3. Social skills deficits
4. Sensory processing problems
5. Executive functioning challenges
6. Problems with focus and attention
7. Restricted range of interests
8. Academic, cognitive, or motor skills deficits

LANGUAGE COMPREHENSION DIFFICULTIES

Transitions, particularly within unfamiliar settings or contexts, can be problematic for students with ASD due to language comprehension difficulties.

Understanding the Problem

Students with ASD who have language comprehension difficulties may not follow transition directions because they do not understand the directions provided. Although they may understand some transition directions that are given on a regular basis or given using ***visual supports*** instead of relying on the student's auditory processing, unfamiliar transitions may contain language that the students have trouble comprehending if ***visual supports*** are not provided to support understanding.

Assessing the Problem

If you think language comprehension difficulties may be affecting your student's ability to make a transition, then check the box in Section 1 of the FBA Checklist for Difficulties with Transitions in the appendix at the end of this chapter: The student does not always understand the transition directions given. Give directions for transitions using ***visual supports*** and clear, concise, and consistent language to assess whether this may be the case for your student. If the student can comply with requests to make a transition with those supports provided but not when the directions are given verbally without such supports, then you can predict that language comprehension problems are affecting the student's problems with transitions.

Supporting the Student

Consider the following strategies and supports if your student is having trouble making a transition due to language comprehension problems:

- If the student can read, then provide written directions for transitions a minute or two in advance to allow the student time to read and process them. If the student cannot read, then give visual representations of the directions when possible.
- ***Use clear, consistent, and concise language*** when giving transition directions.
- Use any of the following strategies when directions cannot be given using simplified language or when the student has trouble even when language is simplified to support the student with understanding the expectation for transition:
    - ***Modeling/request imitation***
    - ***Most-to-least prompting/fading procedures***
    - ***Video modeling***

ANXIETY, FEAR, AND EMOTIONAL REGULATION DIFFICULTIES

Transitions can be anxiety-producing for many students with ASD for several reasons.

Understanding the Problem

Students with ASD may be worried about what activity is coming next either because they know what it is and they do not like it or they do not know what is coming next. They also may get anxious when they are asked to make a transition while they are in the middle of doing something that they really want to finish. If they are not able to cope with their anxiety and fear, then it can result in emotional dysregulation and the occurrence of challenging behaviors, including noncompliance, yelling, crying, or physical aggression.

Assessing the Problem

If you think anxiety, fear, and emotional regulation difficulties may be affecting your student's ability to make a transition, then complete Section 2 of the FBA Checklist for Difficulties with Transitions in the appendix at the end of this chapter. Following are some tips for assessing each item:

2a: The Student Experiences Heightened Levels of Anxiety and Fear When Faced With Transitions Because the Student Does Not Know Exactly What Is Coming Next

If you think this may be the case for your student, then create a ***visual schedule*** that the student uses to check off when each activity is finished and to see what is coming next. If this helps the student comply with transitions more willingly, then you can predict that anxiety and fear about not knowing what is coming next is the root of the problem with transitions.

2b: The Student Generally Has a Strong Desire to Finish Tasks Once They Are Started and Gets Emotionally Distressed if Asked to Stop an Unfinished Task or Activity to Make a Transition to Something Else

Examine the student's ability to make a transition during times when a transition direction is given and the student is not working on any other assignment. Compare the student's ability to handle transitions at these times with times when the student is asked to make a transition while he or she is focused on an activity that is not finished. If the student can make a transition if he or she is not trying to finish an activity, then you can predict that heightened levels of anxiety when the student is unable to finish an assignment before making a transition are causing the difficulties.

Supporting the Student

Consider the following strategies and supports if anxiety, fear, and emotional regulation difficulties are affecting your student's ability to make a transition:

- Give the student a 5-minute warning and 2-minute warning before giving the final direction to make a transition. It may also be helpful to use a visual timer. Do not implement either of these approaches if the student's anxiety increases.
- Support the student with finishing an assignment before announcing the transition direction if possible.
- Create a folder that the student can use for unfinished work, and let the student know when the work can be finished (e.g., put a sticky note on the assignment that says something such as, "I will finish this when I get back from lunch"). See Figure 4.3 for an example.
- Create and explicitly teach the student how to use a personal ***visual schedule*** to help the student understand what is coming next. See Figure 12.1 for sample ***visual schedules.***

SOCIAL SKILLS DEFICITS

Social skills deficits in joint attention can sometimes prevent students with ASD from understanding and, therefore, following a direction to make a transition.

Understanding the Problem

Although it may look like pure noncompliance when students with ASD do not follow transition directions, it could be that they did not even know that you gave a direction due to their joint attention deficits. Students who have significant impairments in joint attention are usually unable to respond to verbal directions that are given to the whole class. You may think that they are able to comply because they may respond some of the time. Yet, their

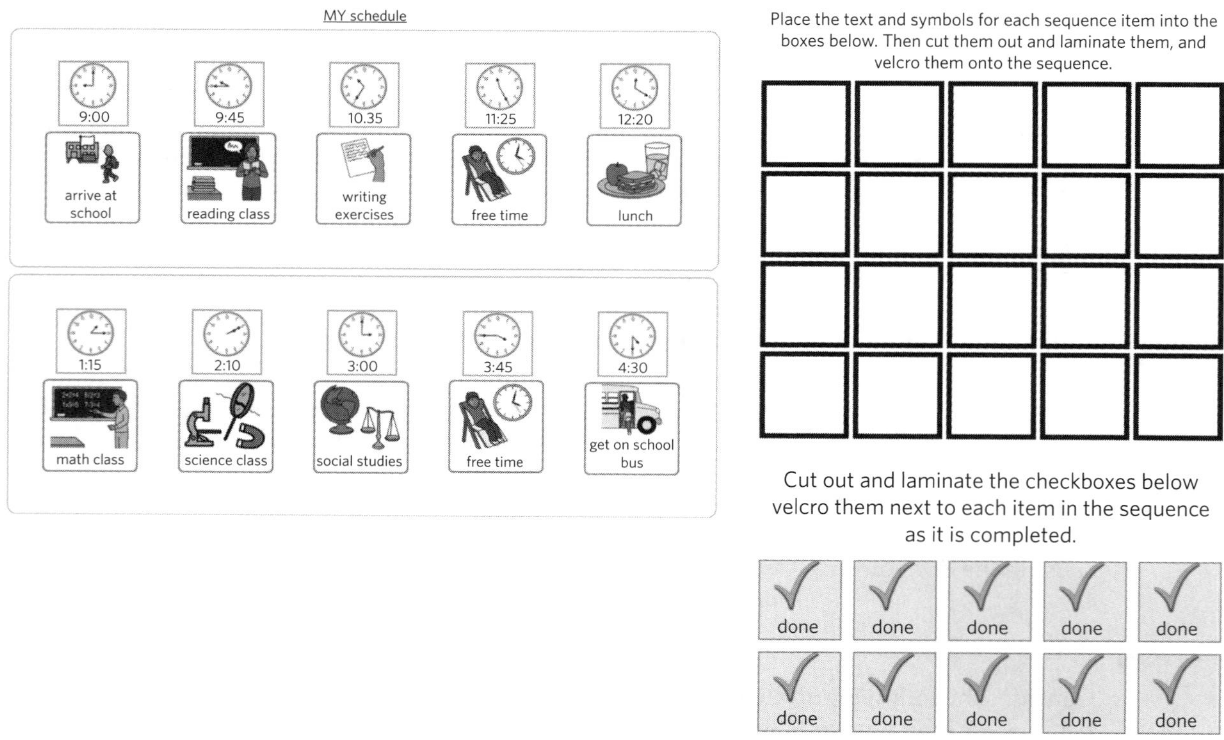

Figure 12.1. Examples of visual schedules.

successful responses usually occur because they have learned the routine, not because they are processing the verbal directions.

Assessing the Problem

If you think social skills deficits (i.e., joint attention impairments) may be affecting your student's ability to make a transition, then complete Section 3 of the FBA Checklist for Difficulties with Transitions in the appendix at the end of this chapter: The student does not follow directions to make a transition when the teacher does not establish joint attention with the student prior to giving the direction. Get eye level and face to face with the student before giving a transition direction to determine whether this may be the problem for your student. Give the transition direction once you have the student's attention. If the student can comply when joint attention is established prior to giving the transition direction, then you can predict that joint attention impairments are affecting the student's difficulties with transitions.

Supporting the Student

Consider the following strategies and supports if joint attention deficits are affecting your student's ability to make a transition:

- Teach the student to respond to his or her name so that you can call the student's name to establish joint attention prior to giving a transition direction. You may or may not know that failure to respond to hearing one's name is one of the red flags for ASD because this is a skill that often needs to be explicitly taught to students who have severe joint attention impairments.

- Use the following ***shaping*** procedures to systematically teach the student to respond to transition directions given to the whole class. Stay at each step until the student is successful without prompting:

    1. Give the transition direction face to face and at eye level, making sure you establish joint attention before giving the direction. Use ***prompting/fading procedures*** as necessary. Provide ***positive reinforcement*** when the student complies.
    2. Stand next to the student, call the student's name, and give the transition direction once joint attention is established. Use ***prompting/fading procedures*** as necessary. Provide ***positive reinforcement*** when the student complies.
    3. Stand about 2 feet away from the student, call the student's name, and give the transition direction once joint attention is established. Use ***prompting/fading procedures*** as necessary. Provide ***positive reinforcement*** when the student complies.
    4. Call the student's name from any location in the classroom, and give the transition direction once joint attention is established. Use ***prompting/fading procedures*** as necessary. Provide ***positive reinforcement*** when the student complies.
    5. Revisit Step 2 after the student is successful with Step 4, but do not call the student's name to establish joint attention. Instead, give a natural cue that lets all students know you are about to give a transition direction (e.g., "All eyes on me." "Everybody stop and listen").

SENSORY PROCESSING PROBLEMS

If your student has sensory processing problems or sensory integration dysfunction, then it is always important to consider if challenging behavior may be related to his or her sensory differences; transitions are no exception.

Understanding the Problem

A student may not follow directions to make a transition to the next activity if the transition routine itself causes sensory overload or if the upcoming activity causes sensory discomfort in some way. For example, some students will demonstrate challenging behavior when told to line up to go to music because of the overload of stimuli they experience in that environment (e.g., singing, playing instruments, moving to the songs). Other students may try to avoid going to art if the materials used cause sensory aversions (e.g., finger paints, acrylic crayons, molding clay).

Assessing the Problem

If you think sensory processing problems may be affecting your student's abilities to make a transition, then check the box in Section 4 of the FBA Checklist for Difficulties with Transitions in the appendix at the end of this chapter: The student tries to avoid going to an activity or location that causes physical discomfort or pain due to sensory processing problems. You need to be fully aware of the student's sensory profile as far as what things cause sensory overload. Write down the transition directions with which the student does not usually comply. Determine if many or most items listed involve the transition to an activity or environment that involves negative sensory experiences for the student.

Supporting the Student

Consider the following strategies and supports if sensory processing issues are causing problems with your student's ability to make a transition:

- Make environmental modifications to respond to the student's sensory needs (e.g., alter the materials used in art, provide headphones for the student to wear during music to minimize the auditory stimuli).
- Teach the student functional communication skills to express the need for a break when feeling overwhelmed or make requests to get his or her sensory needs met (e.g., "May I shut off the lights?").

EXECUTIVE FUNCTIONING CHALLENGES

Complex transition directions may be particularly difficult for students with ASD who have executive functioning challenges.

Understanding the Problem

Some transition directions require that students follow multiple steps in sequential order, and they must do so rather quickly. Students who have executive functioning challenges may be unable to do so. This is even more of an issue when teachers give unfamiliar multistep directions as they are rushing to finish up an activity and make a transition to another. They may talk fast and not necessarily use concise, clear language, which may also increase the difficulty for students with ASD.

Assessing the Problem

If you think executive functioning challenges may be affecting your student's ability to make a transition, then check the box in Section 5 of the FBA Checklist for Difficulties with Transitions in the appendix at the end of this chapter: The student has difficulty with transitions that require the student to plan and execute a sequence of steps. Give only simple, one-step directions, and document the student's level of success. Then give the typical transition directions that may include multiple steps. Compare the student's compliance in each circumstance to determine if the student can comply with simple transition requests but not complex requests that require more advanced executive functioning skills.

Supporting the Student

Consider the following strategies and supports if executive functioning challenges are affecting your student's ability to make a transition:

- Use ***task analysis*** by breaking down transition directions that have multiple steps into sequential one-step directions.
- Use ***visual supports*** to present the steps of the transition direction using ***pictures,*** words, phrases, or sentences.
- Use ***forward chaining*** to teach the student how to use the ***task analysis*** to follow the transition direction.
- Create a ***self-monitoring*** tool the student can use to check off each step of the transition direction as it is completed.

- Use ***video modeling, video self-modeling, point-of-view video modeling,*** or ***video prompting*** to help the student see and remember the different parts of a transition direction that is given at least once a day.

PROBLEMS WITH FOCUS AND ATTENTION

The ways in which students with ASD focus on tasks and shift attention between tasks may pose particular challenges at transition times.

Understanding the Problem

Many students with ASD have difficulty shifting their attention (see Chapter 1). They do not easily stop what they are attending to in order to respond to a direction to do something different because of their intense focus on their current activity. Thus, what may look like a compliance problem is purely an issue associated with this particular ASD characteristic.

Assessing the Problem

If you think problems with shifting attention may be affecting your student's ability to make a transition, then check the box in Section 6 of the FBA Checklist for Difficulties with Transitions in the appendix at the end of this chapter: The student is unable to simply stop engaging in a particular task in which he or she is focused to make a transition to another task or location due to difficulties with shifting attention. Note all of the transitions in which the student does not successfully comply, indicating if the student was or was not focused on another activity at the time the direction was given. Also note the following: Did the student pause or stop to listen to the transition direction? Did the student look away from the task that was being worked on to attend to the transition direction? Did the student's facial expression change when the transition direction was given, or did the student simply maintain focus on the task at hand?

Supporting the Student

Consider the following strategies and supports if focus and attention problems are affecting your student's ability to make a transition:

- Make sure the student is not still focused on a specific task when giving transition directions, which may mean supporting the student in finishing a task prior to giving the transition direction.
- Establish joint attention with the student prior to giving the transition direction.
- Give the transition direction in writing or use ***pictures*** if the student does not read.
- Use environmental cues when preparing to give a transition direction (e.g., ring a bell, turn the lights off and on, clap three times and have the students imitate the clapping).

RESTRICTED RANGE OF INTERESTS

Students with ASD who have a very restricted range of interests can have a difficult time shifting gears and making a transition between activities, especially when they must stop engaging in a highly desired activity.

Understanding the Problem

Teachers may get the most frustrated when students with ASD have challenging behaviors when they are expected to stop a desired activity to make a transition to an undesired activity. They may view this is the child being spoiled and controlling. That is not the case, however, when you consider the restricted range of interests of many students with ASD. If they have intense fascinations and passions and get involved in a task related to one of these, then it is extremely difficult for them to willingly stop the activity, especially when the request is to make a transition to something that is difficult or aversive in some way. It would be like telling someone who loves sweets to stop eating a cupcake and eat some broccoli.

Assessing the Problem

If you think your student's restricted range of interests may be affecting the child's ability to make a transition, then check the box in Section 7 of the FBA Checklist for Difficulties with Transitions in the appendix at the end of this chapter: The student has difficulty making a transition when moving from a highly desired activity related to his or her interests and passions to an undesirable activity. Make a list of your student's special interests. Then take note of the transitions in which the student has trouble successfully complying. Indicate how many involve going from an interest-based activity to a nonpreferred activity to determine if the student's restricted range of interests may be the issue.

Supporting the Student

Consider the following supports and strategies if the student's restricted range of interests is affecting compliance with transition directions:

- Increase the proportion of instructional activities that are based on the student's interests.
- Allow the student to use materials related to special interests while completing nonpreferred activities to increase motivation to make a transition. It may be helpful to give the student a transition object to support the student during the transition (e.g., if the student will be able to use dinosaur pencils at the writing center, then give the student a dinosaur pencil to hold during the transition to that center).
- Use transition objects related to the student's special interests that provide comfort when making a transition to undesired activities (e.g., the student can bring an Incredible Hulk figurine to reading group).
- Use flexible scheduling so that highly preferred activities come after nonpreferred activities as opposed to the other way around. The activities that come immediately after highly preferred activities should still be preferred in some way or, at the least, not highly nonpreferred activities. For example, after using a tablet to play a math facts game (highly preferred), the student makes the transition to lunch (preferred).

ACADEMIC, COGNITIVE, OR MOTOR SKILLS DEFICITS

Academic, cognitive, or motor skills deficits can affect a student's ability to make a transition to activities that call on skills they struggle to apply.

Understanding the Problem

Students with ASD who have academic, cognitive, or motor skills deficits may have problems with transitions when they are asked to make a transition to an activity that involves tasks that are extremely difficult for the student. For example, although a student may be able to solve basic multiplication facts, solving two-digit times two-digit multiplication problems is very challenging. If the teacher does not accommodate for this deficit, then the student may not successfully make the transition to small-group math to avoid facing the difficult work. Students who have fine motor deficits may avoid making a transition to activities that require writing. Making a transition to physical education class may be problematic for those students who have gross motor skills impairments.

Assessing the Problem

If you think academic, cognitive, or motor skills deficits may be affecting your student's ability to make a transition, then complete Section 8 of the FBA Checklist for Difficulties with Transitions in the appendix at the end of this chapter. Following are some tips for assessing each item:

8a: The Student Has Trouble Making a Transition to a Task That Is Academically Difficult

Have a clear understanding of the student's present levels of academic performance. Then note which transitions the student tries to avoid to determine if this avoidance may occur when they are asked to make a transition to tasks that are academically difficult.

8b: The Student Has Difficulty Making a Transition to Tasks That Require Using Fine Motor Skills

If the student has fine motor skills impairments, then consider if the student's transition problems occur when asked to make a transition to activities that require handwriting, drawing, cutting, or other fine motor tasks that may be difficult for the student.

8c: The Student Has Difficulty Making a Transition to Tasks That Require Using Gross Motor Skills

If the student has trouble with gross motor skills, such as jumping, throwing a ball back and forth, or kicking a ball, then playing team sports or other games in physical education classes may be very challenging for the student. Thus, the student may try to avoid making a transition to those classes.

Supporting the Student

Consider the following strategies and supports if academic, cognitive, or motor skills deficits are causing transition problems for your student:

- Use differentiated instruction practices to adjust activities the student is having trouble making a transition to, making sure they involve the appropriate level of challenge.
- Increase the use of explicit instruction when teaching new academic skills.
- Utilize AT to support the student's fine and gross motor needs.

From Assessment to Successful Intervention

Case Study: Nicholas *Nicholas is a third-grade student with ASD who has problems making the transition to the cafeteria. Although he lines up nicely when the teacher gives the instruction to line up for lunch and follows the rules for walking in line, problems begin when the class gets close to the cafeteria. Nicholas begins making loud stereotypic vocalizations and may try to run in the opposite direction before the class enters the cafeteria. When he does enter the cafeteria, he pushes other children while waiting in line, grabs items that are within reach (e.g., grabbing several milk cartons instead of selecting just one), screams, and engages in self-injurious behaviors. Nicholas often runs around the cafeteria after he gets his food, and sometimes he attempts to take his clothes off while running around the cafeteria.*

After 2 months of trying to deal with these issues, his teacher consults with the ASD specialist to seek some advice. They review the FBA Checklist for Difficulties with Transitions to attempt to pinpoint why Nicholas is having trouble making the transition to the cafeteria. They hypothesize that Nicholas is experiencing sensory overload in the cafeteria, and this is affecting the avoidance behaviors when he nears the cafeteria and the significant challenging behaviors once he enters the cafeteria. They also predict that his challenges with executive functioning makes it very difficult to learn the routine for going through the cafeteria line.

See Figure 12.2 for the sections of the FBA Checklist that they checked off, the hypothesis statement that was written, and the intervention plan that was put in place.

Challenging Behavior: Difficulties With Transitions

4. Sensory Processing Problems

☑ The student tries to avoid going to an activity or location that causes physical discomfort or pain due to sensory processing problems.

5. Executive Functioning Challenges

☑ The student has difficulty with transitions that require the student to plan and execute a sequence of steps.

Hypothesis Statement Nicholas has trouble making the transition to the cafeteria, going through the cafeteria line, and making the transition from the cafeteria line to the table because of sensory processing problems. The smells, noise, fluorescent lighting, and excessive movement cause severe sensory overload. In addition, Nicholas has not yet developed the controlled motor planning and executive functioning skills needed to wait in the cafeteria line, move slowly through the line, select the appropriate items at the appropriate times, and check out with the cashier. The excessive prompting Nicholas receives during this activity is adding more sensory stimuli to process, causing even more frustration and discomfort.

Intervention Plan

- Phase 1
  - Use a ***social narrative*** and ***video modeling*** to teach Nicholas the routine for getting his lunch.
  - Create a visual ***task analysis*** that shows the steps of the routine that Nicholas will hold as he walks to the cafeteria to remind himself of the steps he learned.
  - Practice the routine when no other students are in the cafeteria.
  - Allow Nicholas to skip waiting in the line when he gets to the cafeteria to avoid sensory overload prior to getting to the food selection process.
  - Use the visual ***task analysis*** to prompt when necessary instead of giving verbal prompts.
  - Provide noise-cancelling headphones when Nicholas is about to enter the cafeteria.
  - Allow Nicholas to return to the classroom to eat his lunch.
- Phase 2
  - After Nicholas is successful during Phase 1, have him wait in line with just two or three students in front of him.
- Phase 3
  - After Nicholas is successful during Phase 2, have him wait in line with four or five students in front of him.
  - Add intervention procedures to the ***social narrative, video modeling,*** and visual ***task analysis*** for going to the table and eating lunch. Prompt when necessary using the visual ***task analysis.***
  - Allow Nicholas to leave the cafeteria immediately after he is finished eating his lunch.
- Phase 4
  - After Nicholas is successful during Phase 3, have him wait in line like other students.
  - Provide a choice of activities that Nicholas can do after he finishes eating until the class lines up to leave the cafeteria (e.g., listen to music, draw, read a book, play with Legos)

Results

It took 5 weeks for Nicholas to make the transition comfortably and be independent during Phase 1. After experiencing that success, however, he progressed through the next three phases much more quickly; each phase took about 1 week for Nicholas to achieve success. Thus, Nicholas could make the transition to the cafeteria, wait in line, get his food, and eat at a table without engaging in severe challenging behavior within approximately 2 months. He still may engage in stereotypic verbalizations to cope with all the sensory stimuli, but the teacher understands that he needs that outlet and does not consider that a problem to address.

Figure 12.2. Functional Behavior Assessment Checklist and intervention plan for Nicholas.

From Assessment to Successful Intervention

Case Study: Jack *Jack is a sixth-grade student who is having problems with the transition to middle school when it comes to switching classes and managing the starts and stops of working on assignments. His elementary school teacher always allowed him to finish academic tasks before he made a transition to a new activity because of the anxiety he would feel and challenging behaviors he would display when asked to stop something before it was finished. His teachers at the middle school typically allow the students time at the end of class to get started on their homework, with the assumption that they will finish at home if they do not get it completed. Jack screams and gets extremely upset every time the bell rings because he does not have time to finish his work. If the teacher attempts to get him to make a transition to the next class, then he has a meltdown or engages in aggressive behaviors because of his emotional regulation difficulties.*

His special education teacher meets with the team of general education teachers to discuss the problem and come up with an intervention plan. The team looks at the FBA Checklist for Difficulties with Transitions and agrees that the transition problems are primarily related to Jack's anxiety and emotional regulation problems. They also feel, however, that Jack does not fully understand the expectations for starting homework assignments and finishing them at home. Although that was verbally stated at the beginning of the year, he may not have been paying attention when that was stated or he may have needed a much more thorough explanation and supports to learn that process. Thus, he gets very upset when he does not have time to finish his homework, thinking that he should be able to complete it.

Figure 12.3 shows the sections of the FBA Checklist that were checked off, the hypothesis statement that was written, and the intervention plan that was put in place.

Challenging Behavior: Difficulties With Transitions

2. Anxiety, Fear, and Emotional Regulation Difficulties

- ❒ 2a: The student experiences heightened levels of anxiety and fear when faced with transitions because the student does not know exactly what is coming next.
- ☑ 2b: The student generally has a strong desire to finish tasks once they are started and gets emotionally distressed if asked to stop an unfinished task or activity to make a transition to something else.

Other Jack did not learn the hidden curriculum related to starting homework assignments at the end of class and finishing them at home. Thus, he got very upset, thinking he was supposed to finish the assignments before the end of class.

Hypothesis Statement Jack has trouble making a transition from one class to another when he starts a homework assignment and does not have time to finish it. This causes heightened levels of anxiety, which he has trouble regulating. Thus, he may get emotionally dysregulated and engage in verbal or physical aggression when prompted to make a transition to the next class. Jack may not understand this new middle school routine and expectation for starting assignments and finishing them at home because this is not something he did in elementary school. Therefore, he may feel that he is failing to meet expectations when he does not get the assignments completed before the bell rings.

Intervention Plan

- Explicitly teach Jack the expectations related to starting homework assignments at the end of class and finishing them for homework. Do this during a meeting involving his parents so he will not feel anxious about coming home with homework and will have the necessary support to remember to complete each assignment.
- Use ***priming*** prior to giving a homework assignment to remind Jack that he may or may not have time to finish it before the bell rings.
- Create homework folders that Jack can use for each class. When ***priming*** is used, have Jack get his homework folder out as an additional reminder to put the unfinished work inside when the bell rings so he can finish it at home.
- Give Jack the choice of starting the homework assignment or completing the entire assignment for homework if starting and stopping is too anxiety producing for him. If he has enough time to finish, then he may choose to do the assignment in class. If not, then he can choose an alternative activity instead of starting an assignment he will not have time to finish.
- If Jack is almost finished with an assignment when the bell rings, then teach him that it is okay to ask for a couple of minutes to finish before making a transition to the next class. If he asks appropriately, then allow him to finish, accommodating for his anxiety and emotional regulation difficulties.

Results

Jack has responded very well to the intervention plan. He makes the choice whether to start the homework assignment or do an alternate activity. There have been several occasions when he asked for a couple of minutes to finish his assignment before going to the next class. On the most recent occasion, he asked for and was granted more time but then decided to go ahead and go to the next class and finish the work later. This shows that Jack is learning to be less anxious when homework assignments are not completed in class.

Figure 12.3. Functional Behavior Assessment Checklist and intervention plan for Jack.

Challenging Behavior: Difficulties With Transitions

1. Language Comprehension Difficulties

- ❒ The student does not always understand the transition directions given.

2. Anxiety, Fear, and Emotional Regulation Difficulties

- ❒ 2a: The student experiences heightened levels of anxiety and fear when faced with transitions because the student does not know exactly what is coming next.
- ❒ 2b: The student generally has a strong desire to finish tasks once they are started and gets emotionally distressed if asked to stop an unfinished task or activity to make a transition to something else.

3. Social Skills Deficits

- ❒ The student does not follow directions to make a transition when the teacher does not establish joint attention with the student prior to giving the direction.

4. Sensory Processing Problems

- ❒ The student tries to avoid going to an activity or location that causes physical discomfort or pain due to sensory processing problems.

5. Executive Functioning Challenges

- ❒ The student has difficulty with transitions that require the student to plan and execute a sequence of steps.

6. Problems With Focus and Attention

- ❒ The student is unable to simply stop engaging in a particular task in which he or she is focused to make a transition to another task or location due to difficulties with shifting attention.

7. Restricted Range of Interests

- ❒ The student has difficulty making a transition when moving from a highly desired activity related to his or her interests and passions to an undesirable activity.

8. Academic, Cognitive, or Motor Skills Deficits

- ❒ 8a: The student has trouble making a transition to a task that is academically difficult.
- ❒ 8b: The student has difficulty making a transition to tasks that require using fine motor skills.
- ❒ 8c: The student has difficulty making a transition to tasks that require using gross motor skills.

Other ____

____

____

____

Hypothesis Statement ____

____

____

____

CHAPTER 13

Shouting Out

Students who shout out in classrooms can be quite distracting to other students and disruptive to the instruction taking place. The shouting-out behaviors of students with ASD may include yelling out negative comments about the lesson or assignment, yelling at peers, blurting out questions in a loud voice, or verbal repetitive behaviors such as shouting out repetitive sounds, phrases, things they have heard others say, or lines from commercials, television shows, or movies. This chapter discusses four main challenges faced by students with ASD that may explain why they shout out:

1. Social skills deficits
2. Anxiety, fear, and emotional regulation difficulties
3. Sensory processing problems
4. Academic, cognitive, or motor skills deficits

SOCIAL SKILLS DEFICITS

Students with ASD may shout out during class for several reasons that are related to different kinds of social skills deficits.

Understanding the Problem

Students with ASD may shout out during group instruction if they have not yet learned the social rules for raising one's hand and waiting to be called on by the teacher. You may think this is a simple behavioral expectation that is presented as early as preschool and kindergarten, so students with ASD should not require intensive instruction each year to learn the expectations. Teachers usually allow students to shout out some of the time, however, depending on the lesson or activity. It can be confusing for students who have trouble learning the hidden curriculum to know when it is acceptable to shout out and when it is important to raise your hand and wait to be called on by the teacher.

Other students with ASD may shout out to get attention (positive or negative) from the teacher. They may enjoy the predictable negative responses they receive from teachers when they shout out because of their need for sameness. Likewise, if the teacher positively responds to the student's comments or questions without correcting the shouting-out behaviors, then the shouting-out behaviors are getting positively reinforced by the teacher's response each time.

Because students with ASD often have a limited quantity and quality of positive social interactions with peers, they may look for ways to get negative attention from peers by shouting out things to peers or about peers that evoke a consistent response each time. For example, the student may shout out negative comments about another student's behavior or work to get a response back such as, "I did not!" "It is not!" or "Stop it!" Shouting out can also result in positive attention from peers. If the peers laugh when the student shouts out, then that can be very reinforcing for the student because it is an easy way to initiate positive interactions with peers.

Students with ASD who have significant impairments in joint attention and social reciprocity may shout out when they are disengaged during instructional activities. This type of shouting-out behavior usually consists of repetitive verbal behaviors used to regulate themselves as opposed to functional communication.

Assessing the Problem

If you think social skills deficits may be affecting your student's shouting-out behaviors, then complete Section 1 of the FBA Checklist for Shouting Out in the appendix at the end of this chapter. Following are some tips for assessing each item:

1a: The Student Has Not Learned the Social Expectations for Raising One's Hand

Take the time to explicitly teach the expectations for hand raising and waiting to be called on to assess whether this is the case for your student. If the student's shouting-out behavior decreases after doing so, then you can predict that the student shouts out because the appropriate hand-raising behavior has not yet been fully learned.

1b: The Student Lacks the Social Skills to Recognize Appropriate and Inappropriate Times to Shout Out

If your student may be confused about when it is acceptable and unacceptable to shout out, then make sure that you set the expectation that students must raise their hands and wait to be called on at the onset of each and every activity in which hand raising is required. If the student's shouting-out behaviors decrease, then you can predict that the student needs more support to know when it is and is not okay to shout out.

1c: The Student Shouts Out to Get Positive or Negative Attention From Teachers

Collect A-B-C data each time the student shouts out and look for patterns of responses from teachers (see Chapter 3).

1d: The Student Shouts Out to Get Positive or Negative Attention From Peers

Assess the A-B-C data and analyze it to determine if there are patterns in regard to peer responses.

1e: The Student Shouts Out When Disengaged Due to Deficits in Joint Attention and Social Reciprocity

Use A-B-C data, but examine the setting events and antecedents to determine if there is a pattern of limited opportunities for engagement and interaction before the shouting-out behaviors occur.

Supporting the Student

Consider the following strategies and supports if social skills deficits are affecting your student's shouting-out behaviors:

- Use explicit instruction to teach the expectations for raising one's hand and waiting to be called on by the teacher.
- Use ***social narratives*** or ***video modeling*** to support the student's learning during the explicit instruction of expectations for hand raising. Make sure you include when it is required and when it is not required for students to raise their hands.
- Use ***self-monitoring*** to provide a visual reminder of the expectation for hand raising and a place where the student can place a tally mark each time the expectation is met.
- Deliver ***positive reinforcement*** when the student raises his or her hand and waits to be called on or when the student remains quiet during group instruction or independent work.
- Use ***peer-mediated interventions*** to teach peers not to respond to the shouting-out behaviors. It is equally important to also teach them ways to have more positive social interactions with the student to fulfill the student's need for peer attention in a positive manner.
- If the student shouts out, then the teacher should positively redirect the student by using the following ***least-to-most prompts*** hierarchy:
  1. Give a visual prompt (e.g., point to a ***picture*** of hand raising or ***cue card*** that says, "Raise your hand").
  2. Give a gestural prompt (e.g., put a finger on your lips, begin to slightly raise your hand as a cue for the student to raise hand).
  3. Give a verbal prompt (e.g., say, "Please raise your hand").
  4. Use ***modeling/request imitation*** (e.g., raise your hand and have the student imitate).
  5. Make sure you implement ***positive reinforcement*** when the student corrects the shouting-out behavior and raises his or her hand.
- If a student is shouting out as a form of verbal repetitive behaviors due to disengagement, then attempt to increase the active engagement of the student in the lesson or activity.

ANXIETY, FEAR, AND EMOTIONAL REGULATION DIFFICULTIES

Anxiety, fear, or other strong emotions can be at the root of shouting-out behaviors for some students with ASD.

Understanding the Problem

Shouting-out behaviors can increase as a student's anxiety and fear increases. The student may shout out things such as, "This is stupid!" "I'm not doing this!" or simply "No!" when he or she gets anxious or fearful about a specific activity. Also, if the student is having trouble regulating his or her emotions, then the student may shout out as a means of coping with excessive feelings of frustration, sadness, or anger.

Assessing the Problem

If you think anxiety, fear, and emotional regulation difficulties may be affecting your student's shouting-out behaviors, then complete Section 2 of the FBA Checklist for Shouting Out in the appendix at the end of this chapter. Following are some tips for assessing each item:

2a: The Student Shouts Out When Feeling Anxious or Fearful

Collect A-B-C data each time the student shouts out. Analyze the antecedents to determine patterns that may lead you to predict that the student shouts out when certain environmental factors increase the student's levels of anxiety and fear. It is important to know ahead of time, however, what typically causes the student to feel worried, anxious, or fearful. You can find this out by asking the student, family members, and other professionals and by observing the student.

2b: The Student Shouts Out When Emotionally Dysregulated

It would be helpful if the student had an effective means of communicating how he or she feels for you to accurately assess this item. Students with ASD often have a difficult time communicating their feelings, but it is essential because many of these children have emotional regulation difficulties that require intervention. Although they may find it challenging to communicate their emotions, people do not necessarily ask them how they are feeling very often. If asking these students to identify their emotions becomes a regular part of their interactions with teachers, then teachers may find that students are able to learn to do so without much effort.

Of course, you will need to provide ***visual supports*** and examples for each of the emotions to initially teach the students the difference between the various feelings. Discussing examples from their everyday experiences is very important. Many professionals focus on teaching emotions using cards that show different faces representing different feelings. It is important to focus on what types of situations make students with ASD feel certain ways as opposed to relying on commercially prepared emotions flash cards, posters, or picture books because it is well documented that they do not recognize different emotional expressions on faces the same way as typically developing children (Evers, Steyaert, Noens, & Wagemans, 2015; Kessels, Spee, & Hendriks, 2010; Smith, Montagne, Perrett, Gill, & Gallagher, 2010; Uljarevic & Hamilton, 2013). Teaching emotions using rating scales (e.g., The Incredible 5-Point Scale [Buron & Curtis, 2003]) allows teachers to connect emotions to something the student relates to (e.g., a special interest). For example, a student who loves dogs can choose ***pictures*** of different breeds of dogs to represent their different levels of emotion. You can also categorize emotions. For instance, a golden retriever may represent emotions such as feeling happy, calm, comfortable, content, or relaxed. Once the student can share how he or she is feeling at various times of the school day, you can begin to find patterns related to what types of routines and activities may cause emotional dysregulation that leads to shouting-out behaviors.

Supporting the Student

Consider the following strategies and supports if anxiety, fear, and emotional regulation difficulties are affecting your student's shouting-out behaviors:

- Use ***emotional regulation strategies*** such as breathing exercises, calming activities (e.g., physical activities, easy academic tasks, visiting with a preferred adult in the school, listening to music, drawing), and cognitive behavioral techniques (e.g., the student says, "I am okay. This will not hurt me" to him- or herself to regulate feelings of fear).
- Teach the student how to ask for a break to engage in a calming activity.
- Provide ***visual supports*** that support students in identifying their emotions as well as asking for a break when necessary.
- Use ***social narratives*** to teach the student the idea that everyone has feelings, the importance of sharing your feelings with others, and strategies that can be used to deal with different feelings.

- Use antecedent-based interventions to alter the environment to reduce the student's anxiety and fear whenever possible.
- Give the student more choices to help him or her feel more in control of the environment and less anxious and fearful.

SENSORY PROCESSING PROBLEMS

Shouting-out behaviors can occur due to sensory processing problems that cause students to experience sensory overload or insufficient sensory input, especially if students are unable to use functional communication skills to communicate the problem.

Understanding the Problem

If students with ASD are experiencing sensory processing problems, then they may shout out as a result of their discomfort, need for input, or pain. They may be unable to use more advanced communication skills due to their distressed state when they experience severe sensory overload. Thus, even students who have functional communication skills may shout out inappropriately instead of calmly making requests to get their needs met. Students who do not have functional expressive communication skills often resort to shouting out to let others know they are uncomfortable or attempt to cope during times when there is too much or too little sensory stimuli.

Assessing the Problem

If you think sensory processing problems may be affecting your student's abilities shouting-out behaviors, then complete Section 3 of the FBA Checklist for Shouting Out in the appendix at the end of this chapter. Following are some tips for assessing each item:

3a: The Student Shouts Out When Experiencing Sensory Overload

Use A-B-C data each time the student shouts out. Analyze the antecedents to determine if there may be too much sensory stimuli in the environment each time or most times that the student shouts out.

3b: The Student Shouts Out When Needing Sensory Input

You should also use A-B-C data to assess this; however, you will examine the antecedents to determine if the student may shout out most frequently when unable to get sensory input (e.g., when the student is expected to sit down, be still, be quiet, wait).

Supporting the Student

Consider the following strategies and supports if your student is shouting out because of sensory processing problems:

- Make environmental modifications to respond to the student's sensory needs (e.g., decrease sensory stimuli or increase sensory input, depending on the student's profile).
- Teach the student functional communication skills to express the need for a break when feeling overwhelmed or make requests to get his or her sensory needs met (e.g., "May I jump on the trampoline?").

ACADEMIC, COGNITIVE, OR MOTOR SKILLS DEFICITS

Shouting-out behaviors may occur due to frustration with tasks students with ASD have trouble completing due to particular skills deficits.

Understanding the Problem

Students may get extremely frustrated when they are continually given assignments that are too difficult for them, resulting in challenging behaviors such as shouting out. It is often challenging for teachers to know what types of academic activities are appropriate for students with ASD because they often have significant deficits as well as strengths in one academic area. For example, they may have deficits in reading comprehension and great strengths in reading fluency. Thus, it becomes challenging to assign reading activities when there is a huge gap between the student's ability to decode words and his or her ability to comprehend what is being read. The same is true for math: they may have difficulties with solving word problems but perform above grade level with computation skills. Careful consideration of what is included in their assignments is necessary to ensure appropriate levels of challenge.

In addition, it is important to consider different ways that students can learn and demonstrate what they have learned as opposed to differentiating what they are learning and what is being assessed. For instance, it is hard to believe that students with ASD do not comprehend what they are reading because so many of them enjoy the act of reading. The real problem may be the way that teachers assess comprehension. Students are often asked open-ended or multiple-choice questions after they finish reading a selection, which is not always the best way to find out what they actually understand because of their language impairments. Instead, reading comprehension may be assessed by asking students to draw ***pictures*** after they complete a reading selection or giving them opportunities to pause and draw to allow time for processing during the reading activity. They can also demonstrate comprehension by acting out scenes, writing lists of key words and phrases, putting events in order with sentence strips or ***pictures,*** and so forth. Your student's shouting out and other challenging behaviors decrease when you differentiate your assessments, and you can get a more accurate account of the student's abilities.

Assessing the Problem

If you think academic, cognitive, or motor skills deficits may be affecting your student's shouting-out behaviors, then complete Section 4 of the FBA Checklist for Shouting Out in the appendix at the end of this chapter. Following are some tips for assessing each item:

4a: The Student Shouts Out When Frustrated With Academic Work That Is Too Difficult

Keep a record of the particular academic assignments the student is working on when shouting-out behaviors occur. Then examine whether those assignments are appropriately matched to the student's present levels of academic performance or cognitive skills.

4b: The Student Shouts Out When the Fine Motor or Gross Motor Skills Required for a Particular Activity Are Too Difficult

Be sure to consult with the student's occupational or physical therapist to get a clear understanding of the fine and gross motor skills the student has and has not mastered. Then determine if the student may have increased shouting-out behaviors when the tasks are not appropriate to child's motor needs.

Supporting the Student

Consider the following strategies and supports if academic, cognitive, or motor skills deficits are causing your student to engage in shouting-out behaviors:

- Use differentiated instruction practices to ensure activities are appropriately challenging based on the student's varying performance across different academic areas.
- Increase the use of explicit instruction when teaching new academic skills.
- Utilize AT to support the student's fine and gross motor needs.

From Assessment to Successful Intervention

Case Study: Edward *Edward is a kindergarten student with ASD who shouts out many times throughout the school day, specifically during transitions and down time. His shouting-out behaviors usually consist of yelling out reprimands that he has heard his teacher say. For instance, he may shout out, "Amanda, you need to go to time-out!" Then Amanda may say, "I do not!" because she was not doing anything wrong. Then Edward gets a smirk on his face or laughs. Things like this happen four or five times a day on average. The ASD specialist, Mrs. Harris, met with Edward's teacher, Mrs. Logan, to discuss the problem. After listening to Mrs. Logan's description of what occurs, Mrs. Harris said, "Tell me about the positive interactions that Edward has with peers throughout the day." Mrs. Logan paused for a long time and then admitted that he does not really have any positive interactions with peers.*

Figure 13.1 includes the sections of the FBA Checklist for Shouting Out that were checked off, the hypothesis statement that was written, and the intervention plan that was put in place.

Challenging Behavior: Shouting Out

1. Social Skills Deficits

- ❒ 1a: The student has not learned the social expectations for raising one's hand.
- ❒ 1b: The student lacks the social skills to recognize appropriate and inappropriate times to shout out.
- ❒ 1c: The student shouts out to get positive or negative attention from teachers.
- ☑ 1d: The student shouts out to get positive or negative attention from peers.
- ❒ 1e: The student shouts out when disengaged due to deficits in joint attention and social reciprocity.

Hypothesis Statement Edward shouts out random reprimands to peers in the classroom during transitions and unstructured periods of the day to gain attention from peers because of limited opportunities for consistent, positive interaction with peers. He gets positively reinforced because the peers respond every time he shouts out a negative comment, and he continues multiple times each day.

Intervention Plan

Use ***peer-mediated interventions*** in the following ways:

- Teach the peers to ignore the reprimands that Edward shouts out.
- Create many opportunities for positive interaction with peers throughout the day by doing the following:
  - Set up structured partner activities for academic tasks and social games using ***balanced turn-taking.*** Teach the peers how to use strategies such as ***discrete trials, prompting/fading procedures, time-delay,*** and ***positive reinforcement*** to increase the likelihood of successful engagement during these activities.
  - Teach the peers how to ***follow Edward's lead*** to make positive initiations throughout the school day.

Results

It took the peers some time to learn how to ignore the reprimands that Edward shouts out. Edward gradually stopped shouting out reprimands, however, once they were able to ignore him. The teacher is now creating an increased number of opportunities for Edward to positively interact with peers during instructional and noninstructional routines and activities. Peers received the guidance they needed from the ASD specialist to increase the frequency of their positive initiations with Edward, use strategies to encourage responses and interaction from Edward, and look for ways to make positive comments about the good things that Edward is doing in the classroom. Instead of being annoyed by Edward, the peers are learning how much he can contribute and how enjoyable it is to be his friend.

Figure 13.1. Functional Behavior Assessment Checklist and intervention plan for Edward.

From Assessment to Successful Intervention

Case Study: Hannah *Hannah is an 11th-grade student with ASD who participates in general education classes alongside her typically developing peers. Her teachers get together once a month with the special education teacher to discuss any common problems they may be seeing to come up with ideas for addressing them as a team. They were sharing at the last meeting how disruptive it is when Hannah continually shouts out during class, including shouting out answers or questions she may have or indicating she needs help. Her shouting out disrupts others and limits peers' opportunities to share their ideas and responses when she gives all of the answers. The team reviews the FBA Checklist for Shouting Out and decides that Hannah may not understand the expectations for raising her hand and waiting to be called on, even though she is in 11th grade and is very bright. The teachers admitted that they have not explicitly stated the expectation for hand raising because other students already do that. They also admitted that they are probably reinforcing Hannah's shouting-out behaviors because they do accept her responses, answer her questions, and provide assistance. They are so proud of her hard work and achievements and want to encourage her participation and communication. It is time to address the shouting-out behaviors, however, because they are disruptive, stigmatizing, and need to be addressed before Hannah goes off to college where people may not accept her tendency to shout out.*

Figure 13.2 includes the the sections of the FBA Checklist that were checked off, the hypothesis statement that was written, and the intervention plan that was put in place.

Challenging Behavior: Shouting Out

1. **Social Skills Deficits**
   - ☑ 1a: The student has not learned the social expectations for raising one's hand.
   - ☑ 1b: The student lacks the social skills to recognize appropriate and inappropriate times to shout out.
   - ☑ 1c: The student shouts out to get positive or negative attention from teachers.
   - ☐ 1d: The student shouts out to get positive or negative attention from peers.
   - ☐ 1e: The student shouts out when disengaged due to deficits in joint attention and social reciprocity.

Hypothesis Statement Hannah shouts out during class to give answers, ask questions, and ask for help because she is not fully aware of the social expectations for raising her hand and waiting to be called on by the teacher. She is positively reinforced when she does shout out because her teachers accept her responses, answer her questions, and provide assistance.

Intervention Plan

- Use ***explicit instruction*** to teach the expectations for raising one's hand and waiting to be called on by the teacher.
- Use ***self-monitoring*** to provide a visual reminder of the expectation for raising her hand and a place where Hannah can place a tally mark each time the expectation is met.
- Use ***shaping*** by first calling on her immediately when she raises her hand and then calling on her after she waits for one student to answer, two students, and so forth until she can wait like other students.
- If Hannah shouts out, then the teacher should positively redirect using the following ***least-to-most prompts*** hierarchy:
  1. Give a visual prompt (e.g., point to a cue card that says, "Raise your hand").
  2. Give a gestural prompt (e.g., put a finger on your lips, begin to slightly raise your hand as a cue for Hannah to raise her hand).
  3. Give a verbal prompt (e.g., "Please raise your hand").
  4. Make sure you use ***positive reinforcement*** with Hannah by immediately responding when she raises her hand.

Results

The special education teacher met briefly with Hannah one day before first period to review the expectations for raising her hand and provide her with a ***self-monitoring*** tool for each class. The teachers followed the interventions included in the the plan with fidelity, and Hannah quickly learned how to raise her hand and wait to be called on; she no longer shouts out many times during each class period. She may still shout out a few times, but the frequency of that behavior decreases each week.

Figure 13.2. Functional Behavior Assessment Checklist and intervention plan for Hannah.

Challenging Behavior: Shouting Out

1. **Social Skills Deficits**
   - ❐ 1a: The student has not learned the social expectations for raising one's hand.
   - ❐ 1b: The student lacks the social skills to recognize appropriate and inappropriate times to shout out.
   - ❐ 1c: The student shouts out to get positive or negative attention from teachers.
   - ❐ 1d: The student shouts out to get positive or negative attention from peers.
   - ❐ 1e: The student shouts out when disengaged due to deficits in joint attention and social reciprocity.
2. **Anxiety, Fear, and Emotional Regulation Difficulties**
   - ❐ 2a: The student shouts out when feeling anxious or fearful.
   - ❐ 2b: The student shouts out when emotionally dysregulated.
3. **Sensory Processing Problems**
   - ❐ 3a: The student shouts out when experiencing sensory overload.
   - ❐ 3b: The student shouts out when needing sensory input.
4. **Academic, Cognitive, or Motor Skills Deficits**
   - ❐ 4a: The student shouts out when frustrated with academic work that is too difficult.
   - ❐ 4b: The student shouts out when the fine motor or gross motor skills required for a particular activity are too difficult.

Other ____

____

____

____

____

Hypothesis Statement ____

____

____

____

____

APPENDIX A

Characteristics of ASD Assessment

This appendix provides the Characteristics of ASD Assessment, a simple tool you can use to gather information about your student's unique profile. It is best to complete the assessment with the caregivers and professionals who know the student the best.

ASD characteristic	Indicators (check all that apply)
Language comprehension difficulties	❐ The student has difficulty understanding verbal directions. ❐ The student has difficulty understanding written directions. ❐ The student has difficulty understanding academic vocabulary. ❐ The student has difficulty understanding figurative language. ❐ The student is better able to comprehend auditory information when the rate of speech is slowed down. ❐ The student is better able to comprehend auditory information when the speaker uses clear, concise, and consistent language. ❐ The student is better able to comprehend auditory information when it is paired with visual supports.
Deficits in expressive communication skills	❐ The student is nonverbal. ❐ The student primarily uses one-word utterances. ❐ The student primarily uses two- to three-word utterances. ❐ The student primarily uses utterances of a few simple sentences. ❐ The student primarily uses verbal communication to express wants and needs but not for other social and academic purposes.
Anxiety and fear	❐ The student is diagnosed with an anxiety disorder or is taking medication to reduce anxiety. ❐ The student has a specific phobia. ❐ The student worries about disappointing others. ❐ The student worries about upcoming events and activities. ❐ The student worries about getting something wrong.

(continued)

ASD characteristic	Indicators (check all that apply)
Emotional regulation difficulties	❒ The student may get extremely upset very quickly. ❒ The student does not use calming strategies when upset. ❒ The student has extreme positive emotions and cannot effectively regulate them. ❒ The student has extreme negative emotions and cannot effectively regulate them. ❒ The student has meltdowns and is not easily redirected. ❒ The student shows remorse for challenging behaviors displayed during a meltdown.
Social skills deficits	❒ The student has deficits in joint attention. ❒ The student has deficits in social and emotional reciprocity. ❒ The student does not effectively use or understand nonverbal communication (e.g., facial expressions, gestures, body language). ❒ The student has deficits in specific social skills (e.g., turn-taking, sharing, compromising, offering and accepting help). ❒ The student does not pick up on social norms and expectations at the same level as typically developing peers. ❒ The student does not establish and maintain friendships with peers. ❒ The student does not initiate interactions with others for purposes of sharing enjoyment. ❒ The student works alone instead of with peers. ❒ The student spends time alone during unstructured periods of time (e.g., recess, lunch, transitions). ❒ The student says or does things that are offensive to peers or adults. ❒ The student has difficulty taking the perspective of others. ❒ The student has unusually strong connections to one peer without having relationships with other peers as well.
Sensory processing problems	❒ The student is overreactive to certain sensory stimuli (e.g., sounds, smells, tastes, fluorescent lights, clutter in the environment, certain textures, chaotic movement). ❒ The student seeks sensory input (e.g., puts things in mouth, seeks deep pressure, rocks back and forth, jumps up and down). ❒ The student has severe aversions to certain sensory stimuli (e.g., gags when given bananas, screams during a fire drill).
Problems with focus and attention	❒ The student is diagnosed with attention-deficit/hyperactivity disorder (ADHD) or is taking medication. ❒ The student has difficulty focusing during independent work. ❒ The student has difficulty attending during group instruction. ❒ The student pays attention to things in the environment that are not the focus of the instruction or activity. ❒ The student is easily distracted by others or stimuli in the environment. ❒ The student is impulsive or hyperactive. ❒ The student has trouble shifting attention once focused.

ASD characteristic	Indicators (check all that apply)
Repetitive behaviors	❐ The student engages in repetitive motor movements. ❐ The student uses repetitive sounds, phrases, sentences, or scripts. ❐ The student repeatedly engages in the same play sequences. ❐ The student likes to repeatedly watch the same television shows or movies. ❐ The student likes to visit the same web sites to engage in the same activities or repeatedly watch the same video clips.
Restricted range of interests	❐ The student has very limited interests compared with typically developing peers. ❐ The student has a very intense passion about or fascination with a specific topic. ❐ The student has an intense interest in a specific cartoon character or famous person. ❐ The student has very intense interests about things that are not shared interests for most peers.
Need for sameness	❐ The student gets upset when a predictable schedule or routine changes. ❐ The student gets upset when a familiar person is not present when expected. ❐ The student gets upset when a preferred peer is absent or not present for a regularly occurring routine or activity. ❐ The student gets upset when given new tasks. ❐ The student gets upset when new events are going to occur. ❐ The student gets upset when others do not play the right way.
Executive functioning challenges	❐ The student has trouble following multistep directions. ❐ The student has trouble completing multistep tasks. ❐ The student has trouble completing projects that are completed over time. ❐ The student has difficulty with problem solving. ❐ The student has difficulty with time management. ❐ The student has difficulty with organization.
Academic deficits/cognitive differences	❐ The student has deficits in short-term or long-term memory and requires a great deal of repetition and repeated practice to master basic reading, writing, and math skills. ❐ The student has difficulty understanding abstract ideas and concepts. ❐ The student has difficulty making inferences and drawing conclusions. ❐ The student has difficulty with mathematical problem solving. ❐ The student has difficulty with written expression (e.g., generating ideas, putting thoughts into words, organizing ideas, using writing conventions).

(continued)

ASD characteristic	Indicators (check all that apply)
Fine and gross motor skills deficits	❒ The student has difficulty writing legibly. ❒ The student has difficulty using fine motor skills to manipulate small objects and academic tools (e.g., rulers, scissors). ❒ The student has motor planning challenges. ❒ The student has gross motor challenges (e.g., running, jumping, throwing a ball back and forth).
Medical conditions	❒ The student has food allergies or is on a special diet. ❒ The student has seizures. ❒ The student has gastrointestinal problems. ❒ The student has irregular sleeping patterns. ❒ The student has been diagnosed with a mental health disorder. ❒ The student is taking medication to treat seizures, gastrointestinal problems, ADHD, anxiety, depression, aggression, or other symptoms.

APPENDIX **B**

Characteristics of ASD FBA Template and Samples

This appendix provides the Characteristics of ASD FBA Template, a tool you can use for assessing any challenging behavior not explicitly discussed in Chapters 4–13. Two completed examples of this template are shown in Figures B.1 and B.2.

Challenging behavior ______________________

ASD characteristic	Affects the behavior? (yes or no)	Notes
Language comprehension difficulties		
Deficits in expressive communication skills		
Anxiety and fear		
Emotional regulation difficulties		
Social skills deficits		
Sensory processing problems		
Problems with focus and attention		
Repetitive behaviors		
Restricted range of interests		
Need for sameness		

(continued)

ASD characteristic	Affects the behavior? (yes or no)	Notes
Executive functioning challenges		
Academic deficits/ cognitive differences		
Fine and gross motor skills deficits		
Medical conditions		

Hypothesis Statement ____

____

____

____

____

____

____

Intervention Plan

- ____
- ____
- ____
- ____
- ____
- ____
- ____
- ____

Problem Behavior The student smells hair and skin of others

ASD characteristic	Impacts the behavior? (yes or no)	Notes
Language comprehension difficulties	No	
Deficits in expressive communication skills	Yes	The student has minimal independent verbal initiation skills. Although the student can imitate what others say, generating verbal initiations without modeling from others is very difficult for the student.
Anxiety and fear	No	
Emotional regulation difficulties	No	
Social skills deficits	Yes	The student has very few opportunities to interact with peers due to significant deficits in joint attention and social reciprocity. One of the few times throughout the school day that the student interacts with others is when the student smells the hair or skin of others.
Sensory processing problems	Yes	The student has sensory integration dysfunction and seeks sensory input on a regular basis. The student seeks sensory input by smelling things, being involved in movement activities (e.g., jumping, swinging, rocking), and touching (the student enjoys deep pressure activities).
Problems with focus and attention	No	
Repetitive behaviors	Yes	The student engages in repetitive behaviors such as repetitive motor movements, vocalizations, and repeated smelling of various stimuli to seek sensory input.
Restricted range of interests	No	
Need for sameness	No	
Executive functioning challenges	No	

Figure B.1. Characteristics of ASD FBA Template: Sample 1.

(continued)

ASD characteristic	Impacts the behavior? (yes or no)	Notes
Academic deficits/cognitive differences	No	
Fine and gross motor skills deficits	No	
Medical conditions	No	

Hypothesis Statement The student smells the hair and skin of others to seek sensory input due to sensory integration dysfunction. In addition, the student has limited opportunities to engage with peers due to deficits in expressive communication skills and social interaction skills. Thus, the student may smell the hair and skin of others for purposes of establishing an interaction.

Intervention Plan

- Use peer-mediated interventions to teach peers how to initiate and sustain positive social interaction with the student to prevent the student from resorting to smelling their hair or skin. This can be as simple as greeting the student and requesting a high-five or fist bump before the student has an opportunity to smell the peer's hair or skin.
- Use a social narrative and video modeling to teach the student appropriate ways to make social imitations with peers utilizing AAC supports to address deficits in expressive communication skills.
- Use visual supports to explain that smelling the hair and skin of others makes them feel uncomfortable. Provide replacement sensory activities to meet the olfactory input needs of the student (e.g., provide lotion the student can put on and smell, give the student scratch and sniff stickers, keep a collection of free paper perfume samples the student can smell, keep real flowers and plants in the classroom that the student can smell). Create a visual choice board for smelling activities that you can present to the student as preventive measures or to positively redirect the student if the student smells the hair or skin of others.

Figure B.1. *(continued)*

Problem Behavior Running out of the classroom

ASD Characteristic	Impacts the Behavior? (yes or no)	Notes
Language comprehension difficulties	Yes	The student often runs out of the classroom when the teacher is delivering lectures due to difficulties understanding the language. The student is less likely to run out of the classroom when visual supports are provided and active engagement strategies are employed.
Deficits in expressive communication skills	Yes	The student is nonverbal and does not use AAC to compensate for lack of verbal skills. Thus, the student runs out of the classroom instead of communicating to share needs and frustrations.
Anxiety and fear	Yes	The student is currently taking medication for anxiety. Anxiety and fear increases when the student is given new or difficult tasks and when the normal schedule or routine is interrupted (need for sameness).
Emotional regulation difficulties	Yes	The student is unable to regulate his or her emotions when he or she is anxious, fearful, frustrated, or angry. The student's emotions escalate quite quickly and he or she runs out of the classroom.
Social skills deficits	Yes	The student has significant deficits in joint attention and social reciprocity. The student may get frustrated and run out of the classroom when instructional and noninstructional activities require the use of these skills.
Sensory processing problems	Yes	The student has sensory integration dysfunction and is hypersensitive to visual, auditory, and olfactory stimulation. The student may get overstimulated and run out of the classroom.
Problems with focus and attention	Yes	The student has a difficult time focusing to complete independent assignments as well as focusing to engage in recreational activities. The student may run out of the classroom as a result of losing focus and attention.
Repetitive behaviors	No	
Restricted range of interests	Yes	The student does not run out of the classroom when the student in engaged in a highly preferred task related to special interests. The student does run out of the classroom, however, when presented with nonpreferred tasks.

Figure B.2. Characteristics of ASD FBA Template: Sample 2.

(continued)

ASD Characteristic	Impacts the Behavior? (yes or no)	Notes
Executive functioning challenges	Yes	The student is unable to complete multistep tasks without extensive prompting and support. The student may run out of the classroom when this support is not provided.
Academic deficits/cognitive differences	Yes	The student's academic performance is significantly below grade level in reading, writing, and math. The student may run out of the classroom when assignments and activities are not developmentally appropriate (too difficult).
Fine and gross motor skills deficits	Yes	The student has fine motor skills deficits. Thus, the student may run out of the classroom when given writing tasks.
Medical conditions	No	

Hypothesis Statement There are multiple reasons why the student may run out of the classroom, including any of the following:

- Language comprehension difficulties during long lectures without visual supports and active engagement
- Inability to expressively communicate feelings, wants, and needs
- Heightened levels of anxiety, fear, anger, or frustration and the inability to regulate these emotions
- Experiencing sensory overload
- Being given assignments or activities that are not interest based, are new, are too difficult due to academic and fine motor skills deficits, or require multiple steps to complete
- Not having the social skills necessary to engage in the activity

Intervention Plan

- Provide visual supports and use active engagement strategies during lecture-based instructional activities.
- Teach functional communication skills to help the student express feelings, wants, and needs using AAC supports.

Figure B.2. *(continued)*

- Teach emotional regulation strategies to help the student identify when distressed, go to a safe space in the classroom, and engage in a calming activity.
- Make environmental arrangements to respond to the student's sensory profile. Use natural lighting instead of fluorescent lighting, reduce excessive noise and clutter, arrange clearly defined workspaces, and ensure movement of students in the classroom is organized and controlled.
- Make sure academic tasks are developmentally appropriate in regard to the student's present level of academic abilities, utilize assistive technology to address fine motor skills deficits, and tap into the student's strengths and special interests as often as possible.
- Utilize task analysis, chaining, and self-monitoring tools to support the student with maintaining focus and attention and completing multistep tasks.
- Use strategies and teach peers to use strategies (through peer-mediated interventions) to support the student's development of joint attention and social reciprocity skills. This may include following the child's lead, using balanced-turn-taking, modeling/request imitation, and prompting/fading procedures.

References

Alberto, P. A., & Troutman, A. C. (2012). *Applied behavior analysis for teachers* (9th ed.). Upper Saddle River, NJ: Prentice Hall.

American Psychiatric Association. (2013). *Diagnostic and statistical manual of mental disorders, 5th edition (DSM-5).* Washington, DC: Author.

Archer, A. L., & Hughes C. A. (2011). *Explicit instruction: Effective and efficient teaching. (What works for special-needs learners.)* New York, NY: Guilford Press.

Attwood, T. (2004). *Exploring feelings: Cognitive behaviour therapy to manage anxiety.* Arlington, TX: Future Horizons.

Bakeman, R., & Adamson, L. B. (1984). Coordinating attention to people and objects in mother–infant and peer–infant interaction. *Child Development, 55,* 1278–1289.

Baranek, G. T. (2002). Efficacy of sensory and motor interventions for children with autism. *Journal of Autism and Developmental Disorders, 32*(5), 397–422.

Baranek, G. T., David, F. J., Poe, M. D., Stone, W. L., & Watson, L. R. (2006). Sensory Experiences Questionnaire: Discriminating sensory features in young children with autism, developmental delays, and typical development. *Journal of Child Psychology and Psychiatry, 47,* 591–601.

Baron-Cohen, S., Leslie, A. M., & Frith, U. (1985). Does the autistic child have a "theory of mind?" *Cognition, 21,* 37–46.

Bellini, S., & Akullian, J. (2007). A meta-analysis of video modeling and video self-modeling interventions for children and adolescents with autism spectrum disorder. *Exceptional Children, 73,* 264–287.

Browder, D. M., & Snell, M. E. (2000). *Teaching functional academics.* In M. E. Snell & F. Brown (Eds.), *Instruction of severe disabilities* (5th ed., pp. 453–543). Upper Saddle River, NJ: Prentice Hall.

Buffington, D. M., Krantz, P. J., McClannahan, L. E., & Poulson, C. L. (1998). Procedures for teaching appropriate gestural communication skills to children with autism. *Journal of Autism and Developmental Disorders, 28*(6), 535–545.

Buron, K. D., & Curtis, M. (2003). *The incredible 5-point scale: Assisting students with autism spectrum disorders in understanding social interactions and controlling their emotional responses.* Shawnee Mission, KS: Autism Asperger Publishing.

Calloway, C. J., & Simpson, R. L. (1998). Decisions regarding functions of behavior: Scientific versus informal analyses. *Focus on Autism and Other Developmental Disabilities, 13*(3), 167–175.

Canitano, R. (2006). Self-injurious behavior in autism: Clinical aspects and treatment with risperidone. *Journal of Neural Transmission, 113*(3), 425–431.

Cannella-Malone, H. I., Sigafoos, J., O'Reilly, M., de la Cruz, B., Edrisinha, C., & Lancioni, G. E. (2006). Comparing video prompting to video modeling for teaching daily living skills to six adults with developmental disabilities. *Education and Training in Developmental Disabilities, 41,* 344–356.

Cannon, L., Kenworthy, L., Alexander, K. C., Werner, M. A., & Anthony, L. G. (2011). *Unstuck and on target!: An executive function curriculum to improve flexibility for children with autism spectrum disorders* (Research ed.). Baltimore, MD: Paul H. Brookes Publishing Co.

Chaidez, V., Hansen, R. L., & Hertz-Picciotto, I. (2014). Gastrointestinal problems in children with autism, developmental delays or typical development. *Journal of Autism and Developmental Disorders, 44*(5), 1117–1127.

Cicchetti, D., Ganiban, J., & Barnett, D. (1991). Contributions from the study of high-risk populations to understanding the development of emotion regulation. In J. Garber & K. Dodge (Eds.), *The development of emotion regulation* (pp. 15–48). New York, NY: Cambridge University Press.

Clark, E., Olympia, D., Jensen, J., Heathfield, L., & Jenson, W. (2004). Striving for autonomy in a contingency-governed world: Another challenge for individuals with developmental disabilities. *Psychology in the Schools, 41*(1), 143–153.

Constantino, J. N., Davis, S. A., Todd, R. D., Schindler, M. K., Gross, M. M., Brophy, S. L., Metzger, L. M., Shoushtari, C. S., Splinter, R., & Reich, W. (2003). Validation of a brief quantitative measure of autistic traits: Comparison of the Social Responsiveness Scale with the Autism Diagnostic Interview–Revised. *Journal of Autism and Developmental Disorders, 33*(4), 427–433.

Cook, C. R., Grady, E. A., Long, A. C., Renshaw, T., Codding, R. S., Fiat, A, & Larson, M. (2017). Evaluating the impact of increasing general education teachers' ratio of positive-to-negative interactions on students' classroom behavior. *Journal of Positive Behavior Interventions, 19*(2), 67–77.

Cooper, J. O., Heron, T. E., & Heward, W. L. (2007). *Applied behavior analysis* (2nd ed.). Upper Saddle River, NJ: Pearson.

Corbett, B. A., & Constantine, L. J. (2006). Autism and attention deficit hyperactivity disorder: Assessing attention and response control with the integrated visual and auditory continuous performance test. *Child Neuropsychology, 12,* 335–348.

Courchesne, E., Townsend, J. P., Akshoomoff, N. A., Yeung-Courchesne, R., Press, G. A., Murakmi, J. W., Lincoln, A. J., James, H. E., Saitoh, O., Egaas, B., Haas, R. H., & Schreilman, L. (1994). A new finding: Impairment in shifting of attention in autistic and cerebellar patients. In S. H. Broman & J. Grafman (Eds), *Atypical deficits in developmental disorders: Implications for brain function* (pp. 101–137). Mahwah, NJ: Lawrence Erlbaum Associates.

Coyle, C., & Cole, P. (2004). A videotaped self-modeling and self-monitoring treatment program to treat off-task behavior in children with autism. *Journal of Intellectual and Developmental Disability, 29*(1), 3–15.

DiSalvo, C. A., & Oswald, D. P. (2002). Peer mediated interventions to increase the social interaction of children with autism: Consideration of peer expectancies. *Focus on Autism and Other Developmental Disorders, 17,* 198–207.

Dunlap, G., Iovannone, R., Kincaid, D., Wilson, K. Christiansen, K., Strain, P., . . . English, C. (2010). *Prevent-Teach-Reinforce: The school-based model of individualized positive behavior support.* Baltimore, MD: Paul H. Brookes Publishing Co.

Dunn, W., Myles, B. S., & Orr, S. (2002). Sensory processing issues associated with Asperger syndrome: A preliminary investigation. *American Journal of Occupational Therapy, 56*(1), 97–102.

Ellis Weismer, S., Lord, C., & Esler, A. (2010). Early language patterns of toddlers on the autism spectrum compared to toddlers with developmental delay. *Journal of Autism and Developmental Disorders, 40*(10), 1259–1273.

Evers, K., Steyaert, J., Noens, I., & Wagemans, J. (2015). Reduced recognition of dynamic facial emotional expressions and emotion-specific response bias in children with an autism spectrum disorder. *Journal of Autism and Developmental Disorders, 45*(6), 1774–1784.

Farrugia, S., & Hudson, J. (2006). Anxiety in adolescents with Asperger syndrome: Negative thoughts, behavioral problems, and life interference. *Focus on Autism and Other Developmental Disabilities, 21,* 25–35.

Ferguson, D. L., & Baumgart, D. (1991). Partial participation revisited. *Journal of The Association for Persons with Severe Handicaps, 16,* 218–227.

Fleischmann, A., & Fleischmann, C. (2012). *Carly's voice: Breaking through autism.* New York, NY: Touchstone/Simon & Schuster.

Gagnon, E. (2001). *Power cards: Using special interests to motivate children and youth with Asperger syndrome and autism.* Shawnee Mission, KS: Autism Asperger Publish Company.

Gersten, R., Baker, S. K., Smith-Johnson, J., Dimino, J., & Peterson, A. (2006). Eyes on the prize: Teaching complex historical content to middle school students with learning disabilities. *Exceptional Children, 72*(3), 264–280.

Gray, C. (1994). *Comic strip conversations: Illustrated interactions that teach conversation skills to students with autism and related disorders.* Arlington, TX: Future Horizons.

Gray, C. (2010). *The new social story book.* Arlington, TX: Future Horizons.

Gross, J. J. (2007). *Handbook of emotion regulation.* New York, NY: Guilford Press.

Hill, E. L. (2004). Executive dysfunction in autism. *Trends in Cognitive Science, 8,* 26–31.

Hine, J. F., & Wolery, M. (2006). Using point-of-view video modeling to teach play to preschoolers with autism. *Topics in Early Childhood Special Education, 26*(2), 83–93.

Hobson, R. P. (1989). On sharing experiences. *Development and Psychopathology, 1,* 197–203.

Horner, R. H. (1994). Functional assessment: Contributions and future directions. *Journal of Applied Behavior Analysis, 27,* 401–404.

Horner, R. H. (2000). Positive behavior supports. *Focus on Autism and Other Developmental Disabilities, 15,* 97–105.

Iacono, T., Trembath, D., & Erickson, S. (2016). The role of augmentative and alternative communication for children with autism: Current status and future trends. *Neuropsychiatric Disease and Treatment, 12,* 2349–2361.

Kenworthy, L., Black, D., Wallace, G., Ahluvalia, T., Wagner, A., & Sirian, L. (2005). Disorganization: The forgotten executive dysfunction in autism spectrum disorders. *Developmental Neuropsychology, 28,* 809–827.

Kenworthy, L., Case, L., Harms, M. B., Martin, A., & Wallace, G. (2010). Adaptive behavior ratings correlate with symptomatology and IQ among individuals with high-functioning autism spectrum disorders. *Journal of Autism and Developmental Disorders, 40,* 416–423.

Kessels, R. P. C., Montagne, B., Hendriks, A. W., Perrett, D. I., & de Haan, E. H. F. (2014). Assessment of perception of morphed facial expressions using the Emotion Recognition Task: Normative data from healthy participants aged 8–75. *Journal of Neuropsychology, 8*(1), 75–93.

Kessels, R. P. C., Spee, P., & Hendriks, A. W. (2010). Perception of dynamic facial emotional expressions in adolescents with autism spectrum disorders (ASD). *Translational Neuroscience, 1*(3), 228–232.

Kluth, P., & Schwarz, P. (2008). *Just give him the whale!: 20 ways to use fascinations, areas of expertise, and strengths to support students with autism.* Baltimore, MD: Paul H. Brookes Publishing Co.

Koegel, L. K., Koegel, R. L., Frea, W., & Green-Hopkins, I. (2003). Priming as a method of coordinating educational services for students with autism. *Language, Speech, and Hearing Services in Schools, 34*(3), 228–235.

Krakowiak, P., Goodlin-Jones, B., Hertz-Picciotto, I., Croen, L. A., & Hansen, R. L. (2008). Sleep problems in children with autism spectrum disorders, developmental delays, and typical development: A population-based study. *Journal of Sleep Research, 17,* 197–206.

Krantz, P. J., & McClannahan, L. E. (1993). Teaching children with autism to initiate to peers: Effects of a script-fading procedure. *Journal of Applied Behavior Analysis, 26,* 121–132.

Landa, R. (2007). Early communication development and intervention for children with autism. *Mental Retardation and Developmental Disabilities Research Reviews, 13,* 16–25.

Laurent, A. C., & Rubin, E. (2004). Challenges in emotional regulation in Asperger syndrome and high-functioning autism. *Topics in Language Disorders, 24,* 286–297.

Lavoie, R. (2006). *It's so much work to be your friend: Helping the child with learning disabilities find social success.* New York, NY: Touchstone.

Leach, D. (2010). *Bringing ABA into your inclusive classroom: A guide to improving outcomes for students with autism spectrum disorders.* Baltimore, MD: Paul H. Brookes Publishing Co.

Leyfer, O. T., Folstein, S. E., Bacalman, S., Davis, N. O., Dinh, E., Morgan, J., Tager-Flusber, H., & Lainhart, J. E. (2006). Comorbid psychiatric disorders in children with autism: Interview development and rates of disorders. *Journal of Autism and Developmental Disorders, 36,* 849–861.

Lloyd, M., MacDonald, M., & Lord, C. (2013). Motor skills of toddlers with autism spectrum disorders. *Autism, 17(2),* 133–146.

Lovaas, O. I. (1987). Behavioral treatment and normal educational and intellectual functioning in young autistic children. *Journal of Counseling and Clinical Psychology, 55,* 3–9.

Mace, F. C., Hock, M. L., Lalli, J. S., West, B. J., Belfiore, P. J., & Brown, D. K. (1988). Behavioral momentum in the treatment of noncompliance. *Journal of Applied Behavior Analysis, 21,* 123–141.

Mazefsky, C. A., Herrington, J., Siegel, M., Scarpa, A., Maddox, B. B., Scahill, L., & White, S. W. (2013). The role of emotion regulation in autism spectrum disorder. *Journal of the American Academy of Child and Adolescent Psychiatry, 52,* 679–688.

McGee, G. G., Krantz. P. J., & McClannahan, L. E. (1986). An extension of incidental teaching to reading instruction for autistic children. *Journal of Applied Behavior Analysis, 19,* 147–157.

Miller, S. P., & Mercer, C. D. (1993). Using data to learn about concrete-semi concrete-abstract instruction for students with math disabilities. *Learning Disabilities Research and Practice, 8,* 89–96.

Mundy, P., Sigman, M., Ungerer, J., & Sherman, T. (1986). Defining the social deficits of autism: The contribution of non-verbal communication measures. *Journal of Child Psychology and Psychiatry and Allied Disciplines, 27,* 657–669.

Myles, B. S., & Simpson, R. L. (2001). Understanding the hidden curriculum: An essential social skill for children and youth with Asperger syndrome. *Intervention in School and Clinic, 36*(5), 279–286.

Odom, S. L., & Strain, P. S. (1984). Peer mediated approaches to promoting children's social interaction: A review. *American Journal of Orthopsychiatry, 54,* 544–557.

Prizant, B. M., Wetherby, A. M., Rubin, E., Laurent, A. C., & Rydell, P. J. (2006). *The SCERTS® model: A comprehensive educational approach for children with autism spectrum disorders.* Baltimore, MD: Paul H. Brookes Publishing Co.

Provost, B., Lopez, B. R., & Heimerl, S. (2007). A comparison of motor delays in young children: Autism spectrum disorder, developmental delay, and developmental concerns. *Journal of Autism and Developmental Disorders, 37*(3), 21–28.

Rivard, M., Terroux, A., Mercier, C., & Parent-Boursier, C. (2015). Indicators of intellectual disabilities in young children with autism spectrum disorders. *Journal of Autism and Developmental Disorders, 45*(1), 127–137.

Rodriguez, N. M., Thompson, R. H., Stocco, C. S., & Schlichenmeyer, K. (2013). Arranging and ordering in autism spectrum disorder: Characteristics, severity, and environmental correlates. *Journal of Intellectual and Developmental Disability, 38*(3), 242–255.

Rogers, S. J., & Bennetto, L. (2000). Intersubjectivity in autism: The roles of imitation and executive function. In S. F. Warren & J. Reichle (Series Eds.) & A. P. Wetherby & B. Prizant (Vol. Eds.), *Communication and language intervention series: Vol. 9. Autism spectrum disorders: A transactional developmental perspective* (pp. 79–108). Baltimore, MD: Paul H. Brookes Publishing Co.

Rommelse, N. N., Franke, B., Geurts, H. M., Hartman, C. A., & Buitelaar, J. K. (2010). Shared heritability of attention-deficit/hyperactivity disorder and autism spectrum disorder. *European Child and Adolescent Psychiatry, 19,* 281–295.

Rose, V., Trembath, D., Keen, D., & Paynter, J. (2016). The proportion of minimally verbal children with autism spectrum disorder in a community-based early intervention programme. *Journal of Intellectual Disability Research, 60*(5), 464–477.

Scheuermann, B., & Webber, J. (2002). *Autism: Teaching does make a difference.* Belmont, CA: Wadsworth/Thomson Learning.

Scott, T. M., & Caron, D. B. (2005). Conceptualizing functional behavior assessment as prevention practice within positive behavior support systems. *Preventing School Failure, 50,* 13–20.

Silk, J. S., Steinberg, L., & Morris, A. S. (2003). Adolescents' emotion regulation in daily life: Links to depressive symptoms and problem behavior. *Child Development, 74,* 1869–1880.

Simonoff, E., Pickles, A., Charman, T., Chandler, S., Loucas, T., & Baird, G. (2008). Psychiatric disorders in children with autism spectrum disorders: Prevalence, comorbidity, and associated factors in a population-derived sample. *Journal of the American Academy of Child and Adolescent Psychiatry, 47,* 921–929.

Smith, M. J. L., Montagne, B., Perrett, D. I., Gill, M., & Gallagher, L. (2010). Detecting subtle facial emotion recognition deficits in high-functioning autism using dynamic stimuli of varying intensities. *Neuropsychologia, 48*(9), 2777–2781.

Spence, S. J., & Schneider, M. T. (2009). The role of epilepsy and epileptiform EEGs in autism spectrum disorders. *Pediatric Research, 65,* 599–606.

Sugai, G., Horner, R., Dunlap, G., Hieneman, M., Lewis, T., Nelson, M., Scott, T., Liaupsin, C., Sailor, W., Turnbull, A. P., Turnbull, H. R., Wickham, D., Wilcox, B., & Ruef, M. (1999). *Applying positive behavioral support and functional behavior assessment in schools: Technical Assistance Guide 1, Version 1.4.3.* Washington, DC: Center on Positive Behavioral Interventions and Support.

Szatmari, P., Georgiades, S., Bryson, S., Zwaigenbaum, L., Roberts, W., Mahoney, W., Goldberg, J., & Tuff, L. (2006). Investigating the structure of the restricted, repetitive behaviors and interests domain of autism. *Journal of Child Psychology and Psychiatry, 47,* 582–590.

Tomchek, S. D., & Dunn, W. (2007). Sensory processing in children with and without autism: A comparative study using the short sensory profile. *American Journal of Occupational Therapy, 61*(2), 190–200.

Turner, M. (1999). Repetitive behaviour in autism: A review of psychological research. *Journal of Child Psychology and Psychiatry, 40,* 839–849.

Uljarevic, M., & Hamilton, A. (2013). Recognition of emotions in autism: A formal meta-analysis. *Journal of Autism and Developmental Disorders, 43,* 1517–1526.

Van Steensel, F. J. A., & Bogels, S. M. (2011). Anxiety disorders in children and adolescents with autistic spectrum disorders: A meta-analysis. *Clinical Child and Family Psychology Review, 14,* 302–317.

Vaughn, S., & Linan-Thompson, S. (2003). What is special about special education for students with learning disabilities? *Journal of Special Education, 37,* 140–147.

Wehmeyer, M. L., & Metzler, C. A. (1995). How self-determined are people with mental retardation? The National Consumer Survey. *Mental Retardation, 33*(2), 111–119.

Wetherby, A. M., Watt, N., Morgan, L., & Shunway, S. (2007). Social communication profiles of children with autism spectrum disorders late in the second year of life. *Journal of Autism and Developmental Disorders, 37,* 960–975.

White, S. W., Oswald, D., Ollendick, T., & Scahill, L. (2009). Anxiety in children and adolescents with autism spectrum disorders. *Clinical Psychology Review, 29*(3), 216–229.

Wolery, M., Ault, M. J., & Doyle, P. M. (1992). *Teaching students with moderate to severe disabilities.* New York, NY: Longman.

Wolery, M., Bailey, D. B., & Sugai, G. M. (1988). *Effective teaching: Principles and procedures of applied behavior analysis with exceptional students.* Boston, MA: Allyn & Bacon.

Index

Tables and figures are indicated with page numbers followed by *t* and *f*, respectively.